The Workshop Book

The Workshop Book

Scott Landis

The Taunton Press

First printing: July 1991
Printed in the United States of America

A FINE WOODWORKING Book

FINE WOODWORKING® is a trademark of The Taunton Press, Inc.,
registered in the U.S. Patent and Trademark Office.

The Taunton Press
63 South Main Street
Box 5506
Newtown, CT 06470-5506

Library of Congress Cataloging-in-Publication Data

Landis, Scott.
    The workshop book / Scott Landis
        p.   cm.
    "A Fine woodworking book"—T.p. verso.
    Includes bibliographical references and index.
    ISBN 0-942391-37-3
    1. Workshops.   2. Woodwork — Equipment and supplies.   II. Title.
TT152.L36   1991
684'.08–dc20
                                91-12275
                            CIP

Acknowledgments

Frank Klausz one explained the difference between "old-world" and "new-world" woodworkers. According to Klausz, the European craftsmen he learned from would readily admit how much money they charged (and what they earned), but not how they did their work. In America, he said, woodworkers talk freely about their working methods, but won't say how much they make.

This isn't a book about business, but the craftspeople I visited certainly shared their insights and experience, as well as their shops and often their homes, with little thought of their own gain. I had experienced this generosity before, when I gathered information for *The Workbench Book.* But roughly 100 workshops later—in about 25 states and several Canadian provinces—*The Workshop Book* has proven this to be more than a passing phenomenon.

As with *The Workbench Book,* I owe my greatest debt to the craftspeople who appear on the following pages—many of them new and valued friends. Their creativity and unflagging curiosity were a constant inspiration. A few of these contributors deserve special mention: Don Anderson, J. Baldwin, Mac Campbell, Martha Collins, Mark Duginske, Michael Fortune, Roger Heitzman, Barbara Kern, Kelly Mehler,

Peter Murkett, John Nyquist, Richard Schneider, Rob Tarule, Luca Valentino and Norm Vandal. Particular thanks to Jim Rickard and Paul Silke for their help in untangling the intricacies of electricity. I feel lucky to have met Carlyle Lynch before he died and to have had the chance to spend a day talking shop with a gentle master of the craft.

People at a number of museums, libraries and businesses provided valuable insights and greatly facilitated my research: Hallie Bond of the Adirondack Museum; Bob Benz at Billings Farm & Museum; Jay Gaynor, Harold Gill and Mack Headley at Colonial Williamsburg; Don Williams at the Conservation Analytical Laboratory; Valerie Oakley at the Southbury Public Library; Charles Hummel and Greg Landrey at the Henry Francis du Pont Winterthur Museum; Albert LeCoff of the Wood Turning Center; Jeff Storey of Aair Purification Systems; David Scott of Manufacturers Service Co., Inc.; Richard Vonderheide, formerly of the Parks Woodworking Machine Co.; and the Real Goods Trading Company.

I also want to thank the 50 people who responded with enthusiasm to my call for small shops in *Fine Woodworking* magazine. I wasn't able to include them all in the book, but their contribution is nonetheless appreciated.

Thanks also to *Fine Woodworking* editors Dick Burrows, Sandor Nagyszalanczy and Jim Boesel and to David Sloan at *American Woodworker,* who pointed the way to many shops I would not have discovered on my own; to Pam Purrone, Henry Roth and Deborah Cannarella at The Taunton Press; and to Vince Babak for his handsome floor plans.

Whatever success this book achieves is due largely to the contributions of two other craftspeople, who brought so much to *The Workbench Book.* Heather Brine Lambert's drawings, which are scattered throughout the text, set a standard for clarity and accuracy. Having built each fixture, tool chest and wood rack on paper, she knows as much, if not more, about them than their creators. Roger Holmes has once again employed his fine surgical skills to trim the fat and gently prod a mountain of material into life.

Final appreciation goes to Jay Peters, in whose shop and under whose guidance I cut my teeth (but not my fingers), and to Nina, who read and commented on much of the text and photography. She shared in my discoveries, accepted (most of) my obsession and helped keep the sails trimmed.

Contents

Introduction

Late one fall about 15 years ago, on a secluded island in northwest Ontario, I installed my first workshop. With the help of a few friends, I dismantled half of a tumbledown icehouse that once served a commercial fishing camp, long since abandoned. The salvaged lumber and painstakingly unbent nails found their way into the walls of my new shop, which I carved out of the other half. Like the rest of the original icehouse, the 2x4 stud-frame walls were insulated with sawdust and the outer walls were sheathed in tar paper. Brown kraft building paper beneath the interior planking kept the bulk of the sawdust from drifting into the shop as it settled.

Double-glazed windows were out of the question, so I simply removed a horizontal swath of boards along most of the length of the south and west walls and stapled heavy plastic inside and out. I used driftwood and old 2x6s to build my workbench along the wall beneath the windows and to construct a small sleeping loft above the door at the east end of the building. In the winter, the building's footings and shallow shed roof were banked with snow, and toward spring I hung boxes inside the windows to start seedlings.

The shop was nothing fancy, but for the better part of two years I was happily ensconced, making snowshoes, knives and other artifacts of northern life, sometimes writing about the process. The nearest utility pole was about five miles away by water, so I relied entirely on hand tools. I worked mainly during the daytime, now and then (and especially in the winter) supplementing the natural light from the windows with kerosene and gas lanterns. Heat was more than amply provided, even at temperatures well below 0°F, by a cast-iron woodburning furnace that had been set

ashore on the island under rather mysterious circumstances some 30 years earlier. The ganglion heat-exchanger on top of the burner was so effective that I was roused more than once in the middle of the night to quench its ardor. Groggy with sleep, I stumbled down the ladder from the loft to fling open the dull-red door and dump a bucket of snow inside.

I eventually moved on,
abandoning the shop and the island that had been deserted when I arrived. Since then, I have visited hundreds of workshops, almost all of them more sophisticated and better equipped than my own. I worked for a while in six or eight of these shops and shared bench space in a few. But apart from the wilderness workshop that I occupied so long ago, I have never had my own place.

Perhaps I can credit the brief life span of my shop with the fact that I still remember the delicious agonies of decision making that attended every detail of its construction. How wide to make the door and on which side to mount the hinges? How high to make the bench and should I bolt the vise through the top or lag-screw it from below? Where to hang the tools and the other inventory I hoped to acquire in the near future? Decades later, such mundanities may seem trivial, but they were hardly so at the time.

Unsophisticated does not mean crude. Although my workshop was greatly simplified by a lack of electricity and machinery, it was no less thoughtfully organized than many more heavily equipped shops. Likewise, a simple workshop is in no way an impediment to good work. Simon Watts reminded me of how a down-to-earth Nova Scotia boat shop inspired his own "back-to-basics" conversion (see p. 28). The shop's owner, Jim Smith, turned out a fine working skiff

every six days—with the aid of no more than an old bandsaw, an electric grinder and a hand-held drill. Coming from a fully outfitted Vermont furniture shop, Watts found it to be "an absolute eye-opener."

Most of us recognize the value of a clean, well-lit work place, even if we cannot always claim one for ourselves. We wear our shops—as well as our homes—like an old jacket or a favorite sweater, and since most of us spend the majority of our waking hours at work, they ought to fit well. We breath the air and rely upon the light and heat it provides for our comfort, efficiency and survival. If it doesn't reflect our needs and priorities, we are bound to be miserable.

Five years ago, when I embarked upon an exploration of workbenches (which culminated in *The Workbench Book,* published by The Taunton Press in 1987), there was no such consensus of opinion about their importance. Wherever I traveled for that project, I felt compelled to explain—often to politely quizzical silence—what was so engaging and important about so pedestrian an object as a workbench.

The process, as it turned out, revealed a lot about the way the workbench intersects the background and personality of the woodworker who builds and uses it. It also pointed the way to the broader subject of the workshop. Indeed, as a tool, a working environment and a reflection of its maker, the workshop is an obvious extension of the bench. Many of the same functional considerations and traditions that find expression in the workbench have an important role to play in the shop.

To gather the material in this book,
I retraced my steps to a few of the most intriguing and well-considered shops I discovered on my original workbench

hunt. And I visited dozens more, professional and amateur alike. In the process, I took a close look at the basic systems that constitute most modern workshops: electricity, lighting, heating, wood storage, dust collection and sharpening, among others. And I asked the shop owners to explain how they selected and located equipment in order to foster efficient work flow and safety. Our discussions went beyond the normal range of power tools—table saw, jointer, drill press, etc.—to include the workbench and tool chest, as well as the requirements for assembly and finishing. The workshop, I soon discovered, is not a static creature. Like the workbench and the craftsman who uses it, the shop constantly evolves to accommodate the changing needs of its occupant.

I also found that if you ask any six woodworkers about their shop or tools, you are likely to get at least six different answers. At a recent forum on the guitar-maker's workspace, moderator Jeff Elliott noted that the six panelists had a total of more than 130 years of workshop experience and still, he said, "We don't know where to put the bandsaw."

It will be no surprise, then, that the workspaces I've included here vary widely, from snugly efficient basement shops to cavernous cabinet shops. There are lavish, well-appointed shops alongside workspaces choked with salvaged machinery and shoehorned into garages, chicken coops and pantries. I even found some wonderful oddball "shops," among them a condensed tool kit designed to be carried on the back and a turning shop that travels on the bumper of an RV. Some of the shops in this book may approach the ideal, while others border on the improbable. The most creative solutions won't satisfy every palate, but they all share a common ingredient—they work.

This is not a recipe book. Unlike a workbench, a workshop is never built and outfitted from a set of plans. Although lots of information may be gleaned from the floor plans and drawings in the book, they are perhaps more valuable as inspiration than as blueprints. Likewise,

the mention of specific machinery is not intended to recommend one product over another. There is plenty of excellent equipment on the market—new or used, expensive or dirt cheap—and I have made no attempt to evaluate individual brands. For more specific information, either about brand performance or the intricacies of installing, maintaining or overhauling machinery, refer to the sources listed in the Bibliography (see p. 208).

As you think about your shop, don't be intimidated by all the choices confronting you. Many of us feel compelled to research our equipment to death in our quest for quality. Anything less is, well, less than perfect. We tend to disparage those who work in a hovel with a handful of worn-out tools, but let Art Carpenter's biodegradable workshop (see pp. 32-33) be a lesson. Like the bodybuilder's physique, when the workshop becomes a monument to our obsession, it ceases to be a means to an end and becomes the end in itself. For some people I visited, the workshop is obviously their ultimate creative expression. Never mind what goes on inside.

The measure of a workshop,

I found, is far greater than the sum of its parts. Some of my favorite shops are infused with a sense of personality, a character that derives as much from the placement of tools, the music on the radio and the pictures on the wall as from any ingenious jig or fixture. Stripped of that personality, what's left?

I sensed this most strongly when I visited Carlyle Lynch in Broadway, Virginia, not long before he died at the age of 80. I sat in a chair at the foot of Carlyle's bed, listening to his reflections on a rich lifetime as a woodworker and teacher of woodworking. Behind the house, his sprawling two-story workshop lay idle, and he would never work there again.

Between our sporadic chats (Carlyle wasn't up to much more), I wandered through the shop, wondering about the work and life that had once thrived there. Without Carlyle's presence, the benches, chests, and countless fixtures—even the tools and machinery—seemed like so many

bolts and board feet. The future of the shop's contents is uncertain. But whether the tools are kept together or dispersed to other craftsmen who might give them new life, it was clear that the shop could never really be called Carlyle's again.

One final confession:

As I write this book, I am "between shops." My last official workshop was a cavernous space on the second floor of a Toronto industrial building. I was flanked on either side by colorful tenants—a Korean sweatshop to the east, whence emanated the singsong whir of a battery of sewing machines and pungent cooking smells, and a fly-by-night wood-finishing outfit to the west, which generated fumes of much greater concern. Since then, I have shared a group workshop and borrowed space in friends' shops and barns, as the need arose.

Most of my tools are now in boxes, or on loan to friends. My workbench has been rudely decommissioned, its Record face vise removed so as not to interfere with the flow of perforated paper to the computer printer it now supports. A rack of files sits on the opposite end of the bench, and directly beneath them, under the tail vise, is the metal filing cabinet that contains the grist for this book. The whole business is within arm's reach of my chair and computer keyboard.

It's a sordid affair, I'll admit, hardly befitting someone who has spent as much time as I have peering through the windows of other people's shops. But in a way, the odyssey that became this book was a personal quest to discover those elements of the workspace that I will eventually include in my own. As I might have predicted at the start, I stumbled upon no ultimate design, no single solution to the myriad problems of tool selection and organization. But the material I've set between these covers, gleaned from all the shops I visited, will help me greatly when it comes time to recommission my workbench and get back to making shavings. I hope it does as much for you.

A note about safety

Safety must be at the heart of any serious discussion of the woodworking shop, and it was on the minds of many people I visited. High-speed machinery and even hand tools can be dangerous if they are improperly installed, maintained or operated. And basic systems, such as electricity, heat and dust collection can either contribute to a safe and productive environment or they can destroy it. When it comes to building or renovating your workshop, pay particular heed to these systems and make sure to observe safe and accepted installation procedures. Hire professional help if you need it.

Throughout the book, you'll find numerous practical devices and precautions that can enhance the safety of your shop and machinery. But despite all efforts to describe and regulate safety in the workplace, it remains a highly subjective issue. Almost every workshop operation has an element of danger, but the degree of actual risk also depends upon your experience, your state of mind (fatigue and/or haste) and an assortment of other environmental factors (noise, dust and other shop distractions). Just as I would never attempt to paddle my canoe through white water that might be routine to an Olympic kayaker, there are tools others use every day that I get nervous just thinking about. And we all know the dangers of complacency and the overconfidence that comes from mind-numbing repetition.

I recall with a shudder a friend's story about a woodworking shop he operated for the physically impaired. Hearing one of the machines running and noticing that the lights were off, he entered the shop to investigate. He was startled to find one of the clients operating the radial-arm saw in the dark. The operator was blind—but was following every safety procedure he'd been taught. With one hand placed firmly on the work and the other on the saw handle, the risk of injury was actually slight—arguably less than for some cocky cowboys I've seen at work. Mac Campbell said it best when he told me: "The way to protect your hands is to use your head."

"The Carpenter's Shop at Forty Hill, Enfield, 1813," *by John Hill. This 19th-century English joiner's shop is probably typical of the period — plenty of natural light, ventilation and elbow room, but no machinery.*

The Workshop Tradition

The winter, the timber, the wheelwright's continuous tussle, the traditional adaptation, by skill and knowledge —all these factors, not thought of but felt, to the accompaniment of wood-scents and saw-pit sounds, kept me from thinking of the cold... —George Sturt, *The Wheelwright's Shop*

Chapter 1

For years, the makers of period furniture have decried the lack of reliable information about the roots of their craft. Obscure as these origins may be, they are positively transparent compared with those of the shops in which the pieces were produced. A considerable body of woodwork remains from the 17th, 18th and early 19th centuries, but the workshops of those periods have vanished almost without a trace.

To make matters worse, little was written about workshops at the time. Even if interested in the furniture, most writers would have thought it irrelevant to record much about how and where it was produced. And craftsmen didn't make it easy for the few who tried. In an essay describing the compilation of his monumental, 17-volume *Encyclopédie*, Denis Diderot complained that "people who continually busy themselves with something are equally disposed to believe either that everyone knows those things which they are at no pains to hide, or that no one else knows anything about the things they are trying to keep secret. The result is that they are always ready to mistake any person who questions them either for a transcendent genius or for an idiot...." (Diderot's essay accompanied volume five of his *Encyclopédie* and appears in *Rameau's Nephew and Other Works*).

I encountered some of the same obstacles several years ago while investigating the history of the workbench—at once the most fundamental and neglected piece of equipment in the woodworker's tool kit. But as a subject of historic inquiry, the workbench has several characteristics that make it much more accessible than the workshop. Because they are relatively small in comparison to an entire building, enough old benches have been preserved by eccentric antiquarians to provide a discernible record of their evolution. Also, much can be inferred about benches from the nature of the tools used and from the work performed upon them. This naturally reflects specific cultural traditions as well as differences between trades. There are, for example, important distinctions between the design of English and Continental benches, and Japanese workbenches are completely different from those of Europe.

Architecture is likewise steeped in tradition, but the overall structure of the workshop is more often determined by factors that have nothing to do with woodworking. A craftsman might be inspired to build a bench just like the one he learned on, but he would rarely have the inclination or the resources to build his shop to the same specifications. What little evidence we have suggests that shops were at least as frequently adapted from or appended to existing structures. For as long as craftsmen have wielded tools, they have worked at home or in barns, sheds or buildings constructed for other purposes. Unfortunately, after such a space has been abandoned for a few years (much less a few generations) it is typically converted to other purposes and its complement of tools is dispersed.

So how to pick up the scent of a trail gone cold? In my research, I have found three valuable sources of information about the workshop tradition. First is the documentary record, which includes books, paintings, carvings and other ephemera (inventories, probate records, correspondence and so on). Second are historic workshop recreations in museum collections. Last come the precious few surviving 19th-century workshops, suspended precariously between the age of craft and the age of machinery. Each of these sources is fragmentary and limited in its authority, but together they provide a reasonable facsimile of early workshop life.

As leavening to these sources, I encourage readers to reflect upon and respect their own instincts. Some of the most interesting research in the woodworking trades is now being conducted not by historians, but by skilled craftsmen working with similar tools and, in places like Colonial Williamsburg, under similar conditions. After all, the use of hand tools and the properties of wood have not changed much in the last few centuries. Many of the same workshop issues that confront the modern woodworker, such as layout, lighting, heat and storage, must have been of equal concern to colonial craftsmen. We have greater options and resources at our disposal, but I suspect that our instincts and priorities are not unique.

The documentary record

One of the first things made clear by the documentary record is the rigid differentiation that prevailed in Europe during the 17th and 18th centuries among the woodworking trades. As Benno Forman explains in his book, *American Seating Furniture 1630-1730,* separate and unequal guilds were estab-

Trade Secrets

Contemporary documents provide much of what we know of woodworking history. The rigid caste system that segregated the woodworking trades in 17th- and 18th-century England is evident in the first of these extracts, taken from a 1632 decision by the London Court of Aldermen settling a dispute between carpenters and joiners. The second reflects the gradual erosion of that system as joiners encroached on the work of carpenters, taken from A General Description of All Trades (1748). The third notes the emergence of cabinetmakers, who carved a niche for themselves in furniture making. These and other similar references may be found in greater detail in Benno Forman's book American Seating Furniture 1630-1730.

By law, 17th-century London joiners were granted the exclusive manufacture of:

All sorts of Bedsteads whatsoever (onlie except Boarded Bedsteads and nayled together).

All sorts of Chayres and stooles which are made with mortesses or tennants.

All tables of wainscotte wallnutt or other stuffe glewed with fframes mortesses or tennants.

All sorts of formes framed made of boards with the sides pinned or glewed.

All sorts of chests being framed duftalled pynned or glued.

All sorts of Cabinets or Boxes duftalled pynned or glued.

By the 1740s, the distinction between carpenters and joiners was blurring in England, as is shown by the following anonymous comments:

Carpentry and Joinery, that Part especially belonging to House-work (and even Undertaking, or furnishing of funerals) are often performed by the same Persons, though the work of [the Joiner] is much lighter and reckoned more curious than that of Carpenters; for a good *Joiner* can often do both well, but every *Carpenter* cannot work at joinery.

While joiners were becoming architectural woodworkers, cabinetmakers were taking over the furniture trade. Robert Campbell's The London Tradesman *(1747) provides one of the earliest descriptions of the English cabinetmaker:*

The Cabinet-Maker is by much the most curious Workman in the Wood Way, except the Carver; and requires a nice mechanic Genius, and a tolerable Degree of Strength, though not so much as the Carpenter; he must have a much lighter Hand and a quicker Eye than the Joiner, as he is employed in Work much more minute and elegant.... A Master Cabinet-Maker is a very profitable Trade; especially, if he works for and Serves the Quality himself....

One of the earliest workshop views is the so-called Stent panel, a bas-relief woodcarving of a 17th-century joiner's shop from England or northern Europe. Rural economies could not support the rigid structure and specialization of the urban guilds. Woodworkers in such locations typically performed several functions and were perhaps more like the modern generalist craftsman than we might imagine.

lished that clearly delineated the functions and rights of carpenters, joiners and, eventually, cabinetmakers. (These trade organizations were further subdivided into turners, carvers, chairmakers, wheelwrights, instrument makers and so on.)

Joinery is an ancient craft, practiced by the Romans, Celts and Egyptians. It relied heavily on the use of riven or hewn green wood and very little (if any) glue. The staple joint in both the carpenter's and joiner's repertoire was the draw-bored mortise and tenon, which, in furniture, formed the essential component of frame-and-panel construction. Embellishment was usually limited and accomplished with a plane, a scratch stock or chisels.

Cabinetmaking, by comparison, is a relatively recent and refined occupation, which appeared in England and northern Europe during the 16th century. In place of narrow, riven stock, cabinetmakers employed wide, dry boards, usually dovetailed together at the corners. They were more likely to use sawn softwoods, veneers and other decorative elements than were joiners of the same period. With the declining popularity of the draw-bored mortise-and-tenon joint and its great mechanical strength came an increased reliance upon glue.

As you might expect in a frontier environment, the earliest North American furniture was built in the joiner's tradition. London advertisements and colonial inventories listed axes, saws, chisels and other tools that might be equally useful in building houses, as well as furnishings, in the earlier settlements. (According to Forman, smoothing planes were conspicuously absent.) The joiner exercised a kind of vertical monopoly in which he cleared the land, collected the trees, split the wood and built his own shelter and furniture.

Cabinetry, on the other hand, could only thrive in an established and secure community in which sufficient capital was available to invest in dry wood or in green wood that could be set aside for seasoning. Evidence of the first American cabinetmakers does not appear until the late 17th century, with the listing of glue pots and veneering materials in Boston inventories.

The early joiner's workshop might have been closer to the wood yard rather than the parlor, with chunks of log, cleaving and shaving brakes and wood chips in evidence. With dark shadows, marginal heating and dirt floors, they are more likely to have resembled the 17th-century bas-relief shown above than the highly structured workshop dioramas of Diderot and Jacques-André Roubo, which have high ceilings and appear to be uniformly tidy and well lit. (Accompanying the Roubo engraving, shown on p. 8, is a thorough description of an 18th-century French workshop.)

While it may be assumed that colonial woodworkers frequently worked at home or in nearby buildings, the strength of the European guilds was such that, in France, statutes forbade woodworkers from keeping heavy tools at home. Roubo observed that these laws had the benefit of discouraging unqualified individuals from plying their trade. But they trapped enterprising craftsmen in a kind of 18th-century catch-22. Those who kept a bench at home solely to prepare the tools required for their occupation were equally liable to be prosecuted and then denied employment as a result of their lack of tools.

Two of London's most famous high-style, 18th-century cabinet shops have been well documented in recent litera-

An 18th-century workshop

The following text (and bracketed comments) is excerpted from a translation of Jacques-André Roubo's L'Art du Menuisier, *published in Paris between 1769 and 1775. In the original volume, it is accompanied by the engraved illustration shown above, which depicts the interior of an 18th-century joiner's workshop.*

Of all the mechanical arts, joinery [menuiserie] is the one in which there are the greatest number of tools, the perfect knowledge of which is indispensable both for the manner of making them and for that of using them; but before entering into the details I believe that I should speak of the shop or *atelier* where joiners work. This is not to say that every joiner must have premises of a standard type but it is merely intended to indicate the dimensions and equipment which are required.

There are two types of joiners' shops, those which are located in rented houses and those which are especially built with frame construction in the form of lean-to sheds.

The first are suitable for cabinetmakers [ébénistes; Roubo uses this term to apply particularly to those cabinetmakers who produce veneered furniture], all types of furniture makers, and for carriage builders; it is not that the ones of which I have just spoken do not sometimes have very large shops, but what I have said applies in general. For *menuisiers de bâtiments* [those who execute the fine carpentry — such as the paneling — in building construction] ordinary shops are hardly suitable in view of the space which they require; thus the majority of them (at least the most prosperous), and those who undertake large projects, have a shop [boutique] in their own dwellings where they do their small work and a timber-yard in town where they place their stores of timber and in which they have a shed constructed capable of containing a number of benches equivalent to their requirements. There are others who have no shops but who choose premises large enough to lodge them commodiously and to contain their stores of wood and a workshop of reasonable size. This last method is the best because it permits one to keep an eye on everything, which is impossible if one is lodging elsewhere.

When space is limited and one requires a large number of workmen, one makes the shed double, that is, one places benches on both the ground floor and on a second floor. The shop of M. Menageot in Porte Saint Martin is constructed in this manner and is possibly the best built in Paris as much for solidity as for all the facilities which are provided for the workmen.

The shop of a *menuisier de bâtiments* ought to be twelve and one-half feet in height at least, because the timber is ordinarily twelve feet in length and it is essential to be able to dress it and to turn it end over end without being cramped.

Its depth should be from fifteen to eighteen feet in order that there be three feet between the end of the bench and the sill of the shop, nine feet being the length of the bench, and about six feet at the end so that each workman can have a place for his wood and his work.

As for the width, it must be limited by the available space and by the number of benches one wishes to install, which are ordinarily eighteen to twenty inches in width, and that much again is required between each bench; which works out that each worker needs three feet four inches, which dimension determines that of the workshop by simple multiplication.

The window sills of the shop should be of a height equal to that of the benches so that in the case of jobs of extraordinary length one can let the wood pass over the top while working on it, and thus be supported.

There should be several entrances, the number depending upon the width, which will be closed by doors which should open clear to the top in order to facilitate the entry of wood, and which will be glazed with linen so that when they are closed one can enjoy daylight in the interior of the shop.

The space above the sills must also be closed by frames covered with linen which are raised during the day and held to the ceiling by catches which retain them there.

At the top of the front of the shop there should be a pentroof projecting about 18 inches or 2 feet which will serve to keep water out and to prevent damage to the work and tools.

Near the shop there ought to be an enclosure twelve to fifteen feet square in which there is a fireplace with a mantel six or seven feet off the floor and as wide as possible, that is to say, as wide as is convenient, and facing the hearth there is built a little wall or *banquette* of masonry, 15 or 16 inches in height by seven or eight inches thick and four or five feet distant from the bare wall or back side of the fireplace. The top of the *banquette* should be faced by a piece of wood three or four inches thick, which thickness is included in the height of the *banquette*.

This place is called the *étuve* or *sorbonne,* in workmen's language, and serves to melt and to heat glue, to warm and to glue wood, and to dry glue joints during the winter and in damp weather. It is useful also to have a bench in the *sorbonne* in order to be able to pound and to glue joints on it; lacking a bench one uses the top of the *banquette* which is intended for that purpose as well as for retaining the fire and preventing it from spreading.

The *sorbonne* should be quite tight, and yet well lit, so that one can work there as I have described above; it serves also as a place for the workmen to take their meals; that is why one must take the greatest possible care to make it comfortable, especially during the bad season. It must be built very close to the shop and even be contiguous if that is possible so that wood taken there to be heated and glued is not subject to being wetted....

ture. Christopher Gilbert's book, *The Life and Work of Thomas Chippendale,* and Helena Hayward's and Pat Kirkham's *William and John Linnell: Eighteenth Century London Furniture Makers* each include a considerable discussion of the working environment in which the furniture was produced. Their inventories and descriptions of workshop practices help construct a realistic portrait of workshop life. Gilbert's book also contains the floor plan of "Mr. Chippendale's Premises" (shown below).

These are no humble country quarters. Chippendale's compound, which comprised three separate houses, and

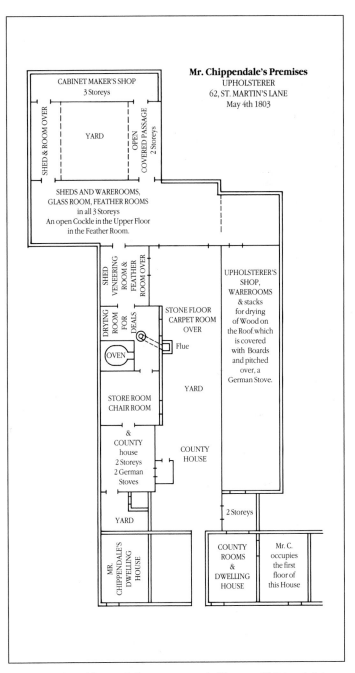

Like many humbler workshop compounds, Thomas Chippendale's home and shop shared adjacent quarters , as shown in this drawing, based on one made in 1803 by the Sun Fire Insurance company.

Linnell's three-story workshop each employed between 40 and 50 workers. (A fire in 1755 gutted the cabinet shop in the rear courtyard of Chippendale's shop, destroying the tool chests of 22 workers.) According to Gilbert, these shops are of "middling size," compared with George Seddon's London shop, which employed 400 men in 1786, although Chippendale and Linnell turned out finer work. Although there is no floor plan of Linnell's shop, the inventory indicates that there were seven "inner benches" in the carving shop and perhaps as many arranged around them, 13 benches in the cabinet shop and three in the joinery shop. There was a separate joiner's tool chest in a large garret and four more benches in the gilding shop. In addition, there were turning tools in both the chair room and the cabinet shop.

Both shops were organized around a central courtyard, in which some timber handling and stock reduction must have taken place. (Chippendale lived in the front of the shop, and Linnell's setup included a sawpit and an office, which do not appear on the Chippendale plan.) They also include several "German stoves," a square furnace used to dry wood and to warm it before gluing or veneering. (Authors Hayward and Kirkham mention that such stoves were used to harden japanning, but they were also widely used for cabinet-shop heating because of their safety.) Not surprisingly, Hayward and Kirkham note that "every available inch of space was utilised in [Linnell's] Berkeley Square workshops," including lofts and staircase landings.

These books help to animate what woodworking historian Frank Hubbard refers to as the "spiritless image" conjured up by most shop inventories. Besides, as Rob Tarule pointed out to me, "you could put together all the 17th-century inventories and maybe get one complete inventory of tools." Tarule, a former Curator of Mechanick Arts at Plimoth Plantation in Plymouth, Massachusetts, now rives and planes green wood in his basement shop. He has spent a lot of time poring over old inventories and has discovered quite a few holes. Many of the most valuable tools were either given away after the woodworker died or were so rough-hewn or worn that they they were overlooked by the appraiser who drew up the list. Large items like built-in workbenches might not be mentioned at all. As intriguing as an inventory may be, it is no more revealing of the actual workspace than is a bill of materials of a piece of furniture.

For "color," we have only a handful of painter's views of early shop interiors, like the one on p. 4, until the late 19th century, when photography got around to recording craftsmen at work (see the photo of an Arts and Crafts machine room on p. 68). Of course, some of the most familiar images come from the great 18th- and 19th-century encyclopedias compiled by Diderot, Roubo and André Felibién and their English counterparts, Joseph Moxon and Peter Nicholson. But workshop illustrations in these books primarily illustrate benches and tools.

One of the limitations of all of these sources is our inability to verify their accuracy. Diderot and Roubo went to great lengths to interview their informants, but we have no way of knowing how closely their illustrations reflect con-

temporary reality. Accurate renditions of specific tools do not guarantee the authenticity of overall room views, which may have been sketched for context more than precise detail. Views may be composites, conveying all the elements the author or illustrator considered important, even though those elements might not have appeared together in an actual workshop. It does seem clear, however, that each author drew heavily upon the work of his predecessors; the English encyclopedists, in particular, borrowed liberally from earlier French publications.

As a document of period craftsmanship, George Sturt's The Wheelwright's Shop is hard to beat. Although the book was first published in 1923, Sturt's shop itself was built in 1795 and then purchased in 1810 by his grandfather. Sturt himself assumed control of the business upon the death of his father in 1884, after only a month of training, and steered the shop into the Machine Age. Fortunately for us, Sturt has described its transformation with the eye of an informed but sensitive participant.

Descriptions of early woodcraft are often tinged with romanticism, and The Wheelwright's Shop is no exception. But Sturt's attachment to the waning craft era is mitigated by his frank portrait of its harsh realities. Working days were long—12 to 14 hours was not uncommon—and conditions were often difficult. There was no machinery in the shop when Sturt took over apart from the great-wheel lathe, which buried the floor of the "lathe house" under a foot of chips. The grindstone stood outside beneath a walnut tree, and in the absence of a bandsaw or circular saw, the felloes were shaped with an ax and adz or were clamped to a bench and sawed with a frame saw. As in the Linnell shop, there was a sawpit on site for preparing lumber.

Within five years, Sturt introduced power to the shop in an effort to save his business. Years later, he noted wistfully that "...there in my old-fashioned shop the new machinery had almost forced its way in—the thin end of the wedge of scientific engineering. And from the first day the machines began running, the use of axes and adzes disappeared from the well-known place, the saws and saw-pit became obsolete. We forgot what chips were like. There, in that one little spot, the ancient provincial life of England was put into a back seat.... 'The Men,' though still my friends, as I fancied, became machine 'hands.'"

The windows of Sturt's shop were merely shuttered openings, bolted at night and wide open to the elements during the day. "With so much chopping to do one could keep fairly warm," he writes, "but I have stood all aglow yet resenting the open windows, feeling my feet cold as ice though covered with chips. To supply some glass shutters for day-time was one of the first changes I made in the shop." Once the machinery had assumed the heavy work, he notes, "men would not and probably could not work at all in such a place; yet it must have sufficed for several generations. My grandfather and my father had put up with it, and so did I until the winter came round again...."

Built on the site of the original 18th-century building, Colonial Williamsburg's reconstruction of the Anthony Hay shop relied greatly on educated guesswork. The Hay shop provided a wide range of woodworking services. Journeyman Mark Hansen, who is in charge of the shop's musical-instrument program, works on a small part for a harpsichord (below). Note the great wheel that drives the lathe and the open fireplace that was the sole source of heat in the original shop.

Historic reconstructions

My most vivid impressions of early workshops come not from documents, but from historic reconstructions of particular 18th- and 19th-century sites. Two of the most intriguing and best-known North American examples are the Anthony Hay shop at Colonial Williamsburg in Virginia and the Dominy workshop at the Henry Francis du Pont Winterthur Museum in Winterthur, Delaware. But because they are, es-

sentially, modern interpretations of historic documents, they sometimes raise more questions than they answer.

Anthony Hay's thriving enterprise employed some of the most prominent cabinetmakers in 18th-century Williamsburg. As the capital of the Virginia Colony, Williamsburg was an important population center, although it was dwarfed in size by Boston, New York and even Charleston, South

Carolina. As is common in small, isolated communities even today, Williamsburg cabinetmakers performed a wide variety of woodworking services. Undertaking, for example, was one of many related activities that became a regular part of shop business. Besides making coffins, craftsmen sometimes became embalmers and even funeral directors. The Bucktrout Funeral Home in modern Williamsburg is the oldest undertaking business in the country and is descended from Benjamin Bucktrout, the second master of the Hay shop.

In his book, *Furniture of Williamsburg and Eastern Virginia, 1710-1790,* Wallace Gusler notes that the "Anthony Hay shop stands unique among colonial cabinetmaking establishments. None other in early Virginia is currently recognized as having produced such quality, and no other workshop in America created such an outstanding group of ceremonial chairs." The modern Hay shop was constructed in the 1960s on the excavated site of the original building, which was erected next to Hay's home around 1756. The original shop operated for about 25 years under three different masters and served a community of about 2,000 people at the time of the American Revolution. (The workshop lapsed into disrepair when its last master, Edmund Dickinson, went off to war. It was turned into a "Publick Armoury" in 1779 and was probably demolished shortly thereafter.)

Archaeology is of limited use when it comes to wood, since the material rots in a few years if exposed to air and moisture. The Hay shop excavation yielded an assortment of hand tools and hardware, but no information about fundamental aspects of shop structure, such as the size or placement of doors and windows or the height of the ceiling, much less the location of benches and tools. In fact, apart from the two-story chimney and the brick foundation, which

was heavily silted with clay, very little of the present shop is based upon archeological evidence. According to Harold Gill, Historian of Historic Trades at Colonial Williamsburg and a member of the Anthony Hay shop reinterpretation committee, much of the Hay reconstruction was "based on a hunch" and "a lot of shots in the dark."

As part of the museum's ongoing reinterpretation program, Colonial Williamsburg's craft shops are periodically updated to reflect changing perceptions about historic "reality." In 1987, for example, musical-instrument making was moved out of the shop extension and integrated with the rest of the shop activity. (There is no evidence of a separate musical-instrument shop, but documents of the period, such as the advertisement shown at left, indicate that at least one of the shop's masters regularly made and repaired instruments.) In its place, a wareroom, which was used mostly for display and sales, was installed in the extension; the space is also used for finishing and upholstery. (This arrangement bears some relationship to the elaborate Chippendale and Linnell shops described earlier.) The extension was added to the original shop in the 1760s and its function is a matter of impassioned debate; the presence of a wareroom suggests an inventory or some speculative work, and there are no documented warerooms associated with Virginia workshops.

During the last major reinterpretation of the shop, Continental or German-style workbenches were replaced with the more historically appropriate English-style benches, which were patterned after the one illustrated in Peter Nicholson's *Mechanical Exercises* (London, 1812). There are seven benches in the shop, including one long bench that separates the visitors' gallery from the work area. Two of them are placed against a wall, but the others stand out in the room, with the face vise situated near the wall and windows. According to Mack Headley, master of the modern shop, "we've moved our benches everywhere you could think of, and this is the best setup." He also noted that, using the current layout, the tail vise on the German benches was too far from the windows for adequate light to reach the work.

WILLIAMSBURG, Jan. 6, 1767.

THE Gentlemen who have befpoke WORK of the fubfcriber may depend upon having it made in the beft manner by Mr. BENJAMIN BUCKTROUT, to whom he has given up his bufinefs.————I return the Gentlemen who have favoured me with their cuftom many thanks, and am

Their moft humble fervant,
ANTHONY HAY.

WILLIAMSBURG, Jan. 6, 1767.

MR. ANTHONY HAY having lately removed to the RAWLEIGH tavern, the fubfcriber has taken his fhop, where the bufinefs will be carried on in all its branches. He hopes that thofe Gentlemen who were Mr. Hay's cuftomers will favour him with their orders, which fhall be executed in the beft and moft expeditious manner He likewife makes all forts of *Chinefe* and *Gothick* PALING for gardens and fummer houfes.

N. B. SPINETS and HARPSICORDS made and repaired.   2   BENJAMIN BUCKTROUT.

Period documents often fill in our knowledge where physical evidence is lacking. This notice indicates that musical instruments were made in the Hay shop.

The Dominy shop was built at about the same time as the original Hay shop in the isolated farming community of East Hampton, New York, near the eastern tip of Long Island. The preserved remains of the shop represent what Charles Hummel called an "accident of survival." In his account of this remarkable collection, With Hammer in Hand, Hummel notes that the shop was used well into the 20th century by more than six generations of Dominy family woodworkers. The surviving record of the shop is housed at the Winterthur Museum in Delaware and includes almost 200 manuscript items and more than 1,000 tools. Hummel's book and the Winterthur installation focus on the three generations of Dominys that occupied the shop during the period represented by the surviving account books, roughly 1760 to 1840. In his preface to the book, Hummel explains that the "objects that [the Dominys] have preserved provide flesh for the dry bones of history by adding dimension to the written word."

Generations of Dominy craftsmen worked in the shop now reconstructed at the Winterthur Museum (at left). The contents of the shop were salvaged in the 1940s before the demolition of the original home and workshop in East Hampton, Long Island (above). The floor plan below shows details of the woodworking and clock shops.

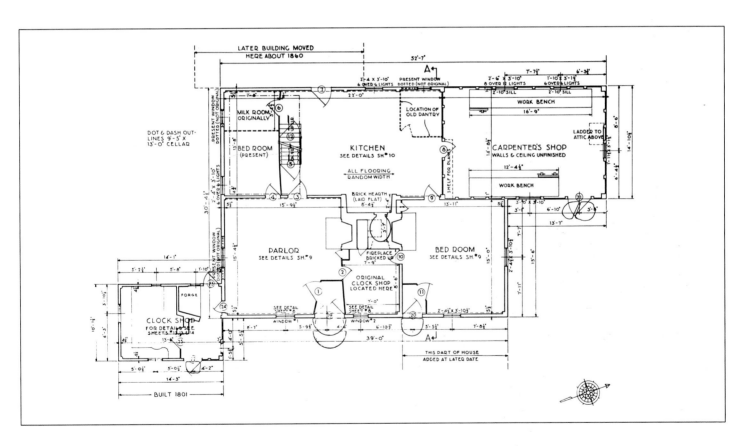

Like the cabinetmakers of Williamsburg, the Dominys were versatile craftsmen who specialized in clockmaking and watchmaking, and also did all sorts of woodworking, construction and repair. The shed-roofed shop was attached to the northwest corner of their home on East Hampton's Main Street. (The building shown in the top right photo was destroyed in 1946 after the premises were surveyed and the contents of the shop were removed.) The core of the house was built in 1715; the front bedroom may have been added at the same time as the shop, around 1745. The clock shop and forge were moved to their own self-contained quarters at the south end of the building about 50 years later.

Rural craftsmen though they were, many of the Dominys' tools were English, probably purchased from New York dealers and delivered to East Hampton by boat. They bear the marks of London, Sheffield and Warrington toolmakers, and many have been hafted with handles of hickory, cherry, beech and other familiar North American species. It is interesting to note the presence, too, of Australian rosewood, lignum vitae and at least two planes made of Ceylonese satinwood. Other tools in the collection were made by local blacksmiths, perhaps in trade, as the Dominys often accepted tools and wood in payment for services rendered.

The Winterthur reconstruction does not incorporate any walls, windows or flooring from the original structure, but most of the tools and equipment are from the shop, including benches, vises and some shelving. Hummel told me that "where shelves existed there was no problem," but the placement of patterns and augers and their relationship to the benches were deduced from contemporary views in Roubo and Diderot. The ceiling height (7 ft. 6 in. to the underside of the log joists) was derived from the original building. A lot of other information came from descendants who grew up in the house, some of whom recalled playing in a loft full of lumber and unfinished furniture parts.

The Dominy and Hay shops functioned with a similar level of technology, but the two installations exhibit some striking differences, which may leave some visitors wondering which version of history to believe. The most obvious difference is their atmosphere. The cheery hearth, large windows and whitewashed wainscoting inside the Hay shop create a warm, inviting ambience and an enticing impression of 18th-century craft life. It would be comfortable to work—or even live—in such a place. By contrast, with dingy, exposed-frame walls, cramped quarters and small windows, the Dominy workshop is decidedly more spartan.

If the Hay shop were rebuilt today, I was assured that it would be done quite differently. It would likely have open-frame, unpaneled walls, and would undoubtedly be much darker. "We're probably a little dressier here than we should be," Mack Headley admitted, "but you wonder what would be the proper setting" for some of the finer work that goes on in the shop. "We are committed to experiencing the same thing," he added, "but it's not impossible that the shop was as nice as this."

Like most buildings of the period, neither shop had any source of power. All work was conducted by hand. (The archaeologists who excavated the Hay shop had hoped to find signs of a water-driven lathe, which would explain why the building was located over a stream, but no such evidence was unearthed.) Until the 19th century, apprentices (or slaves) took the place of machinery in many woodworking shops. They often slept in the shop and were fed, clothed and educated by the master. In exchange, they performed most of the rough, repetitive operations that would nowadays be done with machinery.

In the absence of power, heat and light are of paramount concern. But, as Williamsburg's Harold Gill frankly admitted, "what we know [about such issues] is dwarfed by what we don't know." Cabinetmakers in the Hay shop could have used the fireplace to warm glue and materials, and Dutch ovens appear in some 18th-century shop inventories, but there was no stove in the Dominy shop until the 1840s or 1850s. Apart from the obvious discomfort of winter work in an unheated Long Island shop, how did the Dominys glue and finish their work? Did they keep the door open to the kitchen all winter, or did they haul their furniture into the house?

When I asked Rob Tarule about this, he pointed out that "you can work at 45°F, but you can't glue." For years, Tarule has practiced the techniques of the 17th-century joiner, making board chests and other furnishings with draw-bored mortise-and-tenon joints. The climate in his unheated basement shop simulates that of a cave, or of a 17th-century workshop. It remains fairly constant all year, and his material stabilizes at about 16 percent moisture content. In cold weather, Tarule warms up by pounding nails on a portable farrier's forge for a few minutes. He returns to woodworking for a while and then makes nails again.

Tarule's experience suggests that the Dominys relied more heavily upon mechanical joinery than glue. (They certainly used a good deal of green wood in their turning.) It is also probable that, as Charles Hummel suggested, "their tasks were a lot more structured than we may think." By building some of their furniture from component parts, the Dominys could comfortably perform the aerobic riving in winter and save the assembly and finishing for spring. And, like most rural woodworkers who serviced an agrarian society, they must have engaged in a certain amount of seasonal activity.

Light may be even more important than heat, since we are helpless to work without it. But there is no evidence of lamps, candles or any other lighting devices in either workshop. This is not a serious problem in the present-day Hay shop, where there are large windows and white walls to reflect the daylight. It's not quite like having overhead fluorescents, but as Mack Headley explained, "lighting influences the design." The irregular light and shadows in the shop are well suited to sculpting things that have to look good when lit by a window or candle in a house. "You do the best with what you have," he added.

In the Dominy shop, even with the benches positioned beneath the windows, the dark colors of the interior and the northern exposure must have made it hard to see. But 18th-century woodworkers were used to long days and dim light. The family spent six days a week in the shop and worked from sunrise to sundown. In A. Viires' *Woodworking in Estonia,* there is a description of using firebrands to illuminate the work on dark winter days. This sounds dangerous but may not be too far from the reality of 17th- and 18th-century America.

"The Dominy material is good," Hummel told me, "but it isn't perfect." There are no inventories—only lists of tools bought or bartered—and questions remain about the way the shop was used. Even if everything were known about the

Hay and Dominy shops, it would still be presumptuous to make broad generalizations about thousands of unknown shops based on only two examples.

Still, it's hard not to imagine that somewhere in the countryside another workshop might provide some fresh answers. Indeed, I've heard about one or two recently discovered 19th-century sites, but none are as old or as well documented as the Dominy workshop. "I really do hope that there is something better," Hummel told me. Until an intact, more definitive example is revealed, or a time machine is perfected, we will have to wrestle with these questions on our own.

The living tradition

If we can't return to the 18th or 19th century, the next best thing is finding someone who hasn't left. In my travels, I occasionally heard about some dinosaur of a line-shaft shop that was recently dismantled. Visions of slapping leather belts and well-oiled gears haunt many a woodworker's dreams, but the sad truth is that few of these shops or the old-timers who ran them are still around.

The John Grass shop (shown in the photos below) is one of the survivors. Its motto: "Turning continuously since 1863." The three-story, semidetached brick workshop is located on a narrow street in downtown Philadelphia, where it is surrounded by commercial restaurant-supply outlets. When I visited the shop last winter, there were only two full-time employees (in addition to the current owner, Louis Bower), who seemed so immersed in their work they scarcely noted my presence. The shop is choked with material and blanketed with the dust of the ages, although Bower assured me that the stock "turns over pretty well. It doesn't look like it," he added, "but it does—it has to."

Bower's grandfather was John Grass's partner, and the shop has been in the family for three generations. Bower has worked there more than 20 years, and his veteran employee, John Dailey, has been there for almost 35 years, turning everything from stair balusters and tool handles to countless custom jobs. "I don't know that it's changed all that much," Bower said, but compared with the 10 or 12 employees who once ran the shop, it's a skeleton crew. Bower recalled a happier time when the shop had "a man on every lathe" cranking out ships' rollers and turned flagpoles.

The John Grass wood-turning shop has hardly changed in over a century. Wide leather belts and line shafts carry power to machines engulfed by floor-to-ceiling piles of turning blanks and finished parts.

There is a jointer, a planer, a table saw and three lathes on the main floor, with three more lathes upstairs. On the first floor, one lathe bed runs along the wall of the shop and could turn stock its entire length, if the flotsam were shoveled off. Most of the machinery is original and is driven by flat leather belts run off an overhead line shaft. The only attention the system requires is periodic oil for the shaft bearings, grease for the motors and an occasional new belt. (Leather belts and alligator fasteners can still be had, but they're getting expensive and hard to find.) Power is sup-

plied by a two-phase, 7-hp electric motor bolted to the underside of the main floor. (Another 5-hp motor runs the table saw and planer on the second floor.) The size of a large turkey, the motor cranks the machinery with a quiet, slapping rhythm. Bower told me that it costs less than $100 per month to operate, adding "it's been down there for as long as I've been around."

Falling water has powered mills and machinery for several thousand years. Until the Civil War, when it was eclipsed by

José Abrante turns at a benchtop lathe in the John Grass shop (at left). The horizontal bar above his head engages the belt drive. Samples on the office wall (below) hint at the variety of more than a century of Philadelphia turning.

Ben Thresher and his line-shaft mill are among the last of their kind. Once driven by water, Thresher's machinery is now run by a tractor and power take-off.

steam, water was the principal source of stationary power in America, spawning tens of thousands of small mills all over the Northeast. Several Shaker communities piped water great distances underground to run their machines.

For a brief while at the end of the last century, water and steam lived side by side. But the eventual decline of water as a primary source of local power parallels a similar transition between craft and manufacturing. (The recent revival of both craft and small hydro projects may be more than coincidental.) In today's "post-industrial" society, water power is a comforting reminder of an age in which craft was more than a luxury.

Collapsed mills and breached dams flank the rivers of New England, but on a winding road in northern Vermont, one old woodshop clings stubbornly to its bank. I first saw "Ben's Mill" in a film of the same name, which was produced in the early 1980s. When I visited the mill (shown above) in East Barnet, Vermont, last spring, I drove right past it, never thinking it might house a working shop. With its broken windows and overgrown yard, the haggard structure looked even more disreputable than it did in the film. Clinging to the clapboards beneath the eaves were traces of rust-colored paint that the mill's owner, Ben Thresher, figures are original. "Modern latex wouldn't last that long," he says, and he's sure he never painted it.

The mill has become a Vermont institution and Thresher is a local legend, doling out sturdy country woodwork and droll humor in equal measure. For half a century, he has served the seasonal needs of his farming neighbors—building cordwood sleighs for the winter, wooden cattle tubs in the spring and tool handles all year. The fall before my visit, Thresher pressed 6,000 gallons of cider. It's a no-frills operation, and Thresher would certainly be more at home in the Dominy shop than in many modern furniture studios I visited.

In the film, Thresher notes, "I was just a johnny-come-lately. The real history of it came way before me." Ben's Mill is situated about 2½ miles up Stevens Brook from the Connecticut River, New England's major inland artery. At one time, there were at least four mills in Barnet—including a gristmill, a sash and blind factory and a sawmill on Thresher's side of the village—and three more in West Barnet (two more gristmills and a woodshop like Thresher's).

Ben's Mill has been running since 1848 on the site of an earlier sawmill, and it is the only survivor. The mill hasn't run off water since 1982, when a flood swept away one end of the dam and part of the penstock. Thresher installed a concrete foundation the following year to keep the mill from sliding into its own stream. He calls it his "monument," and says, "it wouldn't be there now if it hadn't been for me. I'm just that stubborn." Although electricity was installed on Thresher's road in 1903, he uses it to power only three bare bulbs, an electric drill and a small motor. In the early days, he recalls, the lights in the shop dimmed when the farmers down the road began their evening milking.

The machinery is now powered by a small tractor, which is belted to the mill's main line shaft. Apart from having to oil the wooden bearings (which used to be lubricated with water) and not having to drain and clean the penstock, operation and maintenance of the mill is about the same as it

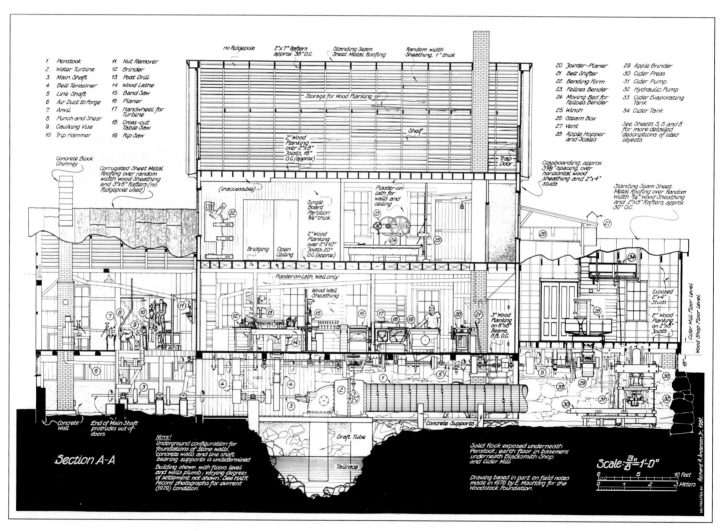

These meticulous drawings of Ben's Mill (shown above and on the following pages) are the product of a joint undertaking, begun in 1976 with an engineering survey conducted by Earl MacHarg and Arthur Nadeau under the auspices of the Vermont Folklife Research Project of the Woodstock Foundation. Work was completed in 1979 by a team of architects, a photographer and a historian, employed by the Historic American Engineering Record. According to Ben Thresher, no effort was spared to make the drawings as accurate as possible. When he pointed out that a 1¹⁵⁄₁₆-in. dia. shaft had been drawn at 2 in., they immediately corrected the error and apologized profusely, saying, 'You see any other mistakes, you let us know.'

was when it was water driven. "Of course it's different work," Thresher says. "It comes out about the same...except you have to buy gasoline."

In the beginning, Thresher put in 16-hour days at the mill, adding, "Maybe I'd be able to do more now if I hadn't done so much then." He relates one particularly chilling episode about an ice floe that jammed the gates open. Thresher waded into the waist-deep water and chopped the ice out with an ax until he could pound the gates shut with a sledge. The next morning, it was -27°F but the dam was full and the mill was running. "I wouldn't do that now," he says.

Nowadays, Thresher doesn't work much in the mill in the winter — it's dark and the walls are uninsulated. But sometime around April (or on an occasional warm winter day), he shuffles down the hill from his house across the road, rolls back the front door and fires up the tractor. For the last ten years, Thresher has worked alone. "I'm used to it," he says. "No arguments that way." On a more serious note, he adds, "I do so many different things that you pretty well lose your time to do [an employee's] work." Shrugging at the trip-hammer in the corner of the blacksmith shop, "That's the best man I ever had," he says. "It won't talk back."

Over the years, the river has proved company enough. The water may be high or low, frozen or flooding, but it's never the same. When the mill was running, water flowed through a gate at one end of the wooden dam and into the penstock. Ben built the penstock in 1949 out of hemlock and tamarack, tough softwoods that last about as long as oak. In its construction, the penstock resembles a horizontal wooden silo, with metal splines in the butt-jointed ends of the boards to keep it from leaking. As the wood swells, the joints seal "just the same as a tub," Ben explains, "and as well."

At the end of the penstock is a horizontal turbine, built in 1911, the year before Thresher was born. The flow of wa-

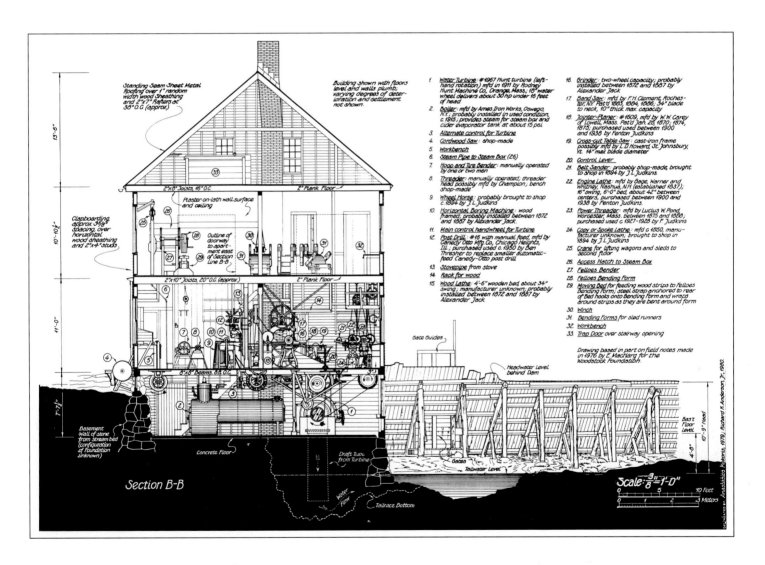

For most of the last 50 years, Ben Thresher has built farming implements and other necessities of wood for his Vermont neighbors with belt-driven, water-powered machines.

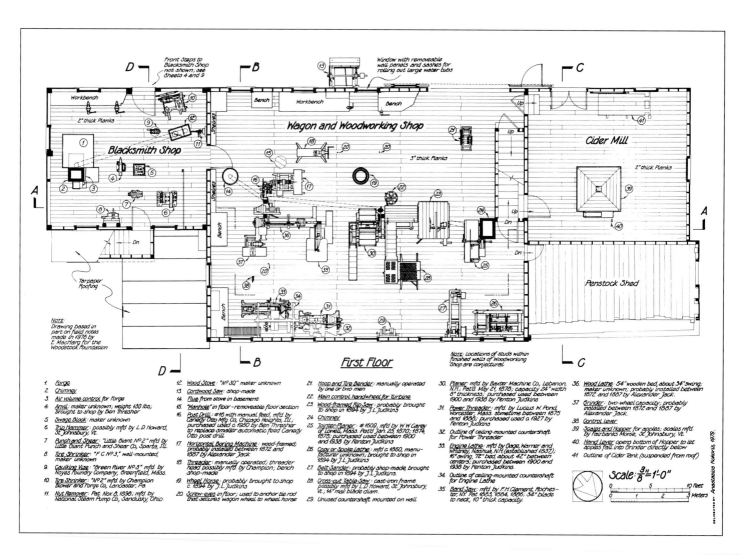

First Floor

1. *Forge*
2. *Chimney*
3. *Air volume control for forge*
4. *Anvil: maker unknown, weight 430 lbs, brought to shop by Ben Thresher*
5. *Swage Block: maker unknown*
6. *Trip Hammer: possibly mfd by L.D. Howard, St. Johnsbury, Vt.*
7. *Punch and Shear: "Little Giant Nº 2" mfd by Little Giant Punch and Shear Co, Sparta, Ill.*
8. *Tire Shrinker: "F C Nº 3," wall-mounted, maker unknown*
9. *Caulking Vise: "Green River Nº 3" mfd by Noyes Foundry Company, Greenfield, Mass.*
10. *Tire Shrinker: "Nº 2" mfd by Champion Blower and Forge Co, Lancaster, Pa.*
11. *Nut Remover: Pat. Nov 8, 1898; mfd by National Steam Pump Co, Sandusky, Ohio.*
12. *Wood Stove: "Nº 30" maker unknown*
13. *Cordwood Saw: shop-made*
14. *Flue from stove in basement*
15. *"Manhole" in floor - removeable floor section*
16. *Post Drill: #16 with manual feed, mfd by Canedy Otto Mfg Co, Chicago Heights, Ill., purchased used c. 1950 by Ben Thresher to replace smaller automatic feed Canedy Otto post drill.*
17. *Horizontal Boring Machine: wood-framed; probably installed between 1872 and 1887 by Alexander Jack.*
18. *Threader: manually operated; threader head possibly mfd by Champion; bench shop-made.*
19. *Wheel Horse: probably brought to shop in 1894 by J.L Judkins.*
20. *Screw-eyes in floor; used to anchor tie rod that secures wagon wheel to wheel horse.*
21. *Hoop and Tire Bender: manually operated by one or two men*
22. *Main control handwheel for turbine*
23. *Chimney*
24. *Wood-framed Rip Saw: probably brought to shop in 1894 by J.L Judkins.*
25. *Jointer-Planer: #1609, mfd by W W Carey of Lowell, Mass. Pat'd Jan 25, 1870, 1874, 1876; purchased used between 1900 and 1938 by Fenton Judkins.*
26. *Copy or Spoke Lathe: mfd c.1880, manufacturer unknown, brought to shop in 1894 by J.L Judkins.*
27. *Belt Sander: probably shop-made, brought to shop in 1894 by J.L Judkins.*
28. *Cross-cut Table Saw: cast-iron frame possibly mfd by L.D Howard, St. Johnsbury, Vt.; 14" max blade diam.*
29. *Unused countershaft mounted on wall*
30. *Planer: mfd by Baxter Machine Co, Lebanon, N.H., Pat'd May 21, 1878; capacity 24" width 8" thickness; purchased used between 1900 and 1938 by Fenton Judkins*
31. *Power Threader: mfd by Lucius W. Pond, Worcester, Mass. sometime between 1875 and 1888; purchased used a 1927 by Fenton Judkins*
32. *Outline of ceiling-mounted countershaft for Power Threader*
33. *Engine Lathe: mfd by Gage, Warner and Whitney, Nashua, N.H (established 1837), 16" swing, 72" bed, about 42" between centers; purchased between 1900 and 1938 by Fenton Judkins.*
34. *Outline of ceiling-mounted countershaft for Engine Lathe*
35. *Band Saw: mfd by F.H Clement, Rochester, N.Y. Pat 1863, 1884, 1886; 34" blade to neck, 10" thick capacity.*
36. *Wood Lathe: 54"wooden bed, about 34"swing; maker unknown, probably installed between 1872 and 1887 by Alexander Jack.*
37. *Grinder: two-wheel capacity; probably installed between 1872 and 1887 by Alexander Jack.*
38. *Control Lever*
39. *Scales and Hopper for apples; scales mfd by Fairbanks Morse, St. Johnsbury, Vt.*
40. *Hand Lever opens bottom of Hopper to let apples fall into grinder directly below*
41. *Outline of Cider Tank (suspended from roof)*

Scale: $\frac{3}{8}$" = 1'-0"

ter is controlled by a cast-iron "cheesecake" gate inside the turbine or by boards shoved in front of the penstock. Next to the penstock in the basement is an old boiler, which Thresher uses to fire a steambox to bend wagon wheels and sled runners or to evaporate cider jelly.

The tailwater beneath the turbine is 16 ft. below the top of the mill pond, a drop (or "head") that generated 29½ hp, or enough to run all the shop machinery at once. (According to Thresher, the 2-ft. long draft tube beneath the turbine added almost as much power as the drop from the pond.) "You could run a 1½-in. dia. bit in the drill press and slow it right down," Thresher explains, "and you've still got the torque."

Thresher pulls the wheel on his bandsaw to jump start it in motion and explains that the machinery "is pretty much like it was 100 years ago." In the last 40 years, he has purchased only two machines—a drill press and a lathe—and the drill press was older than the one it replaced. A horizontal boring machine, more than 100 years old, was moved into the shop from another mill. The elegant cast wheel on the Carey jointer is stenciled "Lowell Mass. 1870." He has two table saws: a sliding saw for crosscutting and a hinged saw for ripping. (The depth of cut is controlled by lifting one end of the hinged top.) "Boy, if I had the lumber that went across that table it'd be quite a pile," Thresher says.

Most of the machinery is situated in the middle of the first-floor workspace, and Ben works across the width of the shop. That way, the material is less likely to interfere with other machines, and he can open a window or the large sliding door to accommodate long stock. There's hardly a tool guard in the building. "OSHA would shut me right down," Thresher says, "only I don't hire anybody." Over the years, the machines have caught him only once, when he snagged his sleeve in the table saw and lost the first digit of one thumb.

What OSHA never got around to doing, time is taking care of. Between spring floods and winter frosts, upkeep on the dam and penstock is enough to make anyone think twice about generating their own power. (Thresher has rebuilt the dam four times.) Still, water is more efficient than just about any other source of power—including electricity, gasoline or wind. It's 90 percent efficient, according to Thresher, and he hated to see it go. Sometimes he still talks as though it hadn't. As I left, he told me, "If it keeps raining, we'll have a good year."

Locating the Workshop

An old mill with ground and upper stories lends itself to handicraft workshops of this nature. Every window looks out onto a lovely common garden, every bench has a posy on it. Nothing could be more delightful than doing rationally good work in such surroundings. —Charles Rowley, describing C. R. Ashbee's Guild of Handicraft in *A Workshop Paradise*

Chapter 2

he first task in putting together any workshop is deciding where to put it. In my travels, I found shops in everything from closets to large buildings in industrial parks. There is no perfect location—one person's dream is another's nightmare. Like choosing a house, your decision regarding a workshop location should be based not on emotion, but on a rational evaluation of your own priorities.

Accessibility and cost are two of the most important issues affecting workshop location. Cost is self-explanatory; as we look at different locations I'll comment on ways to think about spending money and ways to keep expenses down. Access has many facets. There's access to home and family, access to space and services (electricity, water and sewer),

access to supplies and, if you're a professional, access to the market (clients and galleries).

Don't neglect the reciprocal of access—distance. A living-room workshop, for example, provides maximum access to home and family but a minimum of space and distance. Any sawdust you make will wind up in the carpet, your bed and your food. Unless you live alone, your industry will try the most understanding family and neighbors. Marriages have foundered on less and, although I've seen many substantial workshops in residential neighborhoods, you can't expect to blast sawdust onto your neighbor's car or fire up your router after midnight with impunity.

Many woodworkers I spoke to appreciate some distance between the home and workshop. Amateurs and professionals alike feel that the physical process of "going to work" attaches a seriousness of purpose to workshop activities. For reasons of psychology as much as dust control, several woodworkers I visited built outside entrances to their basement shops instead of the traditional interior stairway. If you do a lot of work (and hope to sell it), an old factory or warehouse or a new building in an industrial park across town may provide better access to services, space, suppliers and the market, as well as the necessary psychological distance. Your immediate neighbors may make even more noise and dust than you. But it's tough to keep an eye on your kids from the other side of town. And the more effort it takes to get to the shop, the less likely you are to go, especially for the occasional hour or two of quality puttering that you manage to carve out of your evenings or weekends.

Consider Tage Frid's experience. For 25 years, Frid's shop was located in a small barn only 500 ft. behind his rural Rhode Island home. When the kids were small, he suffered through regular interruptions of his woodworking business and was often tempted to quit work early and join his family's activities. When the kids had grown, Tage sold the house and began renting shop space in a converted textile mill five miles from his new home. Now he begrudges the ten-minute commute he must make, in all kinds of weather, just to do a 20-minute glue job or to wipe another coat of oil on a piece of furniture.

Naturally, your priorities will reflect whether you work in the shop primarily for recreation or to make a living, and whether you work alone or with others. Likewise, your ability to justify (and write off) expenses will be determined by the role of the shop in your life, almost as much as by the amount of money you have in the bank. Consider carefully your options and the trade-offs between them. The decisions you make regarding location will affect your future happiness in the workshop more than any other. Remember also that as your needs and interests grow and change, so will your shop. If you have planned wisely and have access to sufficient resources, your current shop may be able to accommodate many, if not all, of these changes. But if you, like most of us, are limited by vision and finances, you will work your way through several generations of workshops.

The basement workshop

The basement is one of the most common workshop locations. Outside of the southern United States, most houses in North America have one. For many woodworkers, the basement is a natural first workshop. It may require some juggling of household functions and appliances, such as laundry, furnace and freezer space, but most basements can be converted to a workshop with a minimum of expense. The structure is more or less complete, and all of the major services—electricity, water, sewer and telephone—are close at hand. What's more, if you pay attention to insulation and dust collection, you may be able to operate your machinery for years in the basement without irritating your neighbors or your family.

While basement shops offer the obvious advantages of easy access to home and family, they also have a few intrinsic drawbacks. Most of these are structural. Basement walls are generally either poured concrete or concrete block and thus are more difficult to partition or extend than are wood-frame walls above grade. Being wholly or partly underground severely restricts the available natural light and further inhibits additions. And, for aesthetic and practical reasons, you may not like concrete walls in your workshop. It's easier to hang tools and shelves on a wall with wood paneling or drywall, and many foundation walls—particularly in older homes or poorly made new ones—either leak or sweat moisture. To address these problems, many people sheathe their basement walls with 1 in. or 2 in. of foam insulation and heavy plastic. (Sometimes the walls are strapped with 2x4 studs and infilled with fiberglass batts.) This is then covered with wood, drywall or some type of paneling. The additional insulation and paneling also help absorb noise.

Because of the scarcity of windows and doors in most foundation walls, basement shops may be dark and poorly ventilated, with limited access and egress—try moving a 24-in. thickness planer or a chest of drawers through a storm-cellar entrance. What's more, the low ceilings in most basements and the columns that are often used to support the first floor of the house can seriously restrict the movement of materials and the placement of machinery around the shop.

Still, for many woodworkers, a basement shop is an attractive, economical solution. Mac Campbell's is a good example. Campbell (shown in the photos on the facing page) works comfortably and operates a successful furniture-making business in the 1,200-sq. ft. basement of his home in rural New Brunswick. A basement is often the first stop on the road to an above-ground workshop, but Campbell's workspace has moved in the opposite direction. In 1976, when Campbell bought 18 acres of overgrown farmland, the first thing he did was build an above-ground shop in a yard ringed by wild apple trees and encroaching alders. A log home was to follow.

As time passed, however, the dream of a log home gave way to a full, walk-out basement anchored to the hillside with half a ton of steel, a concrete slab and 70 yards of fill. Campbell skidded the shop building on top and set up his tools downstairs while the family moved in above. Because of the switch, the living areas have some peculiarities. The kitchen, which was intended to be the primary work area of the shop, is huge, and its electrical outlets are 3 ft. off the floor. The bedrooms, on the other hand, which were planned for storage and finishing, are small.

The open, rectangular plan of the basement was intended to allow flexibility. Few rural furniture makers can afford to specialize, and Campbell makes everything from custom furniture and antique reproductions to small boxes and cabinets. A 4-ft. wide door allows ample room to move machinery and large projects in and out of the shop.

A concrete floor is one of the oft-cited disadvantages of the basement (or garage) workshop. While this sentiment is by no means universal, it cannot be ignored. A concrete floor

Mac Campbell's basement shop accommodates a full complement of power tools, wood storage and a spray room. A 4-ft. wide door opens onto the backyard and makes movement of machinery and projects easier than for most basement shops.

is hard on the feet and back, and it can be damp and cold unless it is properly drained, insulated and protected with a moisture barrier. Campbell is one of several woodworkers I met who prefer working on concrete; it supports his heavy, industrial machines and is the easiest shop floor to clean. To insulate his feet, Campbell wears good work shoes; to insulate the floor and protect it from moisture, he laid 1 in. of Styrofoam under the slab. If he had it to do over, Campbell told me, he would use 2 in. of foam and cover it with 6-mil plastic to keep the foam from breaking up and creating pockets in the concrete during the pour.

A barrel stove that Campbell made from a kit provides heat for the shop (and some for the house above), fueled by split firewood and a plentiful supply of shop scraps. Three of the four concrete walls are below grade, which provides natural air conditioning in summer and warmth in winter. In ad-

dition, Campbell has strapped, insulated and hung drywall on the walls. With a wood-fired cookstove in the kitchen and secondary electric baseboard heat throughout the building, the total monthly power bill rarely cracks $100. "All of these factors really do work," he says.

Being underground may help conserve energy, but it doesn't leave many options for lighting. Campbell's shop has only four small windows (two of those are in the finishing room), and I couldn't help feeling a trifle molelike. Even the windows he has can be a pain. During the summer, Campbell struggles with direct sunlight from a window behind his bench. Working back and forth across a harsh shadow line is a strain on the eyes, and he sometimes covers the window with newspaper. Most of the light in the shop is provided by overhead fluorescent fixtures and a battery of clip-on and articulated incandescent lamps.

Hoisting the glue-up table

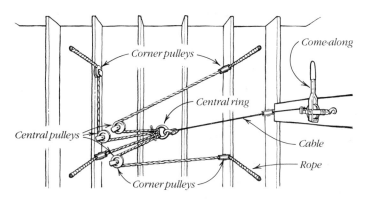

Note: Locate the central pulleys near one corner, so that all four ropes approach the ring from the same direction. A rope at each corner of the glue-up table runs through the pulleys to a central ring connected to the come-along cable. All pulleys are wired to the ceiling joists.

Campbell makes use of ceiling as well as floor space in his basement shop. His glue-up table is raised and lowered with a come-along and stowed against the ceiling. Its legs are secured by wooden battens.

To minimize noise and dust migration upstairs, Campbell omitted the inside stairway that usually joins the basement and the living quarters. A plank subfloor of 2x6 and 2x8 lumber, 2 in. of Styrofoam and ⅝-in. particleboard covered with linoleum or carpeting effectively bar dust and muffle noise from the shop below. (This may seem like overkill, but remember that the original shop stood on piers aboveground, and Campbell made the floor sandwich hefty to keep the cold out.)

In the shop, there is 8 ft. of clearance to the bottom of the 2x12 floor joists, and Campbell left the joists open so he could use the space between them for dust-collection pipes and storage of miscellaneous shop hardware. A 6-in. by 12-in. built-up wooden beam runs the length of the shop and carries most of the jigs and sawblades. "After 13 years," Campbell notes, "every available nook and cranny has got something in it."

Campbell also has made several ingenious ceiling-mounted fixtures to ease crowding on the floor. Systems of ropes and pulleys suspend a steambox and the glue-up table, shown in the photos and drawing at left. The legs of the glue-up table fold inside the frame, and the whole rig is raised and lowered with a come-along attached to a nearby post. "Occasionally you get glue in your hair," he admits, but the ceiling is a convenient, out-of-the-way place to leave glued-up panels to dry. In the winter, it's 20° warmer than the floor of the shop.

Space, or the lack of it, can be a major drawback to basement shops. Enlarging a basement can involve costly excavation and require poking big holes in thick concrete. Despite his ingenuity, space has become a problem for Campbell. "I'm out of floor space and ceiling space in the shop," he says, adding that having the door on the downhill side of the house leaves a lot to be desired when loading and unloading. He considered building a whole new shop—still mainly underground, but with a second floor for a larger, dust-free finishing area. "But I'd have to win a lottery," he concedes, "and I don't buy tickets." In the end, he figures, "The ultimate yardstick is what you get back for what you put out. I'd rather go south for two weeks every winter for the next ten years."

Before climbing out of the cellar, it's worth considering two other steps you can take to enhance the sense of space and make your basement shop—or any shop, for that matter—a brighter and more cheerful place to work. They are so simple that they are often overlooked. First, a brightly painted shop will appear larger, cleaner and more inviting than one with a dark, unpainted, bomb-shelter decor. You can also take a tip from Dwight Barker, a mechanical designer and woodworker in Ambler, Pennsylvania, who has hung two large mirrors on opposite walls of his shop to enlarge the workspace artificially.

The garage workshop

The garage is probably the second most popular workshop location. It offers many of the same benefits of the basement shop without some of the drawbacks. In fact, many garage workshops I visited have been used to work wood for so long that few vestiges remain of their original purpose.

Because it is often attached to or located near the house, the garage retains nearly as much access to family and home as the basement, but with enough physical separation to minimize the intrusion of dust and noise in the living area. Of course, when you move above ground, you also become closer and more obvious to neighbors, who won't be any more receptive than your family to dust, noise and fumes, and may be much less understanding.

Access for materials and equipment in a garage shop is hard to beat. A large door will enable you to drive your plywood and machinery right into the shop and cart your projects out the same way. Since most garages are located above ground on a concrete slab and are built of lumber, they present no real obstacles to insulation or partitioning, and additions are easily added. (Mark Duginske's workshop on pp. 159-160 is an excellent example of a garage that has been entirely overhauled and transformed into a comfortable workshop.) If there aren't enough windows, they can be installed in the walls and roof without major structural disruption. The increased exposure of walls and ceiling in the garage means that you'll spend more money either insulating or heating the shop (or both) than you would in a comparable basement workspace. And the heat you pump into the shop won't take the chill off the house.

There are one or two other ways in which the garage shop may be more restrictive than the basement shop. In most houses, electrical services run directly into the base-

ment, so additional wiring may be required to hook up the garage. Further, few garages are equipped with running water or sewer pipes. Installing them can be expensive; in cold climates at least, it may require substantial excavation. Sure, you can get by without water in the workshop, but not without some inconvenience.

Sooner or later, every garage-shop owner has to decide what to do about the car or cars the structure was supposed to shelter. Some, like Maurice Gordon (whose shop is discussed on p. 59) organize things so shop and vehicles can coexist. Others simply banish the car and enjoy the benefits of a full-time shop.

A room of one's own

Craft is a private enterprise for many woodworkers. After spending their days in high-pressure, public occupations, they approach the workshop as a kind of retreat. As James Whetstone (a part-time woodworker in New Cumberland, Pennsylvania) wrote me, the woodworker's shop "can be a refuge, a place to make his statement, a place where he can actually improve his world."

For many people, especially those on a tight budget or with limited space, a room—or even a closet—at home provides just such a haven for woodworking. What these tiny shops lack in elbow room or privacy, they make up in access. But this arrangement comes at a price. It almost always requires that tools and materials be balanced against other personal priorities. I know one exceptional fellow who built a canoe in his living room; but more often, projects are kept small lest they upset the family equanimity. In fact, although the central location may facilitate access to tools and projects, the tedious unpacking and packing of tools and the

Simon Watts's pantry is a small shop with a large view of the San Francisco waterfront. The large windows, white walls and high ceiling make the shop's 45 sq. ft. feel much larger. Watts opens the window to work on long stock. Cans nailed to the wall (shown above) provide storage for hardware.

Assembling this traveling tool kit (which contains all he needs to conduct a boatbuilding workshop) helped Watts learn how to pare his woodworking needs to essentials.

constant clean up of unfinished projects often discourages work in the living room. (In my travels I've seen several living-room workbenches—handsomely crafted pieces of multi-purpose furniture, designed for occasional use and full-time inspiration.) Wood chips and glue don't do much for the broadloom either, or for the resale value of the house. Given the dilemma, I suspect that many woodworkers eventually give up—either on the shop or the house.

Planing in the pantry   About eight years ago, when he moved to San Francisco from Vermont, Simon Watts faced a daunting task. He had to shrink his shop space from a two-story 2,400-sq. ft. barn in the country to a 5½-ft. by 8½-ft. pantry in a third-floor walk-up apartment. The issue, Watts says, was "how to scale down and still maintain the quality of your space. Machinery is incompatible with small spaces...." This is particularly true in an apartment building, where noise and dust may land you on the street.

"Hand tools," Watts explains, "are the answer." Watts was well prepared for making the transition. For years, he's conducted boatbuilding workshops all over the continent, and he's learned to travel light, winnowing his traveling tool kit down to the essentials. Watts builds more shelves than boats in his pantry workshop (although he occasionally works on boat parts), but the space is useful for all sorts of small hand-tool projects. His power-tool collection amounts to an electric drill. For occasional heavy milling, he rents time in a cooperative shop downtown. "We're going to be doing more and more of this, as we all get older," he says.

In any shop, the workbench is the key to efficient hand-tool use. Watts's shop is mostly bench. His is a simple affair, two side-by-side slabs of 2½-in. thick fir on a trestle base, fitted with a Record face vise. Whatever noise or vibration he creates by planing or chopping mortises is absorbed by the bench itself. Two of the four shop walls are mostly glass—large windows that overlook Alcatraz and the San Francisco waterfront—so hand tools and hardware are stored on shelves in the corners and on the wall opposite the bench. When the sun shines in the Bay area, as it did on the day of my visit, Watts rolls down cloth blinds to diffuse the light. A door opening onto an outside stairwell provides reasonable access for materials.

For some people, the lack of machinery is too much to bear, even in a compact homegrown shop. Aldren Watson's laundry-room workshop, shown at right, is roughly twice the size of Watts's apartment setup. This leaves room for a 10-in. Inca bandsaw and a bench grinder, as well as a built-in workbench along one wall, some wood and lots of tool storage. As a full-time illustrator and writer and sometime boatbuilder, toymaker and modelmaker, Watson prefers the bandsaw to other major power tools. "I wouldn't have a table saw even if I could get one for nothing," he says. "It's just too risky." (Watson designed the closet workshop shown below for someone who had no wall space and no windows.)

Small does not necessarily mean powerless. Aldren Watson's laundry-room workshop has space for an Inca bandsaw. To provide infeed support while ripping long stock, Watson opens the back door of his Vermont farmhouse and inserts a dowel between the jambs.

Out of the closet

Aldren Watson developed this model of a closet workshop for an apartment dweller. The design meets a few of the basic criteria for a hand-tool workshop in a small living space—a solid work surface, some tool storage and minimum impact on the structure.

The benchtop is supported on a triangulated lumber base, which pivots out of the closet on two brackets lag-screwed to the inside of the door frame. A wooden board at the back of the bench protrudes slightly above the benchtop and on both sides to stop the bench against the door frame when the shop is opened for business. A wooden bumper is attached to the back of the closet wall

to protect the wall from the backboard when the rig is closed. To lock the bench in position, Watson fits a wooden crossbar in front of the door molding and uses two hardwood keys to pinch the molding and the door frame between the crossbar and the backboard. (The crossbar and keys are stashed in a small compartment on the inside of the door when the shop is put away.)

Inside the closet and above the bench, shallow shelves flank both sides of the doorway. A plywood tool board spans the open space behind the bench and is attached to the back of both shelf units. A work lamp nests inside the closet when

the shop is closed, and swings out on a wooden arm that's hinged to one of the shelf units. (The closet could be wired for an electrical outlet, or the lamp wire could simply be run outside.)

The pivoting bench can be made to fit any size closet, and when locked in place, it's as sturdy as the door jamb and wall that supports it. (Watson built two tiny sawhorses that pack away between the triangle braces of the model bench base.) "It's not a replacement for a real workshop," Watson points out, "but it's certainly better than no shop at all. If I had to live in an apartment, I'd convert the dining room into a workshop."

A condo shop Larry Smotroff has been carving wood since he was 14 years old, often in a closet or bedroom, so his new workshop (shown below) was a major step forward. It was also a step up, since Smotroff installed the shop in the attic of his two-bedroom condominium in Waterbury, Connecticut. There's almost 200 ft. of floor space, but the slope of the roof takes a considerable bite out of the usable space. (The ceiling is almost 8 ft. high at the peak, but the knee walls are less than 4 ft. high.) Smotroff effected the conversion on a tight budget over a couple of years, making changes and improvements as he picked up inexpensive materials and ideas. "Everybody who comes up here has something to offer," he says. His father suggested making sliding doors in the knee walls, and a friend proposed boxing the bathroom stack with paneling. Except for a few hand-held power tools, the space is intended exclusively for hand tools.

When Smotroff moved into the condo, there was only a narrow plywood runway down the middle of the attic floor, no insulation in the roof and a bare bulb overhead. He put the knee walls in first, ran wire to the outlets, installed two standard bathroom fans above the bench, insulated the ceiling and walls and set up his bench. The fans exhaust dust through the peak vent in the roof. With the fiberglass insula-tion, his neighbors don't even notice the scream of his router. After the structural work was done, he put down the light-colored linoleum floor tiles in sections, moving the bench and other equipment out of the way.

The biggest drawbacks to an attic workspace are access and temperature. Smotroff has to carry all materials upstairs through a walk-in closet in the master bedroom and up a narrow companionway. And even with good insulation and wood paneling, the attic tends to be hot. During the steamiest summer weather, he keeps the large trap door open to the second floor of the house and uses a standard household fan to push the cooler air up from downstairs. He originally hoped to install a skylight and a roof fan, but because of regulations regarding structural alterations to the condo, he opted for the path of least resistance.

"It's been a real challenge," Smotroff explains, to create a comfortable workspace that is both functional and temporary. To protect his investment, he was careful to avoid any permanent fixtures that might not be useful to the next tenants. The critical factor about working in such a tight space, Smotroff adds, is to use a good vacuum cleaner and take your time — "work a little, clean up, work a bit more." That's a foreign habit to many woodworkers, but as he explains, "as soon as I make a mess, I track it down to the bedroom."

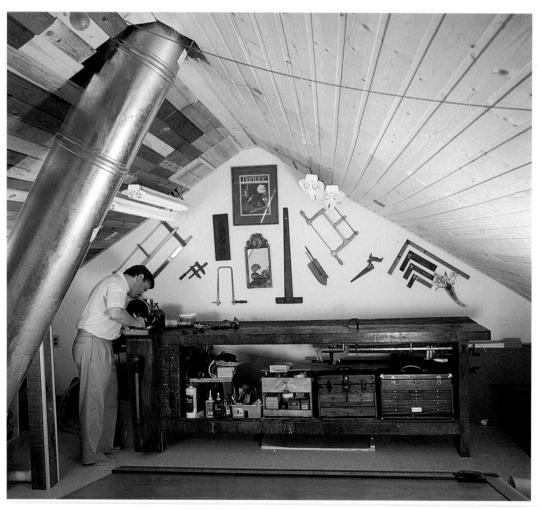

Larry Smotroff's condominium workshop is a cozy retreat for carving and performing other hand-tool operations. A future owner could easily convert the attic space into a spare bedroom or a comfortable den.

All the house a shop

Note: Finishing room and office are located on the second floor.
Air-compressor hose runs to upstairs shop.

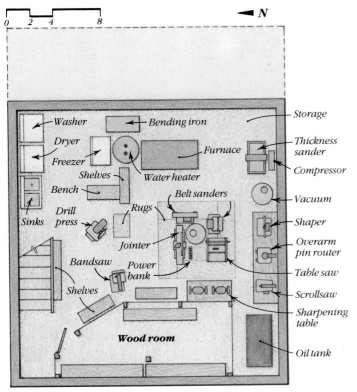

0 2 4 8

◄ N

Basement

- Washer
- Bending iron
- Storage
- Dryer
- Freezer
- Thickness sander
- Furnace
- Compressor
- Shelves
- Water heater
- Bench
- Belt sanders
- Vacuum
- Drill press
- Rugs
- Shaper
- Sinks
- Jointer
- Overarm pin router
- Bandsaw
- Power bank
- Table saw
- Shelves
- Scrollsaw
- Sharpening table
- **Wood room**
- Oil tank

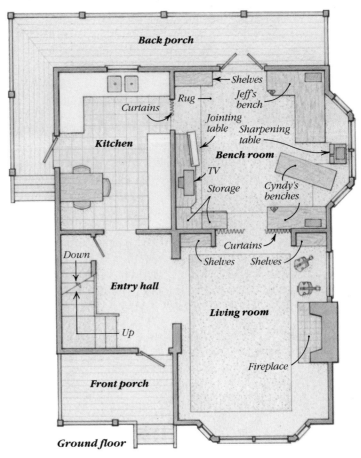

Ground floor

- Back porch
- Shelves
- Rug
- Jeff's bench
- Curtains
- Jointing table
- Sharpening table
- Kitchen
- Bench room
- TV
- Storage
- Cyndy's benches
- Down
- Curtains
- Entry hall
- Shelves
- Shelves
- Up
- Living room
- Fireplace
- Front porch

All the house a shop

A closet or pantry workshop is fine if you can shoehorn your work into a corner of your life and home. For better or for worse, however, work and life are one and the same for some woodworkers. For Jeff Elliott and Cyndy Burton, their home is their workshop.

Elliott and Burton build fine classical guitars in the snug, two-story, Craftsman-style bungalow they share in Portland, Oregon. What was once the dining room, next to the kitchen, is now the bench room. The basement is stuffed with machinery (all the power tools are downstairs) and a humidity-controlled wood-storage chamber. One of the upstairs bedrooms has been converted to a finishing room (used mainly for French polishing), drying room and temporary photo studio. "My bedroom is the library, office and guest room," Elliott says, "we sleep in Cyndy's bedroom." There's a queue of guitars in the upstairs hallway awaiting repair, and finished instruments spill over into the carpeted living room next to the bench room.

Unlike the living-room shops I've seen, it's not the shop that Elliott and Burton roll up in a corner, but their lives. "In our other house," Burton explains, "the shop [bench room] was in a bedroom upstairs. In this case, the shop had to be in the best room in the house—it has windows, heat

Jeff Elliott and Cyndy Burton live their work—their house is their shop. Most of the action takes place in what was the dining room of their two-story, Oregon bungalow. The most comfortable room in the house is now the bench room.

and doors to the outside porch." In many ways, the bench room is a perfect hand-tool environment, with plenty of natural light, a high ceiling and lots of storage. The only major drawback is the south-facing bay window, which casts light directly on the bench tops during the winter. "But in the winter we don't get much sun," they add. With a television set and sound system, the bench room has become their living room. It's also the warmest room in the house, Elliott points out, and is kept between 65° and 70° for good gluing.

Over the years, Elliott has gone from a garage workshop at home, to a storefront shop (where he did retail sales and had several apprentices) and back home again. The years in the public shop, when he did a lot of repair work, were the most lucrative of his 25-year guitar-making career. "I did less building, but made more money," he says. But after 12 years of living in his shop (in three different houses), he now says, "I really don't want it any other way." The home shop is not only convenient and economical, it suits a lifestyle in which the line between work and play has long ago blurred. "It's so much a way of life," Elliott explains, "that having the shop in the home is natural." Burton interjects, "it's also the handiest way to be a workaholic."

The freestanding workshop

Many people begin woodworking by using part of their house—basement, garage, pantry, attic—as a shop. And, as we've seen, quite a few make those conversions permanent. The time may come, however, when you run out of space, or the family runs out of patience, and you've got to find a new location. It may be time to stop sharing space with the television or the freezer or the car and devote an entire building to your woodworking. If you have one, you can convert an existing outbuilding. If you don't, you can build a shop from scratch.

The allure of building from scratch is the chance to design the structure exactly as you wish. Of course, you're restricted by your site, local building codes, your pocketbook and the time and energy you can devote to the project. But theoretically, the possibilities are limitless. At first glance an existing building appears to offer fewer choices. However, given enough ingenuity, energy and/or money, there's not much you can't do with an existing structure—you can move it, gut it, add on to it and so on. At some point, you may ask yourself why you didn't just build from scratch, but by then it will be too late.

Whether you build new or convert, whether the shop is to be large or small, you'll need to consider access, services, heating and/or cooling, lighting, flexibility, insurance and expenses, just as you would for a shop in the basement or garage. All new buildings and most conversions will require addressing the kinds of questions that arise when building or renovating a house, and you may find that consulting an architect can be a big help—particularly if he or she is also a woodworker. At the very least, consult your local building inspector *before* you break ground or start knocking down walls.

A biodegradable workshop

So many shops are built for keeps. Concrete or superinsulated bunkers are not uncommon, with heavy-duty R-values, skylights, solar panels and dust extractors that cost more than a small car. I've seen quite a few that I would be proud to live in.

Art Carpenter's California workshop is a notable exception. With typical wry humor, he told me: "I've arranged things perfectly, so that when I drop dead, everything will decay with me, and I will have left no impression on the ground." Indeed, his rough-hewn, organic workshop and surrounding buildings already show signs of composting.

The 16-ft. by 84-ft. shop was the first thing Carpenter built 30 years ago, when he moved from San Francisco to his present location in Bolinas, a small artist's enclave up the California coast. Across the road from the shop is a saltwater lagoon, where Carpenter sends his apprentices to walk each afternoon in search of inspiration. The bolt-together, scissorlike shop trusses absorb earth tremors without incident, but leaks in the transluscent fiberglass trough that runs down the center of the shop roof require regular attention. (The diffuse light from the overhead panels augments the window light in the shaded shop.)

The shop was followed by a circular house and an assortment of round, yurt-like structures sprinkled about the two-acre property. Carpenter calls them "huts" or "temporary exhibit spaces," for the benefit of local building inspectors. "Some are real buildings, and some are not-so-real buildings," he admits, and they serve various functions—from outdoor toilet to guest sleeping quarters to the office/showroom shown on the facing page. "You do with what you've got," Carpenter says.

In Michael Stone's book, *Contemporary American Woodworkers,* Carpenter is quoted as saying, "When I sit down with my clipboard in my lap fiddling over a new design, I shut out all references to furniture I've seen and concentrate on the functional requirements of the piece." The same could be said of his living and working environment, the utilitarian shells he has thrown up to keep the rain off. Likewise, the five criteria Stone attributes to Carpenter's furniture—function, durability, simplicity, sensuality and practicality of construction—are evident in the design of the structures. The organic, flowing lines of Carpenter's famous "Wishbone" chair, which he builds in less than three days, and his pioneering bandsawn boxes come from the same source. Why do something complicated, he is fond of saying, when simplicity will work as well?

"The [shop] configuration has nothing to do with the space. It has to do with one of the San Andreas cracks over here and the road on the other side," Carpenter explains, pointing to the rivulet that divides the office and workshop. A square or octagonal building might have been nicer, he admits, but the slip of land between the road and the fault was long and narrow.

Inside, heavy machinery is located at one end of the

An elegant work space is no prerequisite to fine craftsmanship, as demonstrated by Art Carpenter's 'biodegradable' workshop. At left, Carpenter glues up some curved chair parts on his all-purpose bench, built from the 2x10s that were used to form the concrete floor. The totem shown below guards the front door. It is one of several carvings around the shop done by Bill Lee, one of Carpenter's early employees.

The simplicity and charm of Carpenter's circular office and showroom hut are characteristic of the buildings in his compound. Built with redwood salvaged from a 19th-century barn, the office is connected by a wooden catwalk to the workshop.

shop, near the front door, and is separated from the benches and hand-work areas by a sliding partition. "The less machinery you have," Carpenter says, "the more freedom you have to play, to make shapes." Many of the schooled woodworkers he meets get spoiled by the tremendous equipment on which they learned. "I didn't," he says. "I just want mine to go. I tinker to get them sharp and running true," but he spends as little time as possible caressing and cajoling his machinery. What obviously began as a necessity—Carpenter started woodworking over 40 years ago, with little money and even less training—has become a virtue.

Carpenter's lifestyle is only a step removed from camping, so I wasn't surprised to discover that the source of heat in the shop "is mainly running around." He uses portable space heaters, if necessary, but mainly, he says, you just get used to living at 50° or 60°. A concrete slab is not cold, he asserts, as long as you've poured it on top of four inches of gravel and a plastic vapor barrier. Lately, he's begun to light the shop with halogen lamps, which last longer, produce more light than tungsten and even help heat the shop. "Every little bit helps," his apprentice chimes in.

That might suffice for human comfort, but what about the wood itself? During most of the year, humidity in the shop hovers around a damp 75 percent. To prepare the wood for building, and during construction, the material is stored in a small chamber fitted with an 8-ft. long electric baseboard heater. Otherwise, the humid coastal climate is ideal for slowly drying wood outside in uncovered, stickered piles. In lieu of a moisture meter, Carpenter simply weighs the wood when it arrives and as it dries. "Talk about primitive!" he exclaims. "I just assume all the wood will be working one way or another for the rest of its life, so I'd better get used to it."

His ideal shop? "I like to open all the doors and bask in the breeze," Carpenter says. "It's a matter of whether you want to live in a sealed case or in the country."

Because they're most interested in what's going to happen inside the shop, most people concentrate on those aspects of the design—how to accommodate machinery, benches, storage and finishing. Often overlooked is the question of where to put the building itself. How does it relate to the other structures on the property? Where is the best spot and the best orientation to make the most of natural light, summer breezes, protection from winter winds, pockets of warmth or coolness? Whether you're building on a suburban lot or alongside a mountain stream, thinking about these questions can make what you do in the shop that much more enjoyable, and can often save you money in construction, maintenance and operating costs.

An excellent example of a workshop integrated with its site is Ken and Barbara Kern's homestead workshop (shown below and on the facing page). It is a multipurpose shop, designed to meet the ongoing demands of a remote, self-sufficient homestead in the foothills of central California.

The overall design and placement of the shop evolved from without and within—both as a function of the site and the organization of the workspace. Its location, several hundred yards from the Kern household, takes into account the site's topography, the relationship to other buildings and activities as well as safety and storage. As suggested by the orientation sketch in the lower right corner on the facing page, Kern considered seasonal weather patterns, the track of the sun and other subtle characteristics of the location.

Kern built the shop in 1978, but it is a product of more than two decades of research in low-tech construction techniques with inexpensive, locally available materials—stone,

earth and wood. It took Kern about 30 days to complete the structure and cost him under $5,000. He folded together ten tons of rock and more than ten yards of concrete to form the 12-in. thick, curvilinear enclosure. By adjusting a couple of turnbuckles, Kern was able to use the same slip form to build every structure on the homestead, from the 434-sq. ft. workshop and 10,000-gallon water tank to a 3-ft. dia. masonry stove. It's nothing fancy, but by any standard of efficiency, it is a model of appropriate technology.

Ken Kern's workshop is integrated not only with its site, but with the multifaceted life Kern lived, as indicated by the range of work it is designed to accommodate. The shop reminds me of an old-fashioned farm workshop, where the farmer mended a broken harrow on the forge one day and built a new wooden gate the next. Inside the shop, areas have been set aside for woodworking, metalworking, vehicle repair and outdoor projects. A 120-sq. ft. carport and loading dock provide convenient entry at the center of the building. The design of the structure and the organization of benches, storage and miscellaneous equipment reveal a careful analysis of workspace functions.

At once practical and iconoclastic, Ken Kern developed his provocative approach to the building trades in a series of books, two of which are listed in the Bibliography (see p. 208). Kern died in a building accident in 1986, but his wife and son are continuing his research.

A woodworking compound The most impressive example of a homestead workshop dedicated exclusively to woodwork that I found belongs to Lewis and Toni Judy of Jefferson, Oregon.

When Ken Kern built his multipurpose shop, he paid special attention to locating the building on its site. The concrete and stone structure relates to the other buildings and functions of the homestead as well as to the topography and climate. (Photo by Ken Kern.)

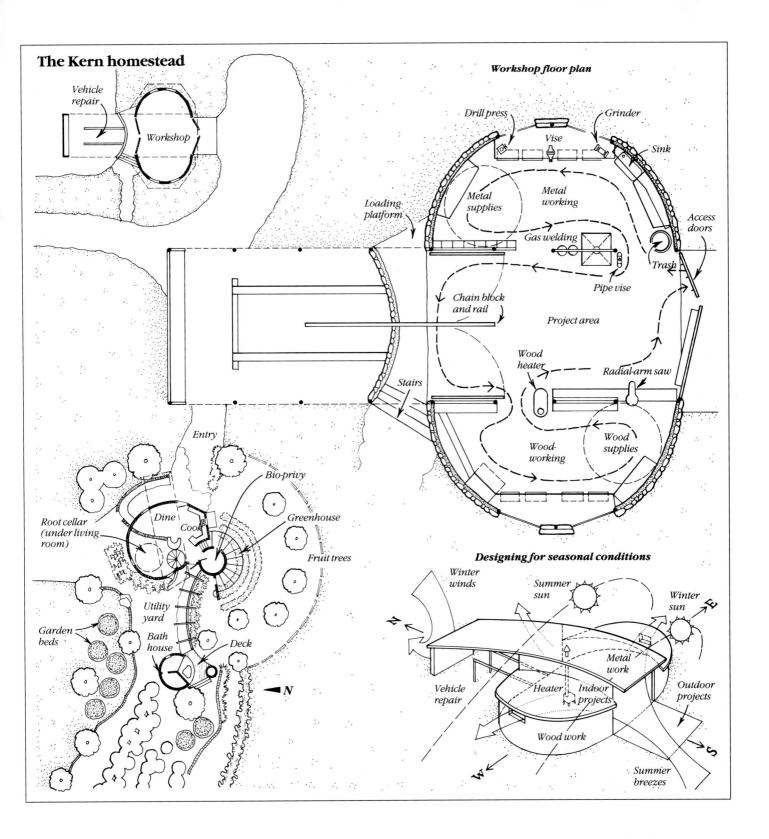

The Kern homestead

Vehicle repair

Workshop

Entry

Bio-privy

Root cellar (under living room)

Dine

Cook

Greenhouse

Fruit trees

Utility yard

Garden beds

Bath house

Deck

N

Workshop floor plan

Drill press

Vise

Grinder

Sink

Metal supplies

Metal working

Access doors

Loading platform

Gas welding

Trash

Chain block and rail

Pipe vise

Project area

Wood heater

Radial-arm saw

Stairs

Wood-working

Wood supplies

Designing for seasonal conditions

Winter winds

Summer sun

Winter sun

E

N

Metal work

Vehicle repair

Heater

Indoor projects

Outdoor projects

W

Wood work

S

Summer breezes

Theirs is a vertically integrated facility, with two wood kilns, a large workshop and finishing area and a new 3,000-sq. ft. gallery, all housed in separate buildings. The shop and gallery cluster are separated from the house by about 20 acres of farmland (planted with garlic, cauliflower, wheat or peppermint by a local farmer) in Oregon's fertile Willamette valley. "We have it all right here," Judy says.

The business began humbly enough in the early 1970s in an 8-ft. by 12-ft. hobby shop, with the table saw, 6-in. jointer and bandsaw they used to build their house. Work on the current shop began in 1975 and has grown incrementally ever since. Beginning in one stall of a large metal bus shed, the shop gradually spilled over into two stalls, then three and, ultimately, consumed the entire 3,200-sq. ft. building.

In their workshop compound, Lewis and Toni Judy take charge of every operation from sawmilling to gallery sales. Their setup includes two Ebac wood kilns and storage space for several thousand feet of lumber, a large workshop and a new gallery. The site plan for the homestead and workshop is shown in the drawing on the facing page.

The place is huge, but the renovation was made more manageable by being done in two phases. In the first, the Judys installed furring strips, insulation and drywall in the walls and roof, added windows and rewired the entire shed with conduit. In the second phase, a built-up wood floor was added at one end for a small showroom, and an overhead sprinkler system was installed. They did all the work themselves, spending about $25,000 on materials. "You couldn't have built a shop that size for that kind of money," Judy says. "It was definitely worth it." And by doing the work themselves, he explains, they were better able to design the place around their own needs.

About five years ago, they built an additional 28-ft. by 28-ft. building for storage and finishing. Shortly thereafter, when Judy began milling local walnut, he added another two 1,000-sq. ft. metal sheds to handle two Ebac kilns and more lumber storage. The last section went up so quickly that Toni didn't even find out about it until a week after it was built.

"I tried to make the shop have a good flow to it," Judy says. "Everything moves. When something's finished it goes out of here. It has a home." That home is now the gallery. When I first visited the Judys about four years ago, the showroom was ensconced at one end of the workshop. It was decorated like a living and dining room, displaying Lewis's woodwork and Toni's stained glass along with other furnishings supplied by local artisans. Apparently I was not the only visitor who was impressed by the arrangement. "That's when our furniture really kicked off," Judy says. By 1989, the business had outgrown the showroom, and they built the gallery (shown on the facing page). When I returned for a recent visit, I mistook the gallery for a new house. As it turned out, I wasn't entirely wrong. The Judys built it as a house, not only for the benefit of marketing their crafts, but also against the possibility that they might someday want to sell it.

Before leaving the subject of freestanding shops, I'd like to point out that they don't have to be large buildings. One of the most memorable shops I visited was a converted garden shed in Phoenix, Arizona. Donald Kinnaman's shop (profiled on pp. 164-165) shows that you can make a shop in a very small, self-contained space, too.

The residential atmosphere of the Judy's "Made in Jefferson" gallery helps sell their furniture and will help sell the building, too, if they ever decide to move.

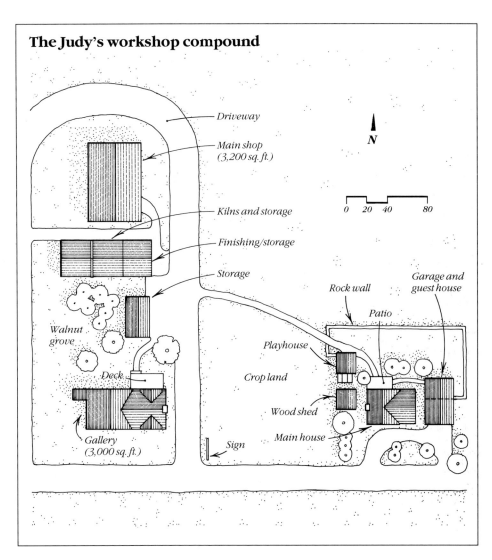

The Judy's workshop compound

Driveway

Main shop (3,200 sq. ft.)

Kilns and storage

Finishing/storage

Storage

Walnut grove

Rock wall

Garage and guest house

Patio

Playhouse

Crop land

Deck

Wood shed

Gallery (3,000 sq. ft.)

Sign

Main house

N

0   20   40   80

Industrial renovation

An age of waning North American industry has provided woodworkers with another option for workshop space. In any city on the continent, you're likely to find relatively inexpensive space in old factories and warehouses. Some, like Tage Frid's renovated mill site (see p. 22), offer bucolic vistas of picturesque countryside. Others, if they have windows at all, offer views of inner-city combat zones.

The trade-offs between the advantages and disadvantages in old industrial buildings can be sharply drawn. In exchange for cheap footage and ready access to three-phase power and hardware and lumber suppliers, you may have to put up with a freight-elevator ride to the third floor and a daily struggle with a half-dozen security devices. (All this after you've spent half an hour looking for a parking spot.)

Space, of course, is a great draw of these old buildings. But you can have too much of a good thing. You may have to rent 1,000 sq. ft. when you need only 500 sq. ft. The space is often cavernous and poorly insulated (if it's insulated at all), and it can cost a fortune to heat or cool. Large industrial spaces may be economical only if shared among several woodworkers or other craftspeople.

Then, there are the neighbors. It can be stimulating and useful to work in the same building with other craftspeople. You can share ideas and equipment and subcontract work. But will you feel comfortable working next door to a guy who's spraying lacquer without proper ventilation? Can you sleep soundly knowing that the live-in sweatshop downstairs is overloading the electrical circuits all night with poorly maintained appliances?

Old industrial buildings, with their 15-ft. high ceilings, vast tracts of space and interesting architectural features, are also enticing because of the possibilities they offer for the creation of a stimulating workspace. But don't get carried away by the romance of it all. One of the reasons you're able to afford the space is because few other people want to tackle its problems.

Curtis Erpelding has succeeded as well as anyone I visited in making the most of space in an old industrial building. Built near the waterfront in downtown Seattle in 1904, the four-story brick building was home to the printing presses of the *Seattle Post Intelligencer.* Today it houses a shelter for battered women and a coffee company as well as Erpelding's shop. The beans are roasted and ground next door to the shop and then transported by vacuum to the upper floors. "They were worried about their noise," Erpelding says, so he wasn't concerned about his own. On the morning of my visit we suffered through the seductive fragrance of French roast. The 300-sq. ft. enclosed office tucked in one corner of the shop is almost half the size of Erpelding's entire previous workshop. "It's bigger than necessary," he admits, "but I was anticipating having to live here."

When we consider space in the workshop, most of us calculate floor footage. Too often we forget to look up. So it's no surprise that a lack of headroom is one of the most common complaints of many woodworkers. Although we're accustomed to an 8-ft. high ceiling in our living areas, it can soon induce claustrophobia in a shop. It's difficult to maneuver a sheet of plywood, not to mention a 14-ft. board or a tall-case clock, under anything less than a 10-ft. high ceiling.

Erpelding's 30-ft. by 70-ft. shop (shown below)has space in both directions. Occupying one-third of the ground floor, it is girdled with epic granite piers that rise 17 ft. to the ceiling, which is strapped with the steel girders that once supported the presses on the floor above. His light fixtures are 12 ft. above the floor, which gives the light a lot of room to diffuse. Two 400-watt, metal-halide Hubbell fixtures flood the space pretty well, although the quality of light is closer to that of an automobile headlamp than to natural sunlight. Dust collection is a minor architectural feat—the pipes ascend like a skyline of smokestacks from the machinery in the center of the shop.

Just as this book was going to press, I discovered that Erpelding had moved his shop across Puget Sound to a 700-sq. ft. garage alongside his house in Bremerton. After a

With a bit of ingenuity and effort, old industrial buildings can be turned into fine work spaces. Curtis Erpelding's downtown Seattle shop has a 17-ft. high ceiling and plenty of room for machinery, a workbench, an assembly area and an enclosed office.

dozen years in industrial spaces, I wondered how he was adjusting to the change. "It's a lot less room than I had downtown," he says, "and I'm struggling with that," but he's forced to use the space more efficiently. "I've been close to my work before," he adds, reminding me of his first city workshop, where he set up clandestine housekeeping in a cubbyhole office down the hall. There are other advantages to country life, too, like the reduced cost of building permits and lack of red tape, but after years of city lights and easy access to goods and services, Erpelding notes, "it's a little too quiet sometimes."

A storefront workshop

One of the benefits of working in an old industrial space is that you won't be disturbed by a lot of casual walk-by traffic. For many professional woodworkers, a shop in an old inner-city warehouse or factory is ideal. It's accessible enough to the designers and architects who are their most important clients, but intimidating enough to discourage tourists and woodworking kibitzers.

For at least one professional craftsman I met, however, being easily accessible to the general public is essential. "People are our best customers," Warren May told me. May builds furniture and Appalachian dulcimers in Berea, Kentucky, one of the country's most popular craft communities.

May's shop (shown on the facing page) faces the sidewalk on a busy corner in Berea's main downtown block. It is flanked by a restaurant and a jewelry studio, with an antique store upstairs. (May also operates his own craft gallery in a separate second-floor walk-up around the corner.) The shop averages about 30 visitors a day over the entire year and more than 50 on a busy Saturday. That would drive many woodworkers to the hills, but May seems to relish life in a fishbowl. "I think it adds a little honesty to my craft," he says. "People like to see people working." Indeed, May's "Williamsburg theme" appeals to many tourists, who wander directly into the shop for an immediate sense of the local craft tradition.

Visitors enter a small gallery at one end of the 1,100-sq. ft. shop, which is separated from the workspace by a wide counter. There they are greeted casually by either May or an employee, who will gladly set aside the carving of a peghead to pluck a few chords or demonstrate dovetailing. Everyone gets talked to and everyone leaves with a brochure.

How does he get any work done? Some of it is done at night, when the store is closed, or during slack times of the day when traffic is light. May arranges his work schedule so that he won't be involved in any gluing or major machining on Saturday, when the shop can be jammed. "The furniture work is more difficult to stop and start," he admits, but 90 percent of his business is dulcimers.

With retail space at a premium, May has pared his inventory of tools to the minimum he requires for dulcimer production. "I'm not a tool freak," he says, "I only have tools to work." Still, the shop is equipped with all the basic power tools, arranged neatly in the back third of the workshop, where their noise and dust will be least offensive to visitors.

Large windows wrap around the two outside walls of Warren May's storefront workshop in downtown Berea, Kentucky. May often works at the front counter, where he conducts business and demonstrates his craft for the public, while his long-time employee, John Kennedy, works behind him in the shop.

Some wood is also stored along the rear wall of the shop and in a new shop that he recently built at home, where May does most of his sanding and all of his spray finishing.

Not everyone is as gregarious as Warren May, and having spent a while selling woodwork at a retail outlet myself, I would think hard before inviting a steady stream of sightseers into my shop—even if they are potential customers. But workshops, like everything else, go through different stages, and a public space may provide some valuable information about the market that would be difficult to glean in a sylvan retreat. With good discipline, organization and clear priorities, it could provide just the contact and exposure you need to turn a profit.

Paying the piper

As you ponder where to put your shop, keep in mind that in the long run the single most important factor may be flexibility. As your needs and priorities change, will a potential location provide room to grow both within and beyond the space? Try to imagine not only where you will fit your current equipment and operation, but also where you might put it in five years. And consider the inevitable: You will probably outgrow the shop and have to move someday. Potential buyers may not think much of the alterations you made to accommodate your shop. Like Larry Smotroff and Lewis and Toni Judy, several people I visited took particular heed of this possibility and made their workspaces convertible—the workshop becomes a den, the gallery a house.

The decision of whether to rent, buy, build or barter will depend upon a host of factors, from the local real-estate economy to your own resources and priorities. But be aware that the transition from a rental workshop to a permanent, wholly owned facility can be very expensive. Overhead soared more than sixfold for one professional woodworker I met—from a $140-per-month rental to a $900-per-month mortgage on a new building. This worked out to a hefty $6.00 per hour increase in his operating costs, which required a 25 percent boost in his prices. Others, like Ken Kern, subscribe to a pay-as-you-go philosophy. For all of his homestead constructions, Kern kept scrupulously free of bank loans, which can more than double the cost of a building over the life of a mortgage.

Wherever you locate your shop, don't forget to investigate building codes and insurance. Unless you plan to run a speakeasy workshop, you'll have to satisfy your local building inspector. Even with careful attention to safety, the risk of fire in a workshop is a serious issue. Increasingly, woodworkers are taking pains to run their shops safely, but the combination of dust, flammable chemicals and miles of electric wiring create an ever-present danger. As their investments increase, more and more woodworkers are buying insurance.

The price of insurance, however, may prove to be a burden too onerous to bear. When Lewis Judy discovered that it would cost him $4,000 per year just to insure his shop building and heavy equipment, he decided to run the risk. "I'm not going to work for the insurance company," he says. But with separate buildings and a sprinkler system, Judy has more protection than most. If your home and shop share the same structure, all of your eggs are literally in one basket, and your rates for everything, household as well as workshop, could go up.

When it comes to planning a layout, a model is almost better than the real thing. You can visualize spatial relationships and evaluate the way windows and skylights will illuminate the workspace. Here, luthier John Monteleone experiments with the layout of his new shop (see p. 65).

Layout

We shape our buildings; thereafter, they shape us. —Winston Churchill

Chapter 3

 ou may or may not have much choice in the location of your workshop. But what you do within its walls is entirely up to you. (Unless, of course, you have to share that space with the family car or three other business partners.) Nothing less than your safety, efficiency and enjoyment hang in the balance.

I wish I could offer one or two ideal layouts that would satisfy most needs. But the factors that affect shop layout—from the height of the ceiling to the size of your wallet and the type of work you do—vary so greatly that any such attempt would be folly. Aspects of layout are sprinkled liberally throughout this book. The selection of machinery, for example, relates strongly to layout, as do wood storage and dust

collection. In fact, just about everything that goes on in the shop has something to do with the subject. What follows is a discussion of the principal considerations involved in laying out any workspace, along with examples drawn from a wide variety of workshops.

Flexibility

Good layout is more than just deciding where to put your equipment. In many shops, it includes planning flexibility into the shop. Limited space or a variety of woodworking projects will make this planning critical in most small shops, while in larger shops or production and specialty shops where the type of work is more predictable, only certain

41

areas need be flexible. As one woodworker wrote to me, "As much as I'd like to bolt things to the floor, I don't because I never know when I'll have to push something over a few inches to allow for some other operation."

Flexibility is most often expressed in the selection and orientation of machinery. In the majority of shops I visited, the table saw occupies a preeminent position in the middle of the floor. A table saw demands space on all four sides—fore and aft, for long boards, and to the left or right for wide panels. By contrast, all the other major pieces of commonly used woodworking machinery—radial-arm saw, jointer, planer, bandsaw, drill press and shaper—require space in only two or three directions and can be placed against a wall.

Arranging the machines around the perimeter of the shop, or even isolating them in a separate machine room, liberates the bulk of the floor space for a constantly changing flow of shop projects. Flexibility is enhanced by folding outfeed tables or portable outfeed horses and rolling tool carts, clamp caddies and assembly tables, an assortment of which are shown in chapters 8 and 9.

As important as flexibility is to most shops, good organization also requires a careful analysis of what kinds of things you do repeatedly and in what order. If you make solid-wood furniture, for example, you are likely to follow a similar sequence of operations regardless of whether you're making a highboy or a chair: You saw and plane rough lumber to dimension, cut joints and shape parts, assemble them, then apply finish. Unless you're really pressed for space, it probably makes more sense to put your table saw or bandsaw, rather than your finishing area, next to your jointer and planer. If you work mainly with plywood, or do a lot of turning, you can also identify an overall order to your work, one you'll usually, if not always, follow. Determining what that order, or workflow, is for you is the first step to finding the best relationships between the components that make up your shop.

Workflow

I've yet to meet a woodworker who felt he or she had too much space. But more space doesn't necessarily mean more efficient space. In fact, the luxury of a large shop may simply provide room to spread out your mess. If a small space forces you to be organized, a large space may have the opposite effect.

This was decidedly not true for Kelly Mehler of Berea, Kentucky, who transformed the 3,200-sq. ft. interior of an old car dealership with a logical attention to workflow rarely found in much smaller shops. (In fact, this *is* a smaller shop for Mehler, who began his business in a 6,000-sq. ft. chicken barn that he rented for $40 a month.) A professional furniture maker, Mehler works mainly on mammoth, second-hand industrial machinery, but the organizational principles evident in his workshop may be applied to any space—however large or small.

Sure, Mehler's shop is luxurious. In its tightest corridor, the machines are still 4 ft. apart. There is a virtual prairie of

unclaimed footage in the main work area. (Not to mention the nearly 800 ft. of sparsely populated showroom at the front of the building.) But Mehler regards all that space as a challenge rather than an excuse, and he distributed his tools and materials according to their function in the process of turning rough lumber into finished furniture.

Material enters the shop by way of an 8-ft. wide overhead garage door that opens directly onto the sidewalk of Berea's main thoroughfare. Lumber is delivered by truck right into the shop, where Mehler unloads it onto rolling carts (for immediate use) or onto the wood racks that line both sides of the entryway. The racks are made of utility-grade 2x4s and are positioned on both sides of a radial-arm cut-off saw.

This is the "break-down" lane, where stock is converted to rough dimensions for particular projects, and Mehler keeps a clipboard handy with his work order and materials list. At the start of a job, wood is pulled off a cart or rack, crosscut on the radial-arm saw roughly to length and bandsawn roughly to width. Scraps and usable "shorts" remain in this area, filed in bins across from the lumber racks until they are used in other projects or burned in the shop stove. This end of Mehler's break-down lane illustrates a solid principle of workflow planning: Don't move heavy pieces of wood farther than you have to. Mehler lugs bulky lumber the shortest possible distance from delivery truck to storage rack and from the rack to where it is broken down into manageable pieces.

Wood racks flank the cut-off saw in the 'break-down' lane of Kelly Mehler's shop. Mehler crosscuts and rips lumber to size here, before moving it into the primary production area of the shop, where the more exacting machine work —dimensioning, joinery, shaping or turning —is done. Beyond the heavy machinery, Mehler does whatever handwork, gluing and assembly is required at one of several workbenches. A fully-equipped spray booth is at the end of the production line. All switches and lights are explosion proof, and the fan exhausts to the outside.

Kelly Mehler's shop: Layout for smooth workflow

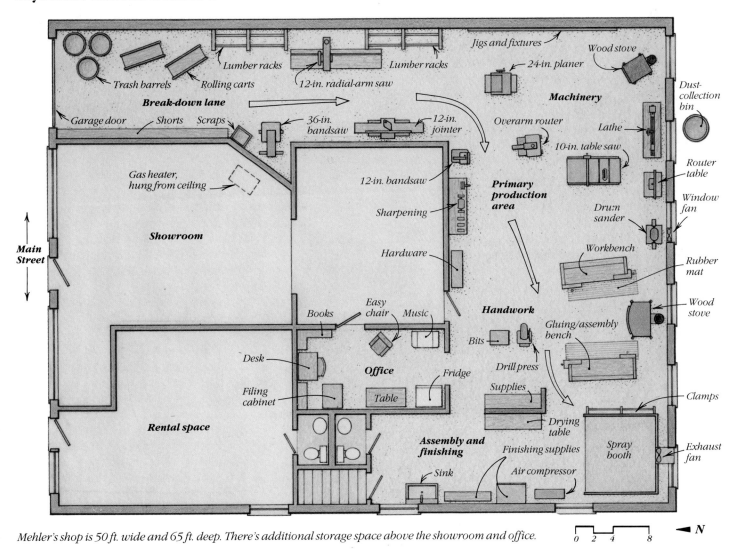

Mehler's shop is 50 ft. wide and 65 ft. deep. There's additional storage space above the showroom and office.

The next operation usually involves jointing a face and edge in preparation for thickness planing or resawing to thinner dimensions. A 12-in. jointer is located conveniently across from the radial-arm saw, between the bandsaw and planer. The classic 36-in. Oliver bandsaw (with a 5-hp motor and a ½-in. skip-tooth resaw blade) and the 24-in. Crescent planer (with a 7½-hp motor) are essential components in these initial conversions. Dust is carried off in a network of stove pipes (sealed at their joints with duct tape) by a 5-hp blower; it is deposited in a large waste bin behind the shop and trucked away.

After the stock is reduced to its rough dimensions, it is placed on a cart and rolled into the primary production area of the shop, where it is ripped and crosscut to final dimension and all the joinery is performed. A Rockwell Unisaw is the heart of this part of the shop, augmented by a four-speed Oliver lathe and an overarm router. Jigs and fixtures live on the wall behind the planer, within easy reach of the table saw.

To save space—one man's warehouse is another's closet—Mehler prefers not to use an outfeed table on the saw, but he is careful to use a portable outfeed roller when he has to rip long stock. When a lot of additional support is required, he uses his workbench, which sits behind the saw and is the same height as the saw table. The table of the overarm router can also be raised or lowered to the same height.

Projects proceed to the workbench for hand joinery, carving and other hand-tool tasks. A drill press is located to one side of the bench, and a portable router table and pneumatic drum sander—one of Mehler's favorite machines—are kept close at hand. The router table, which is just a piece of fiberboard fitted with a clamp-on hardwood fence, has an unusual base—it sits atop a 45-gallon oil drum and is held in place by the weight of the router. (The drum doesn't amplify the router's whine as much as you'd imagine.) In an alcove next to the bench is a sharpening station and hardware depot.

Beyond the primary production area, a second workbench serves as a gluing and clamping station adjacent to the spray booth and finishing area. Mehler keeps the window next to the booth open when he's spraying, so the booth's exhaust fan draws air from outside rather than dust-laden air from inside the shop. (The lacquer dries quickly, so there's little problem with dirt from the unfiltered outside air.) Flammable materials are stored in a metal cabinet in the alley between the spray booth and the sink.

Despite his attention to workflow, Mehler admits that things eventually descend into chaos at some point during a job. The shop, he says, "goes through cycles," and from time to time he stops to straighten it out. To keep things from getting out of hand, he routinely dedicates Saturday to shop-improvement projects.

Mehler heats the shop with wood (there's a gas stove in the gallery), a cheap and available resource in southern Kentucky. The shop can be "coldish" in the winter, he says, but the main wood stove is well-situated near the bench, where it provides heat during the less aerobic exertions required for

careful joinery. It and a secondary stove are also a safe distance from the large sawdust producers in the break-down lane and the volatile chemicals that surround the spray booth.

The primary work areas are well lit by overhead fluorescents and light from large, south-facing windows (which also warm those areas in the winter). Here, the ceiling rises to about 16 ft. at the roof peak, tracing a pleasing catenary curve that contributes to the spacious, airy feeling in the shop. It is one of the architectural reminders of the building's earlier life. A dropped ceiling beneath a large storage loft covers the remaining three-quarters of the shop, including the office and showroom, but there's still 10 ft. to 12 ft. of clearance in the break-down lane.

During the ten years in his current location, Mehler has filled the showroom with furniture and a line of lap desks, quilt racks, desk organizers and other accessories that helped draw cash and customers through the shop. For a while, he dabbled in gallery sales, soliciting crafts from local artisans and hiring help to tend the showroom and keep the books. But as the furniture eclipsed the accessories—Mehler does a wide variety of work, from desks and beds to Shaker-style chairs—he reduced the shop staff from five employees to one and let the showroom go unattended. On the several days I was in town it remained dark, with only a few dusty pieces of furniture on display and the front door locked. It's a luxury to let that much space lie fallow, but Mehler hasn't been spoiled. "I jump in the air sometimes," he says. "I don't know how I got this. I didn't plan it at all...."

Workshop Triangles

Another useful way to consider organizing workshop space is in terms of work triangles, which describe the relationships between several different tools within a single work area. This familiar, motion-study approach is often used by kitchen designers to analyze traffic patterns between the stove, sink and refrigerator—hence the name. (Not all work "triangles" have three sides—some may be squares, trapezoids or circles.) It is equally valuable in developing a workshop layout and amounts to a study of workflow in microcosm.

The workbench triangle Perhaps the most fundamental workshop triangle is formed by the workbench, tool chest and assembly area. The relationship between these elements is apparent in John Nyquist's shop (shown in the top left photo on the facing page). Nyquist, who builds about 30 pieces of furniture each year in his Long Beach, California, workshop, can easily get any hand tool he needs while working at the bench. The tools are arranged in the built-in wall cabinets according to their size, function and frequency of use (similar tools—marking and measuring tools or saws, for example—are grouped together). A low assembly table (in the foreground of the top right photo on the facing page) is likewise accessible to the bench, which may be needed for making final adjustments as the piece is put together.

The importance of the relationship among these three elements—workbench, tool storage and assembly area—

Portable benches and a shop-built router table allow John Nyquist to make flexible use of his shop space. To relieve what he calls 'the masochistic nature of sanding,' Nyquist has made the benches different heights so he can work on his chairs anywhere in the shop without stooping. 'Make it as pleasant as possible,' he says, 'because it doesn't get any better.'

John Nyquist's workbench sits conveniently between the cabinets that hold his hand tools and portable power tools and a 4-ft. by 12-ft. by 2-ft. high assembly table.

should not be underestimated. It is the closest thing to a universal truth in workshop layout. Their relative positions will vary widely, of course, depending on the space and the nature of the work that's performed in it. Where the work is small and refined, as in some musical-instrument shops, hand tools, workbench and assembly stations are within arm's length of each other. At the other extreme, the rolling tool chest in Mac Campbell's shop (see p. 176) makes for a movable work triangle. It carries a large number and variety of tools and is often used at the workbench. But when large case pieces must be assembled, Campbell has to use whatever space happens to be free at the moment, and the cart allows him to roll the tools to the work.

Another good example of a portable work triangle is John Nyquist's chair-production station (shown in the top right photo). Nyquist employs a cluster of assembly and sanding benches made specifically for his chairs in conjunction with a spindle shaper and shop-built router table, both of which are also portable. The space used to make a set of dining chairs this month may be required for a boardroom table or a music stand next month.

Power-tool triangles Power-tool work triangles are at least as variable as bench and assembly triangles. Someone who does a lot of resawing may want an arrangement like Kelly Mehler's, where the bandsaw, jointer and cut-off saw are close together. On a wholly different scale, Francis Pfrank's bandsaw and jointer (shown in the photo at right) are mounted together on a rolling cart, which is stored under his basement stairs when not in use.

Not all work triangles have three sides, or much space between the elements. Francis Pfrank stores a bandsaw and jointer on a rolling cart beneath the basement stairs. The combination works nicely in tandem for small resaw operations—he planes one face on the jointer then resaws on the bandsaw. (Photo by Francis Pfrank.)

A good relationship between wood storage and machinery is even more important in a small shop. In the basement workshop shown in the drawing on p. 46, Frank Jenkins of Groton, Massachusetts, designed the workspace around two major constraints—a dogleg floor plan and a single doorway. Lumber and sheet stock (plywood, particleboard and so on) are stored on two different racks; both are accessible in a straight shot from the door. Sheets are most often ripped to size on the table saw, and they need only be slid out from their position behind a pegboard-covered partition and flopped down on the table saw. Lumber is usually

Frank Jenkins's basement shop:
Handling big stock in a small space

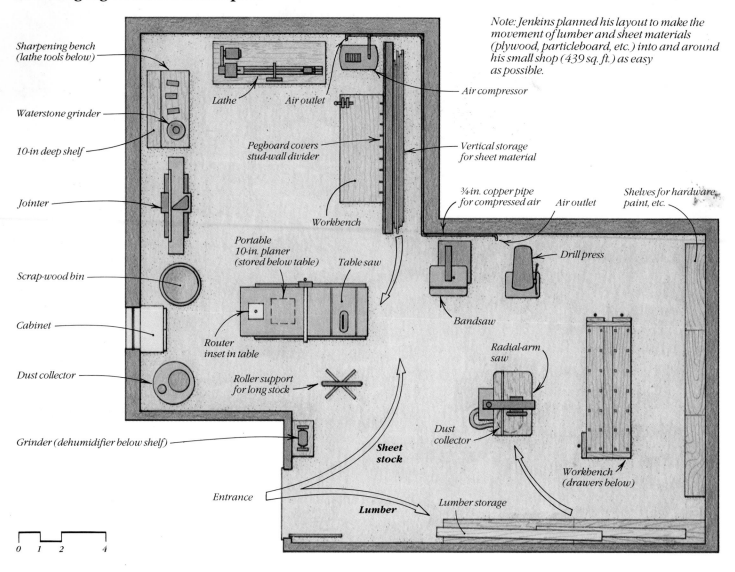

Sharpening bench
(lathe tools below)

Waterstone grinder

10-in deep shelf

Jointer

Scrap-wood bin

Cabinet

Dust collector

Grinder (dehumidifier below shelf)

Entrance

Lathe

Air outlet

Pegboard covers
stud-wall divider

Workbench

Portable
10-in. planer
(stored below table)

Router
inset in table

Roller support
for long stock

Table saw

Sheet
stock

Lumber

Note: Jenkins planned his layout to make the
movement of lumber and sheet materials
(plywood, particleboard, etc.) into and around
his small shop (439 sq. ft.) as easy
as possible.

Air compressor

Vertical storage
for sheet material

¾-in. copper pipe
for compressed air

Air outlet

Shelves for hardware,
paint, etc.

Drill press

Bandsaw

Radial-arm
saw

Dust
collector

Workbench
(drawers below)

Lumber storage

0   1   2   4

first crosscut to length on the radial-arm saw, which is situated conveniently near the horizontal racks. As Jenkins notes, "I found that the most important consideration was not the proximity of the machines, but the way the workpiece will enter and exit each machine."

A power-tool triangle can also be a straight line, which makes for efficient movement between tools. Curtis Erpelding situated his table saw, jointer/planer, thickness sander and bandsaw side by side in a compact line down the middle of his shop (see the photo on p. 38). The machines are oriented so that work is fed across the line (and the shop). That way, Erpelding can push a long board through the table saw without having it bump into the jointer. With this arrangement, Erpelding's shop is wide enough to allow 10 ft. of infeed and outfeed clearance on either side of the line.

Some power-tool triangles are organized for maximum flexibility, to handle a variety of work done by a certain com-

bination of machines. Others, however, are designed for very specific purposes. The photo at the top of the facing page shows a built-in work station for making frame-and-panel cabinets. The lineup, put together by Randall Ores, a California contractor, includes a shaper, a radial-arm saw and two chopsaws. All four tools share the same table and dust collector, and rolling bins beneath the saws hold a large volume of cutoffs. The upper row of cabinets offers convenient storage for sawblades and shaper bits. The whole business takes up more than half the rear wall of Ores's shop.

The photo and drawing at the bottom of the facing page show another compact work triangle in which several tools share the same dust collector and the surfaces of their tables. The 4-ft. by 6-ft. homemade saw table makes it easy to cut large panels in any direction and provides an extended work surface for the adjacent radial-arm saw. A T-square fence serves both the table saw and the router (mounted be-

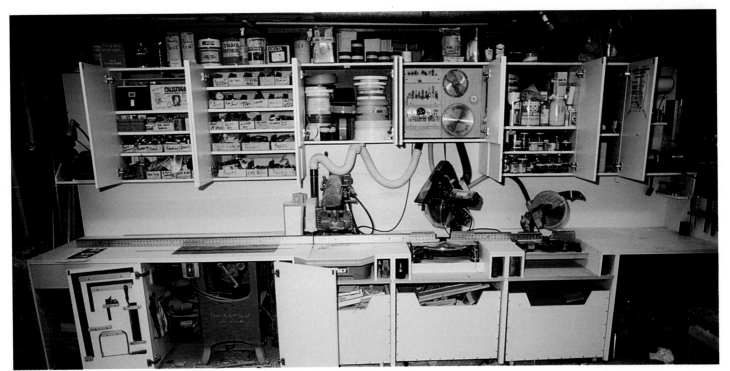

Contractor Randall Ores designed this setup for efficient production of frame-and-panel cabinet components. From left to right is a shaper (visible beneath the benchtop), then a radial-arm saw, permanently set to make 90° cuts, and two chop saws fixed at opposite 45° angles for cutting miters. Rolling wood bins store beneath the saws. Ores operates the chopsaws and dust collector with foot switches. (Photo by Scott Arfstein.)

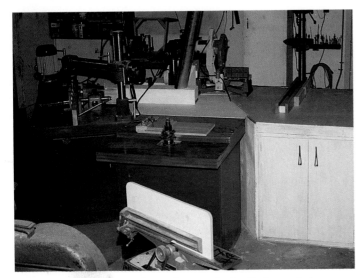

Ike Klassen's machinery cluster shares a dust collector and work surfaces.

neath the saw table) and acts as a crosscut stop for work on the radial-arm saw. The two shapers share a single power feed. The tool cluster, which occupies the center of Ike Klassen's 20-ft. by 24-ft. workshop in Winkler, Manitoba, allows about 10 ft. of clearance on either side of the radial-arm saw blade.

Jeff Elliott's and Cyndy Burton's guitar shop features a similar huddle of power tools in the center of the basement machine shop (shown on p. 48). The table saw, jointer and

Ike Klassen's tool cluster: The whole is greater than the sum of the parts

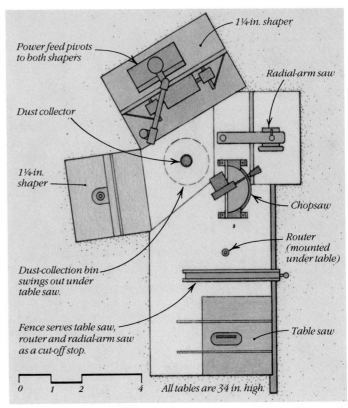

1¼-in. shaper

Power feed pivots to both shapers

Radial-arm saw

Dust collector

1¼-in. shaper

Chopsaw

Router (mounted under table)

Dust-collection bin swings out under table saw.

Fence serves table saw, router and radial-arm saw as a cut-off stop.

Table saw

0   1   2   4   *All tables are 34 in. high.*

Jeff Elliott and Cyndy Burton work on guitar parts at a cluster of small machines in their basement. On the right are an 8⅝-in. Inca jointer and a 10-in. Inca table saw. Two belt/disc sanders form a dogleg at left. The machines share a central dust collector and run off a common electrical panel. The configuration uses space efficiently and also allows Burton and Elliott to work on two machines at the same time.

two belt sanders are surrounded by a ring of machinery, which includes a bandsaw, thickness sander, drill press, overarm pin router, shaper, scroll saw and a small sharpening center. As in Klassen's arrangement, the central cluster of tools share a single dust collector, but Elliott's and Burton's saw table is higher than adjacent tools so that large work is not obstructed. This compact arrangement works well when the machines are used for guitar making, which is almost all the time, but they are small enough to be moved, if necessary, to make room for a larger project.

Dedicated spaces

For obvious reasons, task-specific areas such as the spray booth, drawing table, office or showroom are frequently isolated from the general workspace. But separate areas of the shop also may be designated for such activities as carving, metalworking and gluing up. In many shops, I found small, dedicated zones set aside for tool sharpening, their location dictated mainly by good natural light and running water, or by proximity to the bench area or a particular machine. Turners, for example, frequently locate a bench grinder within arm's reach of the lathe.

Every dedicated workspace, of course, implies a loss of flexibility, and the value of the trade-off depends upon the type of operations you perform in the shop and how frequently you perform them. If you regularly begin your shop routine with a meditative tool-sharpening session, as a few woodworkers I met like to do, a designated sharpening area might make sense, although sharpening stones are easily moved and don't usually require their own bench. Likewise, if your winter shop temperature hovers around 50°F, you may have to set up a separate gluing or finishing room.

It is theoretically possible to divide the entire workshop into a matrix of task-specific work zones, but such an extreme division of space may eventually provide diminishing returns. Many woodworkers speak longingly about an "ideal" workshop in which the machinery would be physically isolated from the bench space. Several mentioned visiting workshops in Europe where machine shops occupied separate buildings. Isolating machines from the rest of the shop has an obvious advantage where a number people share a shop—the machines can be roaring away most of the day and not disturb the concentration of those doing fussy hand work elsewhere.

For most woodworkers, however, complete separation is either difficult, due to lack of space, or undesirable. Michael Fortune, who employs several people in his new Toronto workshop, set aside a room for machinery, but he decided to keep his favorite 10-in. Wadkin Bursgreen table saw next to his bench because, as he explained, "it goes on and off a million times in the course of a day."

Michael Fortune makes furniture, but several other woodworking trades require the same constant interaction between the bench and the table saw or some other machine. This is not true, however, of some specialty trades. In custom-guitar making, for example, milling, joinery, assembly and finishing are discrete, time-consuming activities. Jeff Elliott and Cyndy Burton perform several of these tasks in rooms on different floors of their house (see the floor plan on p. 31).This arrangement also allows one person to machine while the other works undisturbed on a task requiring concentration or a dust-free environment. Although their cavelike basement machine shop might be oppressive if Elliott and Burton had to work there all day, it is perfectly acceptable for the little bit of milling they have to do for each instrument.

If you work alone, separating your machines from the rest of your shop may be more a matter of personal style or habit than one of necessity. For example, you may adopt a cautious demeanor when you approach your machinery, while you feel more relaxed or introspective at the bench. Isolating these functions in physically separated quarters may enable you to develop a safe and more efficient routine; such an arrangement will certainly affect the quality of your work and the enjoyment you get out of it.

Such are the benefits that Robert Weisman derives from his two-room basement workshop in Ann Arbor, Michigan (shown in the photos and drawing on the facing page). The basement was raw when Weisman bought the house in 1980. He staked out the machine room first and used the workbench across from the table saw for all his hand-tool operations. Lack of assembly room or a dust-free environment inspired the adjacent 10-ft. by 14-ft. bench room, which now houses an assembly table, workbench and drawing board.

This arrangement offers some flexibility. If Weisman has a project that requires a lot of machine work, he uses the bench in the machine room. Otherwise, he retires to the hand-tool area after the rough milling is done and completes work at his 8-ft. long Garrett Wade bench and the 27-in. high

Robert Weisman's basement layout accommodates a separate machine room and bench room. Both are brightly painted, well lit and wrapped in Masonite pegboard to provide plenty of accessible tool storage. Even the support post and three sides of the assembly table shown in these photos are covered in pegboard. Note the oversized white shut-off switch attached to the table saw (shown at left). It's an easy target for Weisman's knee or foot, no matter what his hands are wrestling with at the saw. (Photos by Darragh Humphrey Weisman.)

Robert Weisman's shipshape shop

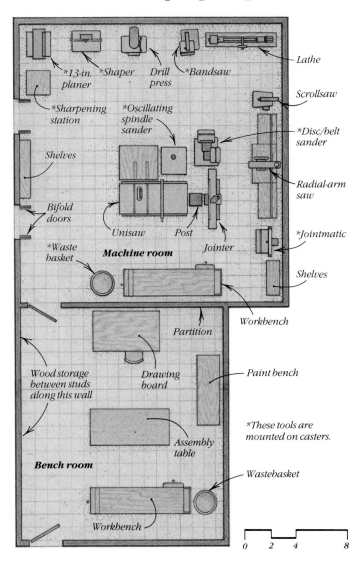

*13-in. planer *Shaper Drill press *Bandsaw Lathe

*Sharpening station

*Oscillating spindle sander

Scrollsaw

*Disc/belt sander

Shelves

Radial-arm saw

Bifold doors

Unisaw Post Jointer *Jointmatic

*Waste basket

Machine room

Shelves

Workbench

Partition

Wood storage between studs along this wall

Drawing board

Paint bench

Assembly table

*These tools are mounted on casters.

Bench room

Wastebasket

Workbench

0 2 4 8

Layout 49

Richard Schneider, a luthier, and Martha Collins, a cabinetmaker, built individual shops on the ground floor of their home in Sequim, Washington. They saved on construction costs and the cost of services while allowing each to tailor a workspace to their different trades and work habits.

assembly table, which has a top made from a Formica-covered solid-core door. "I'm not sure you can have too many benches," he notes.

Having once served aboard a Navy submarine, Weisman appreciates the efficient use of a small space. "I love pegboard," he says, and he practically plastered the walls of both rooms with the stuff. (To ensure that he wouldn't block any holes in the pegboard, Weisman glued ¾-in. thick by ⅝-in. wide strips of pine to the back side of the pegboard, carefully positioned between the peg holes. When the glue was dry, he bored pilot holes for the screws through the pine strips and installed anchors in the cement-block walls.) Recalling another lesson from his submarine service, Weisman notes that the brightly painted ceiling and walls and the flood of fluorescent light create a safe environment and help boost morale (which is especially important in a basement shop).

Shared spaces

It would be hard to find a workspace more thoroughly shared than Jeff Elliott's and Cyndy Burton's home and shop. Their situation is aided or aggravated—depending on your perspective—by the fact that they share their personal lives as well as their work. Their success is due, in part, to patience and mutual respect and, in part, to the kind of work they do and the way they have organized their shop. Each works on only one instrument at a time, so they experience few of the conflicts over machinery and space you might otherwise expect in such a tight space.

Companion shops The photos above and the floor plan on the facing page illustrate a very different arrangement for sharing a workshop, one where the structure and some equipment are shared, but the work areas remain separate. Richard Schneider is a luthier and Martha Collins is a cabinetmaker. Their shop is located on the ground floor of the 3,000-sq. ft. house they built in 1984 near Sequim, Washington, on the north slope of the Olympic mountains. (Collins hired and supervised the construction crew and was general contractor on the job.) Before the move, they operated separate shops on different floors of an old industrial building in Kalamazoo, Michigan. "That's why he married me," Collins says. "I had the air compressor."

When planning the new shop, Collins explains, "We just looked at the shops we were both in and asked 'what's the minimum we can get by with?'" She now wishes they'd built larger. "If I were to do this thing over," she says, "I'd make some space around the building for future expansion." But building on the side of a hill makes additional excavation considerably more costly.

The differences in their work and work habits are reflected in the new shop. Predictably, Collins's cabinet shop is dominated by the table saw and its large outfeed table, with the jointer and thickness planer close by. Other power tools and storage are arranged around the walls. A flexible assembly area is situated behind the saw, near the large exterior doors. The shop is outfitted with a three-phase converter and a separate dust-collection unit, situated outside the north wall. A 10-ft. high ceiling makes moving lumber and sheet stock easy.

The Schneider-Collins companion shops:
Autonomy under a shared roof

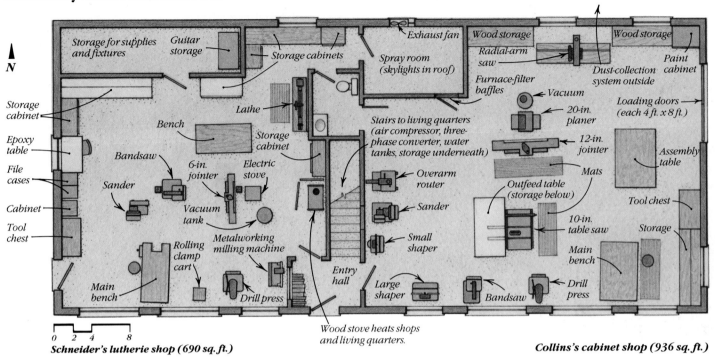

N

Storage for supplies and fixtures · **Guitar storage** · **Storage cabinets** · **Exhaust fan** · **Wood storage** · **Wood storage**

Spray room (skylights in roof) · **Radial-arm saw** · **Dust-collection system outside** · **Paint cabinet**

Furnace-filter baffles · **Vacuum** · **Loading doors (each 4 ft. x 8 ft.)**

Storage cabinet · **Lathe** · **20-in. planer**

Epoxy table · **Bench** · **Stairs to living quarters (air compressor, three-phase converter, water tanks, storage underneath)** · **12-in. jointer** · **Assembly table**

File cases · **Bandsaw** · **Storage cabinet** · **6-in. jointer** · **Electric stove** · **Mats**

Sander · **Overarm router** · **Outfeed table (storage below)** · **Tool chest**

Cabinet · **Vacuum tank** · **Sander** · **10-in. table saw** · **Storage**

Tool chest · **Metalworking milling machine** · **Small shaper** · **Main bench**

Main bench · **Rolling clamp cart** · **Drill press** · **Entry hall** · **Large shaper** · **Bandsaw** · **Drill press**

0 2 4 8

Schneider's lutherie shop (690 sq. ft.)

Wood stove heats shops and living quarters.

Collins's cabinet shop (936 sq. ft.)

Schneider's shop is much more specialized and quite a bit smaller. Apart from the jointer/bandsaw/sander triangle, most of the space is consumed by benches and tool cabinets. The handsome cabinet for hand tools sitting behind Schneider's bench in the photo at right on the facing page has a mate in Collins's shop. She built them both, tailoring each to meet their different requirements (see p. 172 for photos of their tool chests). Schneider would have preferred to place the bandsaw near the window, but opted to locate the primary workbench there instead. "I like the view," he says, "although the glare can be a problem. You have to be careful not to walk away and leave an instrument on the bench in harsh sunlight." More than half of the south-facing wall in both shops is glass, which more than makes up in scenery what it lacks in diffused light. A skylight on the north slope of the roof provides even illumination in the spray room during the daytime.

There is a 7-ft. high ceiling in Schneider's shop and a substantial amount of storage space above the bath and entryway, as well as a 5-ft. by 19-ft. storage room in the back of the shop and floor-to-ceiling cabinets in front of it. A stack of guitars in progress and several decades worth of future guitar stock are stowed on Schneider's side of the shop, along with materials for the turned-bracelet business he and Collins also operate. "My dream," Schneider says, "is to pull everything out of the shop and put down a hardwood floor." It would cost about $2,500, but it would be easier to keep clean—now, everything falls into the cracks of the hemlock underlayment. "But you have to have something you want to do to improve the place," Schneider says. "That's why you live, right?"

The shared facilities between the two shops—bathroom, air compressor and the central stairway to the second-floor apartment—function as a demilitarized zone. The spray room is accessible from both shops, but it's too small for many of Collins's projects. She often oils or brushes on a finish in her shop. A double-barrel wood stove in Schneider's shop vents to the upstairs apartment and pumps heat into Collins's shop by way of 10-in. dia. heat-exchange pipes and a sheet-metal surround. The upstairs register is covered with a double furnace filter to trap migrating shop dust. This heating system is only marginally successful. Schneider reports roasting while Collins's teeth chatter, but his guitar work is comparatively sedentary and less forgiving of extreme temperature fluctuations.

The companion layout has its advantages. "If I need to make a good cut on the bandsaw, I use Richard's," Collins says. "If he needs to do any overhead routing, he uses my machine." Collins also turns to Schneider for help with any gnarly procedures in her work; a quick run next door often solves a problem before it happens. And, lately, Collins has taken over much of Schneider's bracelet production. "The main problem is the music," she adds. She prefers Jackson Browne or Bob Dylan to Schneider's classical guitar repertoire. So each shop has its own sound system.

Life above the shop is another story. "I hate it," Collins says bluntly. Both she and Schneider resent the shop's intrusion on their personal space, and they're tired of eating sawdust. "We've survived for five years," Collins says, "but I look forward to the day when I have a home away from the shop, so I don't have to go to work when I don't want to."

A co-op shop   If it's true, as I was told, that when you "add one person, the situation changes dramatically," what happens when you add ten people to one workspace? To find out, I visited the Wood Studio, a Toronto-based co-op founded nearly a decade ago. While most other group shops I visited are informal associations of people who have decided to share equipment and space, the Wood Studio is a legally incorporated co-operative that holds the lease and owns almost all the machinery.

The ten full-time members and five part-timers are of similar backgrounds, ages and interests, but they are a self-described "eclectic group of people," with four of the ten full-time spaces belonging to women—the largest concentration of female woodworkers I found anywhere. Over the years, shop members have turned out the widest possible range of work—from water skis and doll houses to harpsichords, sculpture and cabinets. Nothing is produced in the name of the Wood Studio, but members often collaborate on projects.

The 6,000-sq. ft. shop (shown in the photos and drawing on the facing page) sprawls the full length of the fourth floor of a defunct woolen mill in downtown Toronto. Two of the limitations of the space are immediately obvious: To get to the shop you must use the freight elevator or climb four flights of stairs; and there is a noticeable shortage of windows and heat (mutually exclusive features in most old industrial buildings).

The central machine area, about 22 ft. wide by 39 ft. long, is set apart from the principal bench area and the rest of the shop by a plywood underlayment and four concrete piers. The remainder of the floor is linoleum over concrete. After making a trip in the freight elevator, much of the wood is stored in an alcove by the fire-escape exit and on a 2x4 platform erected above the planer, jointer and radial-arm saw. (These three tools form a loose work triangle at one end of the machine area.)

At the center of the machine area is a large Italian sliding-table panel saw, which for many woodworkers would be reason enough to belong to the co-op. There is also a Rockwell table saw with a Biesemeyer fence, an 18-in. bandsaw, stroke sander, edge sander, drill press and Myford lathe (the only major shop tool owned by an individual member). At the far end of the shop is a second Rockwell table saw. All the major machines are hooked up to a large, shop-built dust collector.

Each member has his or her own bench space of approximately 10 ft. by 12 ft., the location of which is determined by an ad hoc system that combines fairness and luck. Five of the spaces line the south wall (see the top photo on the facing page), not far from the machinery, the office and bathroom. The others, situated along the west and northwest walls of the shop, are much father away from the action. Often, the apparent benefits of a particular space are mitigated by other factors, such as proximity to the heating fan (noisy) or the location of a support pier (awkward)

Most of the spaces are only partially separated from their neighbors, making the place feel more like one big

The ten full-time and five part-time woodworkers who form the Wood Studio co-operative share a 6,000-sq. ft. shop in an old Toronto woolen mill. The co-operative itself holds the lease and owns most of the machinery. Shown here (from left) are members Andrey Berezowsky, Philip Whitcombe, Bridget Corkery (kneeling), Scott Mohns, Karen Huska, Ted Hunter, Zenon Berezowsky, Anne Gerger and Peter Hall. (Not pictured are full-time members Richard Burroughs, Saryl Jacobson and Fred Knitted.)

workshop than a collection of individual shops. One of the more creative layouts was designed by Karen Huska, (shown at the bottom of the facing page), who elevated her bench on a lumber and plywood platform about 4 ft. above the shop floor. The prospect of climbing yet another set of stairs may not be appealing, but the platform provides a lot more room for storage. Huska keeps an assembly table on the main floor so that large projects need not be toted to the upper level.

To relieve some of the pressure on the shop, part-timers are allotted about half as much space and are generally allowed access to machinery only after 5 p.m. and on weekends. For all but one of the part-timers, the monthly dues pay for storage more than for actual use of the space and equipment. According to the group's spokesman, Philip Whitcombe, "We operate on the basis that most of them won't use it as a workshop."

As you might expect in a shop with fifteen members, storage is a problem. Some members regularly run out of space, although there are several large areas for lumber and panel storage around the shop and the adjacent bench spaces are separated by small sheet-storage bins, shown in the top two photos on the facing page.

To the eight full-time members and two part-timers I met, the place seems pretty much ideal. They have access to well over $50,000 worth of machinery, and by passing work around and hiring each other they are able to draw upon each other's resources to tackle large projects. And most of the current members figure they've learned a lot of what they know from their time spent in the Wood Studio and from each other. As one inexperienced part-time member re-

The Wood Studio:
A cooperative effort

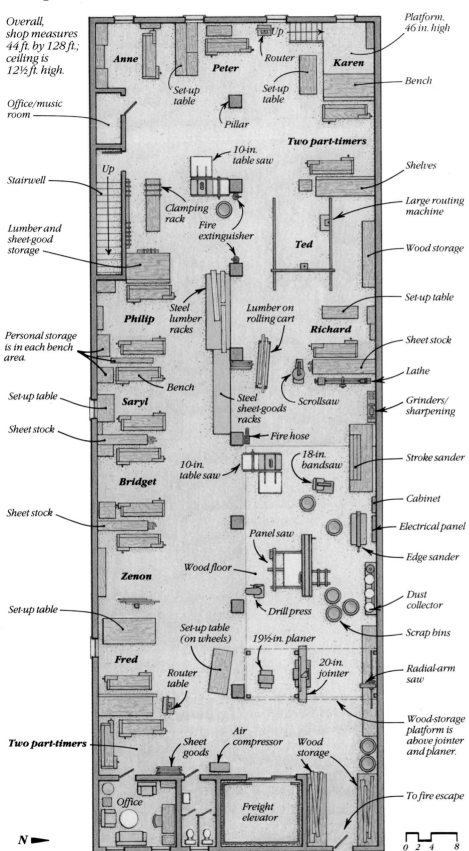

Overall, shop measures 44 ft. by 128 ft.; ceiling is 12½ ft. high.

Anne

Peter

Router

Karen

Platform, 46 in. high

Bench

Set-up table

Set-up table

Office/music room

Pillar

Two part-timers

Stairwell

Up

10-in. table saw

Shelves

Large routing machine

Lumber and sheet-good storage

Clamping rack

Fire extinguisher

Ted

Wood storage

Set-up table

Steel lumber racks

Lumber on rolling cart

Richard

Sheet stock

Personal storage is in each bench area.

Philip

Bench

Scrollsaw

Lathe

Set-up table

Steel sheet-goods racks

Grinders/ sharpening

Saryl

Sheet stock

Fire hose

10-in. table saw

18-in. bandsaw

Stroke sander

Bridget

Cabinet

Sheet stock

Panel saw

Electrical panel

Edge sander

Wood floor

Zenon

Dust collector

Drill press

Scrap bins

Set-up table

Set-up table (on wheels)

19½-in. planer

Radial-arm saw

Fred

Router table

20-in. jointer

Wood-storage platform is above jointer and planer.

Two part-timers

Air compressor

Sheet goods

Wood storage

Office

Freight elevator

To fire escape

N ▶

0 2 4 8

About half the Wood Studio's bench spaces line the south wall of the shop. The 10-ft. by 12-ft. spaces are separated by the benches and partitions, some of which serve as storage bins for sheet stock.

Wood Studio member Karen Huska added a second story to increase her floor space.

marked, "Where else can a guy like me get access to all this machinery for $115 a month? And the wisdom of all these people? It's a gold mine!"

I had a couple of immediate reservations about the ability of the layout and equipment to withstand the population density. Reflecting on the din and dust in the Wood Studio, another Toronto woodworker I met noted that "the place seems so industrial." Every shop makes noise, but in a workspace shared by ten people the place is almost certain to be noisy when you might like it to be quiet. The co-op members considered isolating the machine room with a solid partition, but decided it wasn't worth the effort. In defense of their decision, Whitcombe points out that the most irritating noise comes from routers, which are used in the personal bench areas. Ted Hunter, an original co-op member, noticed that the stereo just gets louder as the years go by. There is one stereo system with speakers all over the shop, which can be locally controlled. A number of members have their own small radios.

"People think you have to take numbers to use the machines," one member said, but in reality the members just work it out, as you might jockey demands on an office copy machine. Clearly, if everyone in the shop is cranking out cabinets full-tilt, nerves and machinery would be stretched to the limit. But this has never happened, because of the variety of work and the fact that there has never been a time when all members were working at the Wood Studio full time. (At the time of my visit, three full-time members supported themselves by teaching.) In another group shop I visited, a rule was established limiting the use of a major power tool to a half hour if in demand by another member.

Common ownership of the machinery has its advantages. In the first place, it discourages abuse: The machines the members screw up are their own, so there's an incentive to be careful. In other workshops, where the equipment is owned separately, people tend to develop a proprietary interest in their own machines, and a tangible void is created when someone departs. And, while one person might put up with an unsharpened cutter or an out-of-square fence—either out of habit, inertia or simply because they don't use the tool very much—someone in the shop is likely to get fed up and fix it.

Of course, it works both ways. Whitcombe explained that most of the machinery operates on three-phase power, with the exception of the single-phase compressor, which is very inefficient. In a shop where one person foots the whole electric bill, he suggests, there would be much more incentive to get a more efficient machine than in a shop where the bills are split ten ways. In a similar vein, the co-op drew up a floor plan to include a spray booth, but eventually decided it wasn't an efficient use of space. Apart from the $5,000 it would cost to install, the co-op would forgo another $2,500 each year for the two part-time bench spaces the booth would consume. Whitcombe prefers a rubbed-on urethane finish anyway.

"If you tried to figure out ways to take advantage of the system," Whitcombe says, "you'd just get bogged down."

The members are united by their commitment to the co-op and the fact that, in a city like Toronto, as in most urban centers, it's one of the only ways to get a fully equipped workshop. "If I were going to set up this shop elsewhere," Whitcombe adds, "I would have to move out of the city." If that happened, I suspect many members would also miss their extended family. "We can get intensely involved with our own stuff," another member said, "and then there's a period when we all come together."

Working in a small space

The Wood Studio's 6,000 sq. ft. works out to 600 sq. ft. per full-time member. That's still a lot of room—two or three times as much as many of us have to play with. The layout issues I've discussed so far—flexibility, workflow, work triangles, dedicated workspaces—are of concern in any shop, but they are doubly important in tight spaces.

There are as many solutions to the problem of laying out a small workshop as there are creative woodworkers. Just when I thought I'd found the most compact or efficient shop, I would discover another ingenious example. In the next few pages are floor plans and photos of seven small workshops. The largest is about 425 sq. ft.; the smallest is only 150 sq. ft. Workshops in smaller spaces certainly exist, and I visited a few (see pp. 28-30), but the ones here are more typical, mechanized shops. They represent the sort of workspace you might find in a garage or basement anywhere across the continent. But that doesn't make them ordinary. In each case, their owner has demonstrated a special ability to shoehorn his priorities into a modest floor plan.

A minimalist shop   At just 12 ft. by 22 ft., Dick Sellew's shop is the smallest professional cabinet shop I saw. "I never thought I could do a kitchen in here," Sellew says, anticipating my question before it is asked. But the cabinets that surround Sellew (shown in the top photo on the facing page) will outfit a kitchen more than 200 sq. ft. larger than the shop itself. Needless to say, there's no room for off-cuts, "and I don't want them!" he quickly adds.

When he set up shop in an old shed in New Marlborough, Massachusetts, Sellew explains, "I wanted to enjoy my work." After 14 years in a San Francisco production shop, he was determined to see how little he needed to get by. He also figured that a low overhead would enable him to build a nest egg. As a result, he spends less on rent than many cabinet shops spend on sharpening (a mere $20 per month), and most of his machines are cut-rate imports. "I can actually make more money here than I could with state-of-the-art equipment and ten other guys." And he lands jobs that bigger shops can't touch.

Apart from his Rockwell table saw, which occupies a space near the door, everything else is arranged around the walls. This leaves as much room as possible in the center of the shop for assembly. Instead of a shaper, Sellew mounts a large router in a shop-built router table that sets up on sawhorses. When not in use, the setup packs away in a cabi-

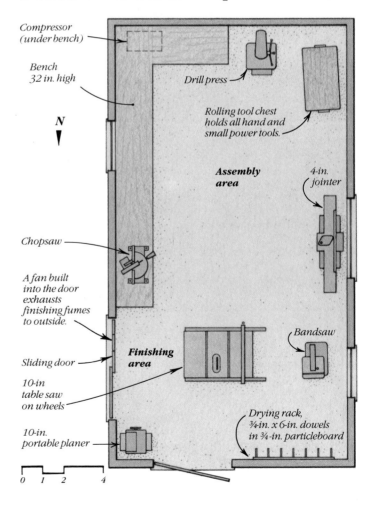

Dick Sellew handles surprisingly big projects in his tiny workshop. The cabinets clustered around him (at left) go in a kitchen that's 200 sq. ft. larger than the shop itself. When weather permits, he moves his planer outdoors. The wood storage shed (the building on the left in the photo below) is almost as big as the shop.

Dick Sellew's minimalist shop

Compressor (under bench)

Bench 32 in. high

Drill press

Rolling tool chest holds all hand and small power tools.

N

Assembly area

4-in. jointer

Chopsaw

A fan built into the door exhausts finishing fumes to outside.

Sliding door

Bandsaw

Finishing area

10-in. table saw on wheels

10-in. portable planer

Drying rack, ¾-in. x 6-in. dowels in ¾-in. particleboard

0 1 2 4

net. A chopsaw fixed to a table along one wall does the cut-off work of a radial-arm saw. An assortment of six table-saw sleds, or trays, is used to perform a variety of crosscut and miter operations. Planing and edge-joining are done on a 4-in. jointer and a portable 10-in. Ryobi planer. When the weather is nice, he puts the planer on a telephone cable spool and works outside.

Open rafters and a gable roof provide storage space (Sellew has to climb on the table saw to retrieve his edge-bander from the rafters) and room to swing long boards. Wood is stored in an adjoining shed. Three radiant electric panels on the ceiling heat the shop quickly and consume virtually no space; their white surfaces also reflect light. Sellew sprays finishes right in the front of the shop (he admits the hazardous nature of the practice); he simply rolls the table saw out of the way and turns on a fan to blow the fumes outside. A wall-mounted rack near the front door holds pieces while the finish dries.

"To be honest, I didn't think it would be as easy as it's been," he says. "But even in a 6,000-sq. ft. shop, I'd assemble in a space no bigger than this." Shoveling planer shavings into the woods, he calls over his shoulder: "I've got it pretty simple, now...it could be the best life ever."

A pint-sized production shop   Paul Potash planes no lumber outside and dumps no shavings in the woods. His 420-sq. ft. cabinet shop is located behind his house in an upscale southern California suburb, and is designed to be neither seen nor heard (see the photos and drawing on the facing page). The back of the shop borders an alley and faces a row of neighboring backyards. He feeds piles of sheet stock into the shop through an unobtrusive slot in the wall (shown in the photo at center left on the facing page), which helps maintain the low profile his location requires. Two high windows on the same wall remain closed most of the time to keep the noise and dust inside — a constraint he's learned to live with. Potash uses an electrostatic air cleaner, described on p. 111, instead of a vacuum dust collector.

Small size and all this discretion don't seem to have hindered production. Potash once built cabinets for three kitchens and six bathrooms at the same time. As in many workshops, rolling power tools enhance flexibility, but Potash's shop also benefits from a thoughtful investment in machinery. The Holz-Her 1203 vertical panel saw, the smallest in the Holz-Her line (shown at bottom left on the facing page), is the heart of the system. It takes up very little floor space and, used in conjunction with the table saw, mortiser and edge bander, gives Potash an efficiency rarely found in a small shop.

Sheet goods are stacked along the wall next to the loading slot. From there, they can be flipped onto the table saw or scooted around to the panel saw with a minimum of effort. The workbench and built-in tool cabinet make an effective assembly station. The 10-ft. high ceiling makes it easy to move sheet goods around the shop and even allows Potash to stand on top of the bench to assemble a carcase without having to crouch. Most hand tools are kept inside the bench or wall cabinets to protect them against the waves of sea breeze that wash over Potash's ocean-side neighborhood.

Fifty-six years of woodworking

While preparing this book, I ran a notice in Fine Woodworking *magazine asking for ideas from readers who work in small spaces. Four of the seven shops profiled in this section were sent in response to my query. Many others had a interesting comment or story to tell, and one of my favorites is this excerpt from Robert Markee's letter. Markee, of Iowa City, Iowa, also contributed the design for the rotary clamp rack shown on p. 180.*

"Even though he died when I was about twelve years old, [my father] left a large impression on me. He was a toolmaker, gardener, hunter and fisherman. He left a rather large collection of hand tools, which I still have.... I have had a shop of my own for about 56 years, starting with my father's

things.... My first power tool was a belt-driven head that could use an abrasive wheel or a saw blade or a drill chuck on it, the second was a scrollsaw mostly of wood. It cost about $1, I think. In about 1935, I got a very old, small metal lathe, but I had not the tools or the skills to repair it.

"By 1937, enough money was saved to purchase a new Atlas metal lathe for about $100. The banker thought I was foolish to spend that kind of money...but I was able to learn enough with it to get a job in a tool room as a lathe hand. This foothold enabled me to advance and spend the rest of my working career at good pay and interesting work. The old Atlas brought about $500 when I entered the army in 1943. Enough said about the banker.

"In the late 1950s, I started a small business repairing contractor's transit levels.... After paying taxes, I share the money with my wife. It is never used for household expenses. With this money I also have purchased many tools. Many clamps, etc. were made from available materials. Extra wood is kept on hand as well as a wide collection of nails and screws. No attempt has ever been made to sell shop projects.

"Many people look at all the things down there and wonder how I did it. After all, it's taken 56 years to get to this point. They also ask what will happen to all this when I pass by and leave it to my wife or daughter. Shucks, it won't bother me for a moment.

"Would I change anything? Of course, but nothing major: a built-in sawdust collector and a spray/welding booth, but I'll never get either done.... I have the usual high blood pressure, cholesterol, gout and all the other things from modern living. I hope to continue full-tilt down the road of life, leaving a trail of projects and shavings to the very end...either in the shop or in the garden."

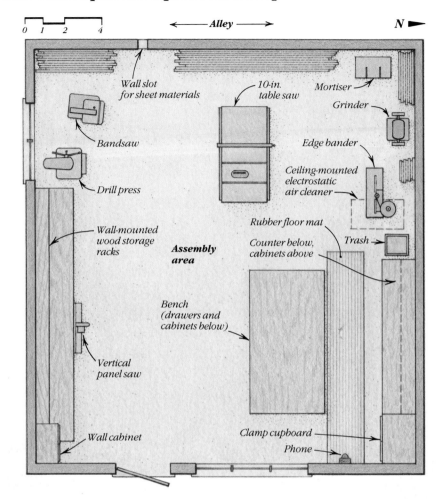

Paul Potash's pint-sized production shop

0 1 2 4

← Alley →

N ►

Wall slot for sheet materials

10-in. table saw

Mortiser

Grinder

Bandsaw

Edge bander

Drill press

Ceiling-mounted electrostatic air cleaner

Wall-mounted wood storage racks

Rubber floor mat

Assembly area

Counter below, cabinets above

Trash

Bench (drawers and cabinets below)

Vertical panel saw

Wall cabinet

Clamp cupboard

Phone

Paul Potash's small cabinet shop, in a comfortable California suburb, is well-camouflaged behind his house. Even the material slips quietly into the shop through a specially made slot in a wall.

A Holz-Her 1203 vertical panel saw makes Potash's small shop feasible —a standard, horizontal panel saw would take up half the shop. A rack on the wall behind the saw holds solid wood.

There's lots of room for storage in the bench drawers and nearby cabinets. The laminated maple tops overhang the bases to allow room for clamps and an electrical-power strip.

An eclectic retirement shop A workshop for an active retirement often serves all sorts of demands. Don Anderson of Sequim, Washington, is a retired Kodak chemist, and he designed his shop to handle everything from woodwork and photography to stained glass, ceramics and plastics. "It's an organized mess," he says. The four separate workrooms are in a 20-ft. by 26-ft. garage, and the shop is separated from the rest of the house by a covered breezeway, which provides extra room for storage and overflow workspace.

When he moved in, Anderson had to dismantle the shelves in the garage with a crowbar and a hacksaw. Learning from the experience, he designed his shop to be fully convertible. All the partitions are screwed in place and can be removed easily. Even the sand-pit foundry in the floor can become a grease pit for auto repair. A wood floor underlays the bench room and the darkroom; the machine area and projects room have a concrete floor. The projects room has four benches and a photographic port in the wall, which converts the space into a camera obscura.

Anderson's power tools are basic, but adequate to his hobby needs. An 8-in. Sears Craftsman table saw, a jigsaw and grinder are housed in the machine room, while his 6-in. Craftsman lathe and drill press are installed in the bench room. Wood is stored in a separate cubicle next to the bench room and along the walls of the machine room. To eliminate the need for permanent shelving and to keep tools accessible, he hangs many of them on cords (more than 50 at last count) around the shop. "I was taught to lay a plane on its side," he says, "but bench space is frequently not available, so I just hang it up."

Anderson extends the capacity of his tools and workspace with some homey, but effective, accessories, such as the little drill-press table shown in the photo below. Occasionally, work overflows the shop, to his pipe-clamp stump or one of four portable, lap benches (shown below right). The lap benches are carried into the house (or any place in the shop) for work on miniatures. "Anything I want to do, I can probably work out a way of doing it," he says.

Don Anderson's retirement shop

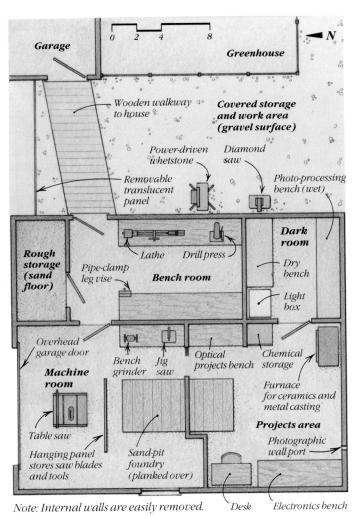

Garage

Greenhouse

0 2 4 8

N

Wooden walkway to house

Covered storage and work area (gravel surface)

Power-driven whetstone

Diamond saw

Removable translucent panel

Photo-processing bench (wet)

Lathe *Drill press*

Dark room

Rough storage (sand floor)

Pipe-clamp leg vise

Bench room

Dry bench

Light box

Overhead garage door

Bench grinder *Jig saw*

Optical projects bench

Chemical storage

Machine room

Furnace for ceramics and metal casting

Table saw

Hanging panel stores saw blades and tools

Sand-pit foundry (planked over)

Projects area

Photographic wall port

Note: Internal walls are easily removed. *Desk* *Electronics bench*

Don Anderson gets the most out of simple equipment in his retirement workshop. The plywood box shown here allows him to drill pieces on a table without removing the drill-press vise. As the floor plan at left shows, five separate areas in his converted garage serve a range of hobbies. And when he runs out of space in the garage, he can move outside to his pipe-clamp stump 'bench' or into the house, where he works on miniatures with the aid of several lap benches like the one below. (Photos by Ross Hamilton.)

Maurice Gordon's computer-aided shop design

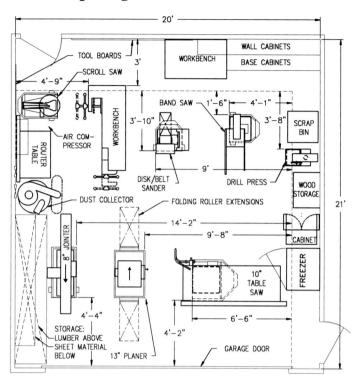

Set up for work

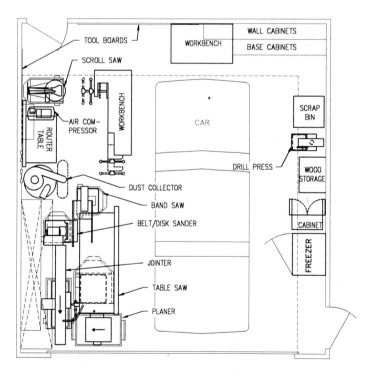

Knocked down for parking

Maurice Gordon's garage shop is a tour de force of planning. With the help of a computer design program, Gordon figured how to combine workshop and car parking in the same space. The printouts at left show it packed up for parking with room for hand-tool work (top) and set up for work (bottom). (Photo and printouts by Maurice Gordon.)

Sharing the shop with a car When Maurice Gordon's only major tools were a Shopsmith and a Sears table saw mounted on casters, it was relatively easy to share space with the family car in his Houston garage. The situation became more complex, however, as his woodworking turned professional and he replaced his tools with single-purpose machinery.

In 1988, Gordon considered his needs—a full-function shop with sufficient space around the stationary equipment and room for one car when the shop was not in use. That's a tall order for a 420-sq. ft. attached garage. Gordon used a computer-aided design (CAD) program to organize his power tools, benches, fixtures and storage. By moving outlines of his machinery around on the computer screen, he was able to figure out where to put the tools to make room for the car. (The tools that need to move are on rollers.) Using the overlay feature of the AutoCad program, he also designed a lighting plan for the shop.

The arrangement is not perfect—the garage door must be opened to saw large sheet stock or to surface long boards—but it would be hard to improve. Active and stored tool locations are painted on the cement floor like notes to a stage crew, enabling Gordon to set up the workshop or to knock it down in five minutes.

A well-organized basement shop Organization and storage are more than a luxury in most basement workshops. Jim Whetstone's shop in New Cumberland, Pennsylvania, is as highly organized and economical in its use of space as any I've seen. As the floor plan below shows, Whetstone located his major power tools near the centerline of the shop. Three workbenches surround the machinery, and wood storage is at the far end of the shop. This arrangement allows him to rip 4-ft. by 8-ft. sheets of plywood on the table saw and cut 14-ft. lumber on the radial-arm saw. It also provides space to lay out, construct and finish a variety of projects.

The ceiling and partition between the shop and the rest of the basement are of drywall construction, which makes for easy maintenance and sound insulation and aids fire prevention. Electrical boxes hang from the ceiling to keep cords off the floor. For safety and convenience, Whetstone color coded the circuits — red for lights and orange for equipment. To promote order and style, he painted his cabinet cases and door frames green and the doors blue. I was impressed by the number of clever storage ideas he had come up with, one of the reasons he's able to cram so much in such a small space and to keep it neat. Several of these are shown in the photos on the facing page.

The shop appears to be complete, but according to Whetstone, it has evolved a little bit each year since it was built in 1974. "It is not finished," he explains. "No true woodworker with a reverence for wood, order and quality is ever satisfied with his workplace. It will grow as I grow."

Jim Whetstone's basement shop: A place for everything...

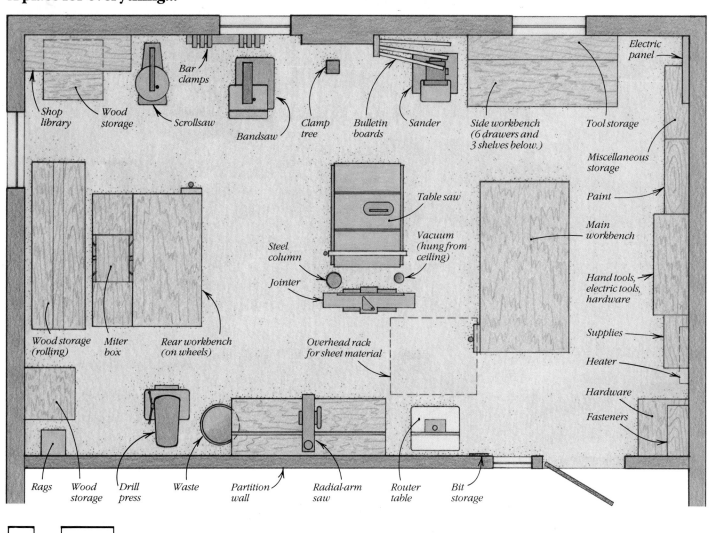

Shop library · Wood storage · Scrollsaw · Bandsaw · Bar clamps · Clamp tree · Bulletin boards · Sander · Side workbench (6 drawers and 3 shelves below.) · Tool storage · Electric panel · Miscellaneous storage · Paint · Table saw · Vacuum (hung from ceiling) · Main workbench · Steel column · Jointer · Hand tools, electric tools, hardware · Wood storage (rolling) · Miter box · Rear workbench (on wheels) · Overhead rack for sheet material · Supplies · Heater · Hardware · Fasteners · Rags · Wood storage · Drill press · Waste · Partition wall · Radial-arm saw · Router table · Bit storage

0 1 2 4

Jim Whetstone gets a lot of mileage out of his small basement workshop by making sure there's a place for everything and that everything is in its place. He has come up with some creative ideas for storage, shown in the photos at left. The 34-in.-sq. rack (shown at far left) pivots down from the ceiling to provide access to sheet goods; drill bits are stored in a handy, ceiling-hung rack above the drill press; handscrew clamps are stored on a 4x4 'tree' and three cork bulletin boards, which display plans and patterns are hinged to a single post. (Photos by James Whetstone.)

C. Wayne Joslin made the most of the basement in his 80-year-old home. The compact carving studio itself is carved out of an old cistern. Joslin jockeys his machinery around the main workshop to pack it all in. Two wings on either side of the radial-arm saw table fold down for easy storage.

C. Wayne Joslin's shop: A little here, a little there

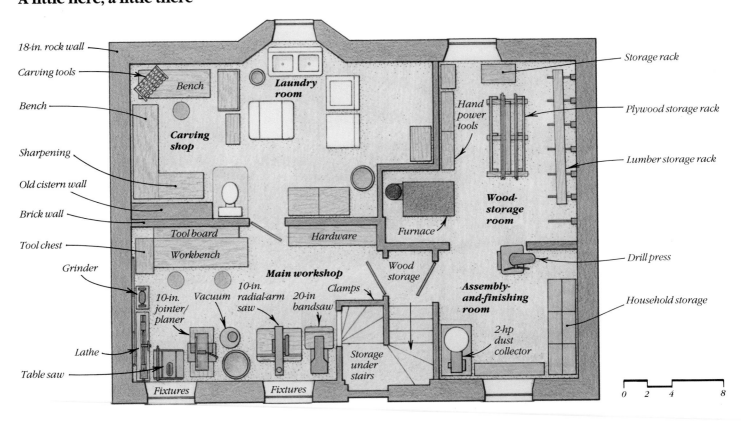

18-in. rock wall

Carving tools

Bench

Sharpening

Old cistern wall

Brick wall

Tool chest

Grinder

Lathe

Table saw

Bench

Carving shop

Tool board

Workbench

10-in. jointer/ planer

Vacuum

10-in. radial-arm saw

Main workshop

Fixtures

Laundry room

Hardware

20-in bandsaw

Clamps

Fixtures

Wood storage

Storage under stairs

Hand power tools

Furnace

Wood-storage room

Assembly-and-finishing room

2-hp dust collector

Storage rack

Plywood storage rack

Lumber storage rack

Drill press

Household storage

0   2   4   8

Dividing to conquer Most of us face a very simple problem—too much stuff in too little space. Without knocking down walls or selling off tools (the first option is usually impractical, the second unthinkable), there seems to be little hope. C. Wayne Joslin's shop, on the facing page, has expanded over 20 years to fill virtually every available corner, and some that were won by laborious effort.

The shop is dispersed in four basement rooms of Joslin's 80-year-old home in Cambridge, Ontario. Joslin notes that "efficiency of storage opposes flexibility. The more organized everything is, the less scope there is for change...." By dividing his workshop into several discrete function areas, he was able to use spaces that would, on their own, be too small to house an entire shop.

Thus, by pulverizing the 18-in. thick walls of a rock cistern, Joslin created an 8-ft. by 11-ft. carving shop. The 10-ft. by 13-ft. furnace room holds wood and hand-held power tools, while the adjacent household storage room is used for assembly and finishing. The main shop area is reserved for a workbench and the most frequently used machinery—compact Inca tools predominate.

The divided layout is well suited to Joslin's work. A prize-winning carving he recently finished was six years in the making—not the sort of project that could take up prime bench space. It remained accessible, but not in the way, on a corner of the carving bench. The machinery in the main shop presents a different problem. "I can't just whip downstairs and run a board through the planer," he explains. Only the radial-arm saw can be used where it stands. The other equipment must be set up and knocked down, and the sawdust cleared before the family tracks it through the laundry room.

On a recent visit I made to Joslin's shop, it struck me as more comfortable and less crowded than I expected. "I don't even think of it as crowded," he said. Joslin has learned to live with the limitations of his divided basement shop, developing fastidious work habits and an assortment of useful storage fixtures (some of which are discussed in Chapter 8).

A vertical layout According to Dave Evenson, of Cumberland, Wisconsin, "the vertical dimension is as important as the horizontal in a small space." While some woodworkers make all their tables and machines the same height to provide outfeed support, Evenson was more interested in unobstructed access in his 150-sq. ft. basement shop. The table heights on his benches and machines are staggered, allowing him to feed stock over and under adjacent equipment, as shown below. Stock is fed to the router table beneath the 44-in. high benchtop and above the dust collector. The table

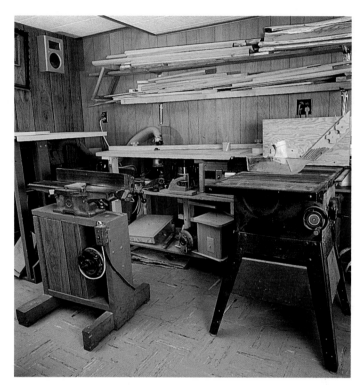

Dave Evenson varied the heights of his machines and benches when laying out his small basement shop.

Dave Evenson's vertical layout

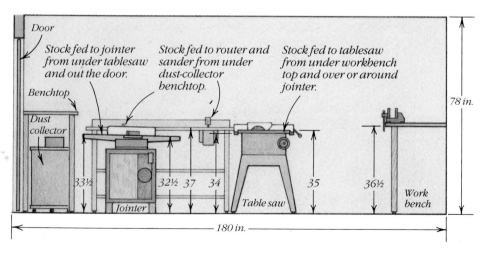

saw is higher than the jointer fence and lower than the workbench extension that covers the shop vac. The jointer feeds below the table-saw extension. The base he made for the jointer is not level, and the angle provides even more clearance. "I'm sorry to say it was an accident," Evenson told me, but it's one mistake he's glad to have made.

"A small shop tends to dictate the size of projects," Evenson says. He's built three or four pieces of furniture, but works mainly on picture frames, toys, boxes and musical instruments. Evenson buys 8 ft. air-dried lumber from a local mill (or splits it out of firewood) and cuts it into 4 ft. lengths outside, using an electric chainsaw or circular saw. Bench space is always at a premium. He keeps a chunk of countertop on top of the lathe bed most of the time and uses the router table and table saw (with bit and blade lowered) for auxiliary work surfaces.

Planning the workshop layout

There are woodworkers who shun the drawing board, favoring "spontaneous" design right at the saw, motor running. You can lay out your shop the same way—simply move your stuff in and start working. But if you've ever chopped tails on both parts of a dovetail joint, you'll appreciate the value of good planning. With all of the elements involved in putting together a shop, which is a lot more complicated than a piece of furniture, you'd be well advised to start with a pencil and paper, and a good eraser. Designing, like writing or dancing, is meant to *look* natural and easy, but it rarely is.

Before you start sketching floor plans, it's a good idea to make a few priority lists. Take a tip from kitchen designers and begin with your equipment. Make a list of every tool (large and small) you currently own or expect to buy, and rate its importance. Consider not only how much space each tool requires for efficient operation—what's the most you'll

need and how little you can get by with—but also how often you use it and for what sorts of operations. This exercise may reveal some surprising, even unpleasant information. The size or expense of a tool may bear little relationship to its importance in your shop. For example, if you use a bandsaw only for occasional resawing of heavy timber, you may be better off consigning it to the wood shed than having it consume valuable shop space. And perhaps the money you were saving for a thickness sander would be better spent on a new set of planer knives or a scraper. (You might be able to rent time on a sander.) Make sure to consider which tools are often used at the same time, so you can develop clusters of work triangles with an efficient overall workflow.

Take an inventory of materials and hardware, and review how they typically get used up. If lumber or plywood arrives regularly and is used promptly, you may want a temporary storage location close to the machinery, like Kelly Mehler's break-down lane. If you are overrun by a mountain of precious lumber that you rarely use but hate to part with, you might take a hard look at other storage solutions, or consider a behavior-modification program. (Friends have tried the latter on me, so far with no success.)

The priority lists will generate all the information you need to begin your design—from power requirements to dust collection. The process should also serve as a catalyst for asking basic questions about your work habits: What temperature are you comfortable working in? What sort of light do you prefer, and how does it vary with different operations? Do you spread your work out or burrow in? Are you neat, or are you a slob? If your dream shop is somewhere in your future and you are currently working in another space, take the opportunity to examine the ways in which the current shop aids or hinders your work. By analyzing your daily routine—how many trips you make to the bench, how many times you start the saw—you'll add valuable layers of infor-

A model can bring a shop layout to life. John Monteleone's is so vivid, it's easy to imagine how the space will work.

mation to the plan. Keep your list handy and amend or enlarge it as new projects arise, or as you visit other shops.

There are several good ways to develop a floor plan. You can outline the perimeter of your shop on a sheet of paper and simply sketch in the equipment, but a method that allows you to move things around easily and try out many different possibilities is likely to give you the best results. You can cut out pieces of paper or cardboard to represent each tool and move them around on a floor plan until you get it right. Be sure to represent the equipment and the shop space to scale. Carefully consider the direction of feed for each machine and the amount of space required for each operation. A few inches can make a big difference.

Like Maurice Gordon, an increasing number of woodworkers use a computer and design program to do the same thing. By printing out different versions, they can compare many possibilities. Gordon used an AutoCad program to work up his floor plan. He entered each machine, bench and other workshop fixture as a separate component in the drawing, so that it could be manipulated without affecting the overall floor plan. The program's 256 overlay functions made it easy to develop lighting, electrical and dust-collection plans, just as an architect would use transparent drawing overlays. The program is pricey, and Gordon uses it in his "real-life" engineering business, but less expensive (and perhaps less elegant) drawing programs are available that would work fine for a workshop floor plan.

After the floor plan, you might draw some elevations — if not for the entire shop, then at least of some walls. As I mentioned earlier, vertical layout is an important factor in the efficiency of any floor plan, particularly in a small space where the heights of adjacent tools and work surfaces are critical. Elevations will wean you away from the flat plan and get you thinking in three dimensions. This is a necessary transition and will enable you to develop a total shop plan that accounts for things like storage, shelving and windows.

If you have trouble thinking in three dimensions, try making a model. After working for years in a decrepit, dockside machine shop on Long Island, luthier John Monteleone wanted to be sure that his new workshop would be worth the wait. He began, as many people do, by manipulating cardboard cutouts on a board, but was soon frustrated. "You have to use a lot of imagination," he says.

So he started making models — benches first, built to a 1-in. scale. "Things started out simple," he says, "then I got enthused!" He measured each tool and cut the corresponding model out of pine on the bandsaw, sticking the parts together instantly with cyanoacrylate glue and spray accelerator so clamping could be accomplished with hand pressure. He spent several days in the process — almost two hours on the thickness sander alone. His results are shown on the facing page and on p. 40. Monteleone was inspired in part by his father, who built a scale model of New York City for the 1939 World's Fair.

This may appear excessive, but to Monteleone, who is best known for his elegant arch-top guitars and mandolins, it seems a small down payment on the investment in a new shop. His current plan includes a 30-ft. by 40-ft. freestanding structure, with a 750-sq. ft. storage loft. The advantage of the "doll-house" construction is the ease with which parts can be moved around and their three-dimensional relationship assessed. Moreover, you can vary the overall orientation of the building and the location of windows and doors to simulate the effects of sunlight on the interior during different seasons or times of day.

For years, Monteleone has relied on the ramshackle appearance of his waterfront shop to keep the riffraff out. "In the early days," he explains, "I was concerned with the quality of my craft. I still am, but that was *all* I was concerned about." As he has grown older and more established, he finds himself more interested in the quality of life. "I don't need a beautiful place to do what I do," he says, "but it sure would be nice!"

Machinery is often the largest investment of both money and space in a workshop. Combination machines save space and simplify shop-layout decisions. This classic belt-driven Parks Planing Mill Special combines a table saw, 12-in. jointer, 22-in. bandsaw, hollow-chisel mortiser (converted to a drill press), swing cut-off saw and shaper — all powered by a 5-hp electric motor. It was manufactured in Cincinnati, Ohio, before World War II; Parks went out of business in 1989.

Machinery

I have at my disposal what the whole world demands; something which will uplift civilization more than ever by relieving man of all undignified drudgery. I have steam power. —Matthew Boulton, partner in the Boulton & [James] Watt factory

Chapter 4

For years, I worked wood almost entirely by hand. I built my first log cabin with a bucksaw and an ax, borrowing a chainsaw for one fretful day of cutting door and window openings. Later, in my first workshop, I made perfectly serviceable snowshoes, canoe paddles, knife handles and small boxes without benefit of electricity or gasoline.

When my woodworking joined the 20th century, I entered gradually, testing the water, as it were, with one toe. The first power tool I spent any time with was the Parks Planing Mill Special (shown on the facing page). With its heavy cast construction, leather belts and cavalier lack of safety devices, the Parks is itself a transitional creature, not wholly emerged from the age of steam, when woodworking machines were run off line shafts and a missing finger or limb was just part of the price of progress.

For me, the Parks was an ideal guide to the age of machinery. It had all the basic equipment I would later encounter in more sophisticated forms, yet it was never so accurate or refined that I could expect it to bring more to the work than I was capable of myself. It was a kind of latter-day apprentice (quite a luxury for a novice woodworker) employed to do most of the stock reduction and rough joinery, which would be refined and finished by hand.

Although I've lost track of that old Parks—the friend who owned the machine eventually sold it and moved forward, technologically, by several decades—it recalls fond memories. The Parks introduced me to the wonders of the

table saw, bandsaw and jointer, three of the most basic time-saving and muscle-saving devices in the business. I used it to build my first workbench, which was also my first major woodworking project. With its slapping belts and unguarded blades, the Parks also taught me respect, if not fear, of power. Firing the machine up, I imagined prop-starting an old single-engine airplane. I learned to throw the switch and retreat for about ten seconds, until the ascending whine of the engine leveled out at its operational rpm.

Machinery has become so much a part of the modern workshop that it's easy to forget that it comes with a price. This may be measured not merely in dollars or even fingers and eyes, or in displaced workers, as the 19th-century Luddites predicted. But with every operation assumed by a machine, we distance ourselves from our work and our material. As David Pye so aptly observed, machinery replaces the creative "workmanship of risk" with the more predictable "workmanship of certainty." Eventually, we risk becoming tool managers, not woodworkers.

It is tempting to draw a simple conclusion from all this and forgo the use of power tools entirely. It would be difficult, however, to make a career of it, and I know of no full-time professionals (and only a handful of amateurs) who do not rely on some form of power. In fact, I've met a number of virtuosos who use machines almost exclusively and to great effect. Even the traditional chairmakers and boatbuilders I visited use them in moderation.

Around the beginning of the century, such luminaries of the Arts and Crafts movement as C. R. Ashbee and Gustav

Stickley argued that basic machinery should be employed to free the craftsman from drudgery and conserve his energy for more creative tasks. By the close of the century, it could certainly be argued that machinery has got the better of us, amateurs and professionals alike. Although many woodworkers begin with hand tools (often in a junior-high-school woodshop class), they soon "graduate" to table saws, jointers and routers. Then, after a few years of working as the machines dictate, they find themselves longing for a smoothly planed surface or a more flexible routine.

The fundamental question about machinery is not whether a Powermatic is better than a Delta, or whether to buy an American machine instead of a sleeker European or cheaper Asian import. The question is rather how machinery fits with the kind of woodworking you do and the reasons you do it. Tools are seductive—every time you get a new one you wonder how you lived without it. But before rushing headlong into debt in search of the machine that will make you a better craftsman (if you find it, let me know), try to make certain that you won't regret your indulgence in the morning. Think carefully about the things you make, the materials you prefer, the room in your shop, your proximity to neighbors, your tolerance for noise and dust, and the size of your budget. For every major purchase you contemplate, balance the return against the investment—will it increase your profit or enhance your pleasure?

Finally, remember why you started woodworking. If the process is as important to you as the product, think twice about the merits of any machine or production shortcut that promises to deliver the finished result in half the time. As James Krenov notes in his book, *The Fine Art of Cabinetmaking*, despite the small selection of power tools with which he began, "I did get things done...the pieces weren't primitive because of the way the shop was equipped—it's just that they might have been finished a bit sooner...I learned more then than at any time before or since."

Selecting machinery

I asked many woodworkers about their choice of machinery. Mac Campbell's response was typical: "The first and most important consideration is, 'What tool will most reduce the grunt work?' Some sort of sawing machine comes first." Campbell's first power tool was the Sears table saw that he used to build his shop. His next acquisitions were a 4-in. Sears jointer and a Taiwanese drill press. Then, in a radical departure, he rented a three-ton, 24-in. babbitt-bearing planer for about $300 per year, which he eventually purchased for the accumulated rental fee.

To keep from being buried alive by machinery and overhead, many woodworkers I met, especially in industrial areas, rent time on someone else's large sander, thickness planer or other equipment. In Halifax, Nova Scotia, the Atlantic Woodworkers Association provides its members with an unusual service. For a nominal fee, the organization rents small specialty items that are not usually in constant demand, such as a Lamello biscuit jointer, a Makita long-bed electric planer and a finger-jointing jig. Although the program has been slow in catching on, it offers an appealing alternative to the endless accumulation of equipment so many woodworkers face.

Campbell's initial machinery acquisitions parallel the history of technology. The first patent in North America for a mechanical invention was issued in 1646 to Joseph Jenks of the colony of Massachusetts for his improved sawmill and scythe. This was followed by patents on planing machines (for stock reduction and preparation) and later, mortising and tenoning equipment (for joinery).

Similar types of machines still form the backbone of most woodworking shops. A typical complement in the shops I visited would include a table saw and/or radial-arm saw, a bandsaw, jointer, planer and drill press. Then, depending on the type of work, come lathes, stroke or belt sanders, shapers, mortising machines and jigsaws. Most shops also contain a panoply of small bench and hand-held tools—grinders, pad and belt sanders, routers and drills. These tools probably do as much work as any major machine, and they save at least as much time and energy. In a growing number of shops, the computer is assuming a significant role, not only in managing books and correspondence, but in planning production and even in design (see "Microchips in the workshop," on pp. 84-87).

Woodworkers' interests and talents differ too much for me to go comfortably beyond these general observations and recommend specific combinations, sizes or brands of machinery. But as you read through the book, you'll see all kinds of woodworking done with all kinds of tools, both hand and machine. I hope that the following real-life examples will prove more useful to you than any particular list of tools or comparison of brands that I could come up with.

No matter what piece of equipment you're looking for, I suggest you follow advice I heard from Tage Frid. "The worst thing you can do," he said, "is buy cheap or underpowered machines—an underpowered machine is dangerous." There's a constant risk of an overloaded motor, kickback and burned blades. And, you have a tendency to compensate by pushing the work too hard, further taxing the motor and blades and risking an accident. Frid recommends a 10-in. table saw (1-hp motor), an 8-in. jointer (1- hp motor), a 12-in. planer (2-hp motor) and a 20-in. bandsaw (1-hp motor). Anything smaller he considers a toy. And he considers these motors to be minimum sizes. For serious production, a 3-hp or even a 5-hp motor would not be too large for a 10-in. table saw. Larger motors run cooler because they're under less load and they draw less current.

It's a good idea to make considered, informed choices when buying machines, but things often happen otherwise. "Wouldn't it be nice," Mac Campbell reflected, "if someone actually was organized enough to think about what is really needed, instead of seeing something and thinking: 'I can come up with enough money for that machine'...which is actually the way it happens." I've seen plenty of examples of what ingenuity and hard work can do for machinery that wasn't optimum, but was available. Some people do wonders with machines Frid would surely consider toys; others make machines the size (and vintage) of mothballed battleships hum like Swiss watches.

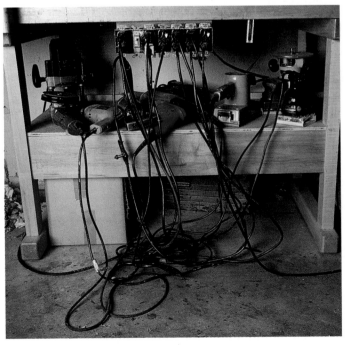

Although they occupy only a fraction of the space of their larger, stationary cousins, hand-held power tools are indispensable to most modern workshops.

The Delta Unisaw, with its 10-in. blade, tilting arbor and heavy cast-iron tables, is the workhorse of American-made table saws.

Saws Of the basic types of stationary woodworking machines, saws present the greatest variety. If you want a machine to flatten boards, you'll need a jointer; if you want to thickness boards, you'll look at planers; for boring holes, drill presses. But if you want to saw wood, you can choose between three very different machines: the table saw, the radial-arm saw and the bandsaw. I've met woodworkers who swore by one or the other, and those who owned one (or more) of each, so I think it's worth saying a few words about them.

A table saw is as essential as a workbench in many shops. In fact, some woodworkers do so much at the table saw that its convenient flat surface functions as a workbench and assembly table. The modern table saw is a very versatile machine. With a miter gauge and rip fence, it's capable of crosscutting and ripping large roughsawn boards to length and width as well as accurately executing quite a few basic joints. It can do even more when augmented with aftermarket and shop-built jigs and fixtures. (I saw a lot of Paralok, Biesemeyer and Vega rip fences in shops.)

However, a table saw usually isn't the best tool for any one particular job. A panel saw does a better job of crosscutting sheet stock. A tenoner is better at cutting tenons. A bandsaw works much better for resawing and ripping rough

Safety at the saw

If you work long enough around sharp tools and high-speed cutters, they're liable to catch up with you sooner or later. Most old carpenters and sawyers I know have their share of scars — or missing fingers — to show for their experience. But that doesn't mean you can't take some precautions to reduce the likelihood of an accident or, if one occurs, to improve your chances of making it a minor one.

All workshop power tools carry an element of risk. But the table saw seems like an accident waiting to happen. Among the more than 1,000 respondents to a 1983 survey in *Fine Woodworking* magazine, the table saw was responsible for 42 percent of all injuries reported. (The jointer earned a distant second place, at 18 percent, followed by the radial-arm saw at 7 percent and the bandsaw at 6 percent.) Many

of these accidents occurred while ripping stock that was either too short or too thin, warped or knotty. Crosscutting accidents were much less common, but certainly not unheard of. This is due, in part, to the popularity of the table saw — it was the first choice of most woodworkers I visited — but the nature of the tool demands respect.

Elusive guards
Table-saw manufacturers and users seem to share a phobia about blade guards. In a sobering number of shops, standard factory guards are nowhere in sight. When asked, many woodworkers reply that these guards obstruct visibility and are either so clumsy or inadequate as to be more dangerous than none at all. If you agree, take heed of the *Fine Woodworking* survey findings: "Hardly anybody...reported a serious table-saw accident that

occurred with a blade cover, kickback pawls and splitter all in place."

In the last few years, a number of aftermarket saw guards have been introduced that warrant more serious consideration. Kelly Mehler uses a Brett-Guard, manufactured by HTC Products, Inc. (see Sources of Supply on p. 210), and has come to feel funny if he works at a saw without one. "As soon as I put it on, I immediately relax," he says. "It's safer and it feels better. It doesn't do everything, but it does *a lot.*"

The Brett-Guard, shown at left on the facing page, is supported by two steel rods, which are raised and lowered by a handscrew mechanism that bolts to the edge of the saw table. The mounting plate can be attached to either side or to the back of the machine, to suit a variety

of sawing operations. Although the clear plastic housing affords an excellent view of both blade and work, Mehler does all his measuring — setting the depth and angle of cut and the position of the fence — before he positions the guard in place. (The Delta Uniguard, shown on the saw in the photo above, is another increasingly popular aftermarket guard.)

Faced with the cost of a sophisticated unit like the Brett-Guard or the Biesemeyer BladeGuard (shown on p. 103), several woodworkers have built their own. The BladeGuard and Charlie Mastro's shop-built guard (also shown on p. 103) combine cutter protection with an effective dust-collection pickup. Michael Strong, of Bellingham, Washington, made the simple guard shown at right on the facing page after he was cited stock. In fact, other than ripsawing boards to precise dimensions, it's hard to think of a woodworking task that can't be done better on some other machine. But how many of us can afford to buy seven different machines?

There are a lot of table saws on the market, ranging in price from hundreds to thousands of dollars, and in size from tiny to huge. The 10-in. models (designated by the diameter of the blade) are by far the most popular among serious amateurs and in small professional shops. Like Mac Campbell, a lot of woodworkers cut their teeth, so to speak, on an inexpensive Sears table saw, then move up to a 10-in. Delta Unisaw, the Ford or Chevy of table saws. Several North American manufacturers, such as Powermatic and General, produce comparable machines, and in recent years a host of Far Eastern knock-offs of these machines have appeared, sometimes copying the original right down to the paint job. The differences between these trade saws are often subtle and a matter of personal preference, such as whether the tilting arbor angles the blade away from the fence (as on the Powermatic) or toward it (on the Unisaw).

Many woodworkers conserve space by using combination machines or, more often, simply by choosing smaller, more portable equipment. Small does not necessarily mean cheap or shoddily built. The 10-in. Swiss Inca table saw costs about as much as the leading "trade" machines, but it is a favorite among several amateur and professional woodworkers I visited because of its small size, light weight and precise operation. (The Unisaw, for example, weighs about four times as much.)

The Inca table saw has two main drawbacks: the 10-in. blade won't fully retract beneath the table surface, and the tilting table can be difficult to use on plywood and other large stock. (Most trade saws have a tilting arbor.) These disadvantages are partially offset by the mortising attachment on the outboard side of the Inca's arbor. In the end, the choice you make should reflect your own priorities. Production cabinetmakers and professional furniture makers or house builders would likely find the Inca restrictive, while craftsmen who have only occasional need of a table saw might appreciate its lightweight, quality construction and be willing to work around its limitations.

As the single most popular machine in the workshop, and perhaps the most dangerous, the table saw is the source of more accidents than any other tool. Below is a discussion of some of the things you can do to improve your odds when you face the table saw.

Michael Strong's shop-built blade guard works better for ripping than crosscutting, when the Plexiglas shield tends to obscure the end of the cut. To accommodate different sizes of stock, the shield is hinged at the back to an adjustable wooden shaft.

Kelly Mehler likes the Brett-Guard for its ease of adjustment and good visibility. He always uses outfeed or sidefeed support when ripping long stock to keep from levering the guard out of position.

for numerous infractions by his local safety inspector. Strong recognizes the incentive it provided to add guards to his machinery, which he admits he should have done long ago. Even if he doesn't use the guards all the time, their very presence makes him more cautious.

Splitters
A splitter is almost as important as a guard, since it keeps the kerf from closing behind the blade and greatly reduces the risk of kickback during a ripping operation. Several manufacturers make them. Delta's, for example, is standard equipment on their Uniguard, but it can also be purchased from Delta as a single part.

You can also make a good splitter yourself. The one shown in the drawing on p. 72 was designed by Bill Ketelle, the head of wood technology at Cerritos Community College in Norwalk, California. In addition to protecting against kickback, Ketelle's splitter incorporates a guard that prevents accidental contact of a hand or a piece of wood with the blade. You can make a simpler splitter by mortising a vertical plastic or hardwood finger behind the blade in a wooden throat plate. With or without a splitter, a wooden

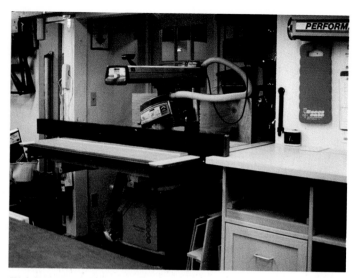

Kirk Kelsey cuts joints and rips heavy stock on his 10-in. Sears radial-arm saw. The saw's table, fitted with a Paralok fence, extends on tracks pirated from a bifold door and can be locked just over 5 ft. from the blade to rip large panels. (Kelsey inserts leaves in the fully extended table to fill in the open space and keep it from twisting.) The infeed table to the right of the saw is hinged and can be flipped up for access to the cabinet below. (Photo by Kirk Kelsey.)

Despite the table saw's versatility, many woodworkers, particularly those with limited space, prefer a radial-arm saw that fits comfortably against a wall. For Kirk Kelsey, who works in a narrow (11½-ft. wide) basement in Seattle, a radial-arm saw was the logical choice. Kelsey found that a good radial-arm saw can perform crosscutting and mitering tasks as well as any table saw, and with meticulous attention it can be made to rip stock and cut joints with precision. While I have always considered the radial-arm saw to be more appropriate for construction work than for furniture or cabinetmaking, Kelsey is one of several woodworkers I know who rely on it for a wide variety of stock-reduction and joint-cutting operations that are usually done with the table saw.

Kelsey employs a Paralok fence, shown on his saw at left, to improve rip-cut precision and reduce setup time, and he built a hinged-top infeed table to the right of the saw for extra support. A recently added power feeder enables him to do heavy production ripping of 8/4 purpleheart. "I don't tell anybody I don't have a table saw," he says, "and they never know it." (When Kelsey has to cut a lot of sheet stock, he uses a homemade vertical panel saw, shown on pp. 80-81, which he keeps in the garage.)

---

or plastic throat plate that fits the blade closely is also good protection against kickback, since it leaves no place for small offcuts to jam. (Ketelle also recommends using small blades—an 8-in. blade in a 10-in. saw, for example. Though the smaller blade will cut more slowly, it won't vibrate as much and chances of kickback are reduced.)

Keeping your distance

The key to preventing a table-saw accident is keeping your hands away from the blade, without losing control of the work. There are a host of homely shop devices—push sticks, feather boards, crosscut sleds, and the like—that can greatly improve your accuracy, control and safety, and no shop should be without them. More and more woodworkers are also using commercial hold-downs, like the Shophelper wheels shown at right, or

other brands of antikickback stock feeder.

Regardless of how many guards, splitters and hold-downs you have, perhaps the single most important safety feature at any power tool is the switch. It must be readily accessible from any reasonable operating position. Foot-operated and enlarged switches are popular since they will allow you to turn the saw off without letting go of the work. Make sure that the switch cannot be easily flipped on by accident, and as an extra security measure (especially if there are children around), install a master switch or a key lock on your machinery. (See Chapter 5 for more on switches.) Finally, it's a good idea to wear ear protection as well as a face shield and/or dust mask when you're using any power tool.

Bill Ketelle's splitter/guard

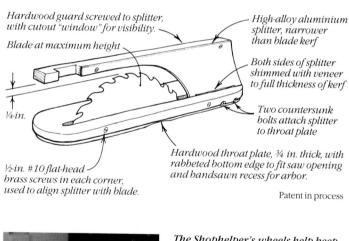

Hardwood guard screwed to splitter, with cutout "window" for visibility.

Blade at maximum height

¼-in.

½-in. #10 flat-head brass screws in each corner, used to align splitter with blade.

High-alloy aluminium splitter, narrower than blade kerf

Both sides of splitter shimmed with veneer to full thickness of kerf

Two countersunk bolts attach splitter to throat plate

Hardwood throat plate, ¾ in. thick, with rabbeted bottom edge to fit saw opening and bandsawn recess for arbor.

Patent in process

The Shophelper's wheels help keep the stock where it belongs—flat on the table and against the fence. The wheels rotate only in a clockwise direction to keep the stock from kicking back on a table saw or radial-arm saw. (Shophelper sells different colored wheels that rotate counterclockwise or in both directions for other machine applications.)

Radial-arm saws typically cost much less than comparable table saws, and they take up a lot less space than a full-size, 10-in. table saw. But in more and more workshops, I found the radial-arm saw pushed aside by an even more compact power tool, the miter saw (or chopsaw). Designed to make rapid and accurate angled crosscuts in narrow stock, the chopsaw is a fairly specialized tool—it won't rip stock or crosscut wide boards. Although it is ideally suited to house framing, it can be very useful to anyone who must repeatedly trim narrow stock to a precise angle. Several woodworkers I met use one or more chopsaws, sometimes in addition to a radial-arm saw or table saw. (Randall Ores, whose setup is shown on p. 47, keeps two chopsaws set to opposite 45° angles and uses a radial-arm saw for 90° crosscuts.)

In quite a few workshops—notably all the chairmaking, boatbuilding, turning and guitar-making shops I visited—the bandsaw is the sawing machine of choice. While its forte is curved work and resawing, a good bandsaw can be an effective tool for ripping and for cutting a variety of joints, including tenons, lap joints and dovetails. In fact, if I had to choose only one saw, it would probably be a bandsaw. It is the only tool that can comfortably handle the irregular chunks of green wood I occasionally tackle and the boat-repair work I like to do. I also prefer its thinner blade and slower speed for ripping stock. A bandsaw is quieter and safer than a table saw or radial-arm saw and wastes less wood in the kerf. Because I don't do production woodwork and only occasionally use plywood, the bandsaw is more flexible and appropriate for me than any type of circular saw.

People who have only occasional use for a bandsaw might be satisfied with a 14-in. model, but many of the woodworkers I met prefer an 18-in. or 20-in. machine. (Bandsaws are described by the measurement of the throat, the horizontal distance between the exposed blade and the upright post.) Those, like Mac Campbell, (shown above, right) who have managed to obtain an old 36-in. industrial saw are reluctant to part with it, despite the amount of shop space it consumes. By adding another wheel, manufacturers have been able to make small bandsaws with large throats. These three-wheel bandsaws are capable of handling a wide cut, but in relatively thin stock; they are more appropriate for light work and cutting scrolled patterns than for resawing heavy timber.

Peripatetic tools

Where space permits, large machines are usually assigned a permanent spot in the shop layout. Planers and jointers, for example, are often positioned along an outside wall, where they won't interfere with the general flow of projects and material. But where a variety of tasks must be performed and space is in short supply, ease of movement is a top machine priority. Most shops have at least one or two machines or carts mounted on casters, and you'll see quite a few of them throughout the book. (A number of clever portable workstations are shown in Chapter 9.)

Since the table saw, unlike the planer or jointer, requires open space on all sides, it is the major tool most often

Aided by spot lighting and a magnifying lens, Mac Campbell is able to make very precise cuts on his renovated 36-in. bandsaw.

The wheelbarrow-style base on Peter Murkett's table saw is stable but portable. Murkett disconnects the dust-collector pipe (located beneath the saw) and wheels the saw away on casters attached to the large trestle. The switch for the dust system (on the side of the table) hangs on the wall when the machine is in transit.

designed to travel. Delta makes a foot-operated, mobile base for their heavy-duty Unisaw (as well as other bases designed for smaller equipment). For smaller table saws and other shop equipment, many woodworkers prefer to make their own rolling bases.

Peter Murkett purchased the 10-in. Atlas table saw shown above to make a split-laminated railing for a specific job, but it proved so useful that it won a permanent spot in his shop. Still, it must be moved now and then to make way for assembly of large projects or to set up shop on a job site. The size and portability of the saw also reflect Murkett's ambivalence about power tools. He only recently installed the AC power necessary to run them, and hasn't quite come to terms with them yet.

Power tools that are easily moved enhance flexibility and efficiency. Rather than lugging materials back and forth across the shop between project and tool, a small, portable machine can be carried or rolled to wherever the action is. Below, Cliff Friedlander demonstrates one of the numerous operations performed by his new Wirth Machine II horizontal mortiser (available from Woodworker's Supply of New Mex-

Cliff Friedlander mounted his Wirth Machine II horizontal mortiser on a round table pedestal that he rolls around the shop. The machine is powered by a 3-hp Bosch plunge router, which is easily removed and used on its own.

ico). The table travels 12 in. horizontally and the power unit moves 6 in. vertically, enabling the machine to be used for a variety of mortising, tenoning and duplicating functions. At only 30 lb., it is exceptionally portable. Friedlander mounted his on a wobbly metal table base, which seems to be sufficient and is easy to roll around his 560-sq. ft. cabinet shop. The Wirth Machine costs about one-third as much as other more substantial "industrial" units, but it lets Friedlander to make and sell mortised face-frame cabinets competitively with dowel-jointed or plate-jointed cabinets.

Specialized tools

The more specialized your work, the easier it is to justify specialized (also called dedicated) machinery. Like anything else, equipment designed to perform only one task almost always does that job better than a multipurpose machine. Specialized equipment doesn't come cheap—most of it is built for industrial applications—but for many woodworkers, the investment pays off in the long run.

A stroll around Walter Phelps's cavernous window-sash shop in southern Vermont (shown on the facing page) is like a visit to an industrial machine showroom. His is the biggest one-man shop I visited (about 4,000 sq. ft.), with the dedicated machinery of a small factory. Phelps has four industrial French-made shapers, acquired when Rossignol closed its ski plant in Burlington. He rebuilt the machines, turning the spindles down to accept the multihead cutters that he uses to produce a complex tenon joint on his European-style window sash. "The machines are big and heavy and don't have too many amenities," Phelps notes. They are almost ho-hum alongside his SCMI L'vincible shaper and Alternax oscillating chisel mortiser. The line of three-phase machines snakes around the shop in a purposeful production sequence, almost every tool dedicated to one or two specific operations. At the end of the queue are two Marunaka super surfacers (shown at top right, facing page) with which Phelps produces a silky finished surface.

"I've kind of bootstrapped my way up in equipment," Phelps says. "I've definitely gotten carried away with it all." The week before my visit, he put the finishing touches on his dust-collection system (see p. 102). The project took three years to complete and when it was all done, he admits, "a part of me wanted to walk away."

Phelps invites superlatives the way he collects machinery. Using only clear pine and mahogany, he makes some of the finest custom window sash in the business. He also traveled as far as anyone I'd met in terms of tool technology. When Phelps began making traditional window sash in 1979, he made all of it by hand at the bench, using antique molding planes. Having mastered the art, his search for new challenges led him to acquire the machinery that would transform his business. At the time of my visit, his old workbench and an unfinished saw cabinet were the only neglected tools in the shop. Did he miss the pace or the intimacy of the hand work, I wondered? "No," Phelps replied, "I like to produce really nice, clean work—and lots of it. Priorities change."

The biggest little sash shop: Almost all of the industrial-size machinery in Walter Phelps's one-man shop is dedicated to just one or two tasks in the production sequence for making custom window sash. At the end of the line, Phelps tends two super surfacers, mounted in tandem. Their razor-sharp knives (above the work on one machine, below on the other) smooth the top and bottom of each piece of sash in a single pass.

"A lot of the things have been done here in the name of efficiency. Others I just don't like to do," he added, noting that technology is driven by the sometimes contradictory desires to work less, but to work better. Where other woodworkers I know acquire dedicated machinery in order to hire somebody else to manage it, Phelps enjoys doing the work himself. More than that, he can't bear the thought of someone fouling up the machines he has so painstakingly rebuilt. "I like doing the work," he explains. "Each time I put a stick of wood in one end and it comes out the other, I say 'ahhh'...."

The overhead is a little scary. "You wouldn't go out and invest $200,000 to earn what I earn. You'd be better off buying a Dairy Queen," Phelps says. But, by buying and rebuilding used machinery, Phelps spent much less. And he spent it incrementally, rather than all at once. "It just happened," he says. "That's the way most woodworking shops get going."

Not all specialized machines are big and expensive; I saw a fair number of smaller, shop-built machines likewise dedicated to specific functions. Tom Phillips uses the rig shown at right to shave round tenons on parts of the crooked "twig" furniture he builds in upstate New York's Adirondack Mountains. Because every stick is different and there are no flat reference edges, Phillips is unable to use conventional tenoning machinery for this operation.

The tenoner actually represents the fourth generation in the evolution of Phillips's chairmaking technology. He began whittling the tenons by hand ("tenyons" he calls them), graduated to a hollow auger powered by a brace and bit, then used a multispur tenon cutter in a ½-in. drill before arriving at the tenoner, which works like an electric pencil sharpener of Bunyanesque proportions. Plunging each stick freehand into the spinning maw of the tenoner is an awesome operation that Phillips won't let his apprentice touch—the machine is capable of flinging a misplaced stick across the shop. In fact, he plans to replace the 3-hp motor with a smaller one or gear it down from its present speed of 1,700 rpm to about 600 rpm. "You don't relax for a minute," Phillips says. If he does, the machine will wake him up smartly with a rap on the knuckles or by spitting the stick out. Phillips works on short runs of chairs to fend off complacency. "I don't get slaphappy and I don't develop an ulcer using it."

Tom Phillips can build 200 'twig' chairs in a winter with the aid of this dedicated tenoner—an electric motor fitted with Bignell cutters in ½-in., ¾-in. and 1-in. diameters.

Multipurpose tools

At the other end of the spectrum from a machine as narrowly focused as Phillips's tenoner are the multipurpose combination machines that promise to deliver an entire machine shop in a few square feet. Like the proverbial jack-of-all-trades, they are often accused of doing nothing well. But these machines are an attractive alternative for many woodworkers who are limited by space and budget. All combination machines require some adjustment between tool functions, but judging from the number of satisfied owners this is not necessarily a sacrifice.

With machines like the Parks Planing Mill Special (shown on p. 66) and the Wagon Shop Special, also manufactured by Parks, ca. 1921-1927 (shown below), there is a long tradition of serious combination tools. An old Parks brochure trumpets a 1920 testimonial from an Illinois cabinetmaker: "A Parks is a money saver to any contractor. I save 1½ men for

12 months of 25 days each, 9 hrs. per day. At 70¢ an hour this is $40.50 a week or $486 a year.... If you offered me $2,000 for my machine and I could not get another Parks I would certainly say 'No.'" I've been unable to locate an earlier price list, but in 1942, the list price of the Parks Planing Mill Special was $745.

Today, you can find a multipurpose machine to suit any budget, from the low-priced Shopsmith (shown at left on the facing page), to a number of more expensive European machines. The heavy-duty, Belgian-made Robland X31 (which weighs half a ton and costs over $5,000) or the moderately priced Italian-made Zincken (shown at right, facing page) provide table saw, jointer, planer, shaper and horizontal borer. More limited combination machines are also available, like the Inca 550 10¼-in. combination jointer/planer and the Robland XSD 31, which combines a 12-in. jointer and planer.

The Shopsmith is probably the most popular combination machine in the North American hobby market. For

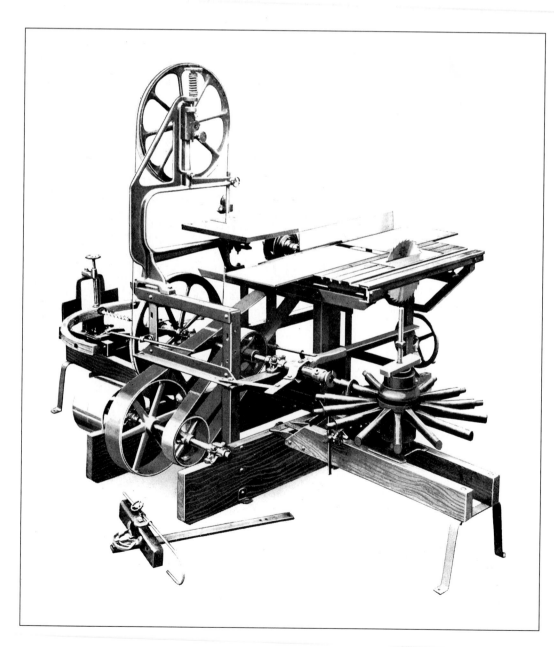

The Parks Wagon Shop Special included a circular saw, a 22-in. bandsaw and a 12-in jointer, along with special attachments for boring felloes, tenoning spokes and rounding rims. A complete wagon shop in less than 50 sq. ft., the Wagon Shop Special ran on 4-in. wide, 'high-quality' babbitt bearings and a 5-hp motor and sold for about $250 in the 1920s — including blades, bits, bushings and leather belts.

In production since about 1952, the variable-speed Shopsmith Mark V has become the standard American combination machine. While the multipurpose aspect is most popular with hobbyists, professionals use it for special tasks. John Nyquist (shown above) employs the machine to bore a variety of holes in his chair parts.

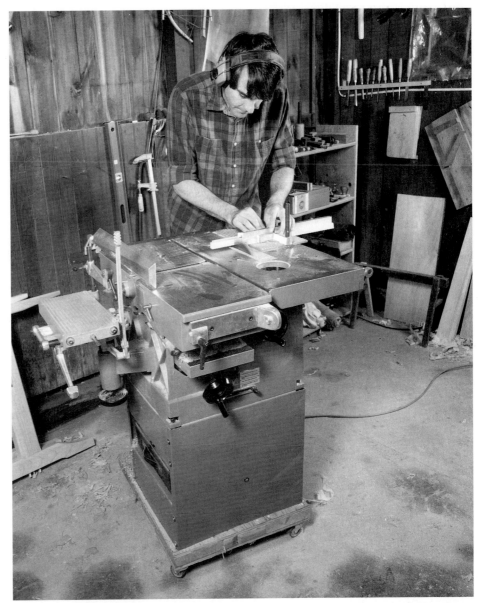

The Zincken Compact 21 is a mid-price alternative to the Shopsmith and other more expensive European combination machines. Its five modes (220mm table saw, 210mm jointer and planer, shaper and horizontal borer) are powered by a 1½-hp motor and belted pulleys. A single lever shifts pulleys to engage the desired tool.

about as much money as a Delta Unisaw, it delivers five basic tools: table saw, lathe, drill press, horizontal borer and disc sander. Like the Black & Decker Workmate®, it is usually written off as a lightweight, amateur piece of equipment. But at least one professional I met uses two old Shopsmiths almost exclusively for chair work. "Everybody laughs when they see the Shopsmiths," John Nyquist admits, "but really they're the most practical. Most of the machine *is* Mickey Mouse, but it makes a great little drill press and horizontal boring machine." Nyquist's chairs require four end-grain boring operations, which are difficult to accomplish on a conventional drill press because of the central post and the side-to-side tilting table. The Shopsmith table tilts forward and, because of the machine's parallel-tube design, long chair legs can

pass directly beneath the head, as shown in the photo above left. In addition, with the throat plate in the table removed a chair leg can be clamped vertically below the bit to cut end tenons.

Perhaps the ultimate multipurpose machine I saw is the computer numerically controlled (CNC) Alberti milling machine shown on p. 86. "Big Al" is a hybrid, a combination machine dedicated to cabinetmaking but capable of performing all the routing and boring operations with computer-animated precision. Priced at more than $80,000, it's not exactly the sort of machine you'd stick in the basement, but it points the way to a new era in machine tools for at least one sector of the industry.

Rebuilt and shop-built machinery

Before you assume a second mortgage to purchase the tool of your dreams, consider two viable alternatives—restoring old equipment and building your own. Many professional woodworkers have discovered they can get superior performance by purchasing industrial equipment of an earlier era. Much of it is huge and well built and runs on three-phase power. (Three-phase power can be brought into the shop directly or converted on site. Three-phase conversion is described in Chapter 5.) If you've never moved a large machine before, the prospect can be intimidating. But you needn't be an Olympic weightlifter or an engineer to do the job. In many towns you can rent an inexpensive pallet lifter—the poor-man's forklift—which will move a heap of equipment with a lot less strain on back and brain than any amount of pipe, rope and come-alongs.

Walter Balliet designed and built this ornamental lathe out of scrap iron. The bed and legs come from an old metal-spinning lathe, the headstock was salvaged from a Garvin milling machine and the gear box combines an oil-burner motor with parts from a post-hole digger. A tool-and-die maker by trade, Balliet, who lives in Collingswood, New Jersey, spent six years building the lathe in his basement machine shop and added the rose-engine attachment later.

Like Walter Phelps, Kelly Mehler gravitated toward machines he could afford, cast-offs from the declining rust-belt industries of the Midwest. (Mehler's Kentucky workshop is described on pp. 42-44.) "If you're not averse to creative mechanical work and intense cleanup, furniture-factory auctions and machinery outlets can provide good, serviceable equipment," he says. After decades of scrounging, however, real bargains are getting harder to find. Mehler cautions,

After years of tinkering and reconditioning, original parts are hard to find on Roger Heitzman's Sears table saw. The direct-drive motor was the first to go, and Heitzman welded a new stand to accommodate the belt-drive conversion. Later he added the fence (a shop-built copy of a Biesemeyer) and sealed the open frame of the base for dust collection. Finally, he added the router-table wing and fold-down extension tables on the side and back.

"You have to be careful, some of the old machines are antiques." Sloppy babbitt bearings or a burned-out motor may be worth replacing; warped tables and broken castings may not.

Between rebuilt and shop-built is a category you might call adapted machines. Lots of woodworkers tinker with their equipment. Some soup it up, like a hot-rod, so the resulting tool does the same job, but better. Others start with a stock machine, but alter it to perform a different or more specialized task. Still others just keep replacing worn-out parts until it becomes impossible to tell where the original machine leaves off and the shop-built creature begins. That's a fair description of what happened to Roger Heitzman's 12-in. Sears table saw, shown at left. Part by part, the saw has been so thoroughly overhauled that only the table and tilt mechanism are original.

Unlike most woodworkers I know, who keep metal work at arm's length and tackle machinery repair and restoration only under duress, Roger Heitzman of Scotts Valley, California, relishes the challenge. Heitzman has built six major pieces of shop equipment, including the articulated duplicating carver, the three-wheel bandsaw and the edge sander shown below.

If this strikes you as obsessive or intimidating, as it did me, consider that the machines were added one by one, as they were needed for a particular job. "I was a starving student when I built my disc sander," Heitzman explains. "I didn't have a choice." That is no longer the case. As Heitzman's custom-furniture business has become increasingly successful, his motivation has changed. "I just like making stuff," he says simply.

About ten years ago, Heitzman built the three-wheel bandsaw to replace an old Sears saw and provide some re-

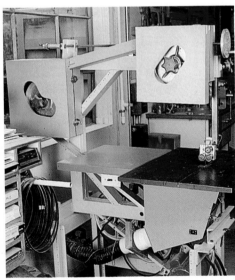

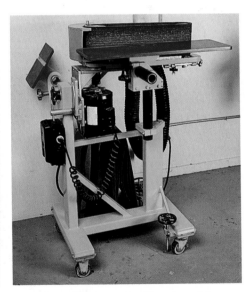

Roger Heitzman has filled his shop with homemade machines. The three-wheel bandsaw (above, center) was one of his first. The counterweighted arm on the carving machine at left covers the 40-in. by 60-in. table surface (the full size with both wings of the table open). The carver is built for a 1½-hp Rockwell 6900 router. Phenolic wheels and levelers keep the edge sander (above right) from rolling around. Aluminum bumpers on the feet protect its hot-rod paint job. (Photos above by Sandor Nagyszalanczy.)

To build his machinery, Roger Heitzman uses a variety of materials that can be worked with woodworking tools. Here, he uses a plunge router, a carbide bit and a simple plywood jig to machine a square edge on a chunk of aluminum. (Photo by Sandor Nagyszalanczy.)

A pair of shop-built machines

Many of the shop-built machines I saw on my travels were either too specialized or too complex to be of much use to other woodworkers. Two notable exceptions, however, are shown here; the sketches show the salient construction information if you want to build your own.

Panel saw

Kirk Kelsey, of Seattle, Washington, installed the vertical panel saw shown below and on the facing page in his garage to relieve some of the pressure on his 220-sq. ft. basement shop. Sheet goods are unloaded in the garage and ripped or crosscut into manageable dimensions before they enter the workshop. Kelsey modified his design from a plan in a book by Don McNair, *Building & Outfitting Your Workshop*, by enlarging the back panel and extending the bottom rail to provide better support for ripping 8-ft. sheets. He plans to add a lip to the front edge of the rail, which would prevent thin sheets of plastic laminate from slipping off. A few quick-action hold-down clamps mounted to the carriage rails would help hold the stock in place, too.

Construction of the saw is straightforward, and most of the parts were available at Kelsey's local hardware store and lumberyard. It took him less than a week of evenings to complete and cost less than $150. The biggest single expense, apart from the saw, was the sliding-door tracks used for the carriage. "Two-by-fours didn't agree with me," Kelsey says, so he used quartersawn Douglas fir, 1¼ in. thick and 4 in. wide, to construct the frame instead and beefed up the inside edge of the carriage rails with additional 1x3s. He used screws, instead of nails or bolts, and didn't glue anything. The carriage assembly hinges at the bottom so it can be flipped down to set up material or clear any problems.

Kelsey bolted a 7¼-in. Sears cut-off saw through the base plate to threaded inserts in the plywood saw carriage. As a counterweight to the saw, he fed a length of chain

Kirk Kelsey keeps his shop-built vertical-panel saw is the garage, where he uses it to reduce large sheets to size before lugging them to his basement shop. (Photo by Kirk Kelsey.)

saw capacity. It has a 30-in. throat and a 13-in. depth of cut. Aside from the wheels (salvaged from an industrial cart and trued in place) and the table (from an old drilling machine), there are no off-the-shelf parts. The frame is made of channel iron, chopped up and welded together.

The saw works well, although it's a bit fussy for resawing, even with a 1-in. blade and a 2-hp motor. Later on, Heitzman added speed-reducer wheels for cutting metal. He's used the tilting-table feature only once, and if he designed it again, he would not put the motor directly below the blade, where it receives the most dust. Heitzman reckons it was a good idea to start with a simple machine that runs at low speeds and is not subjected to heavy loads. "I would never want to build a jointer," he says, "although...you gotta 'tweak out' once in a while."

What makes Heitzman's machinery accessible to metalworking-illiterates like me is his reliance on aluminum and brass and other soft metals and plastics that can be worked with conventional woodworking tools. "I don't farm anything out," he says. One of his favorite materials is laminated phenolic resin (Micarta), which he stocks in several different thicknesses. Micarta machines nicely and is stronger and more stable than most wood products. He uses it for machines, the blast gates on his dust-collection system and for a variety of other workshop tools and fixtures.

Heitzman admits that the carving machine snowballed "to the point of absurdity." He began, as usual, with a need—to

Kirk Kelsey's vertical panel saw

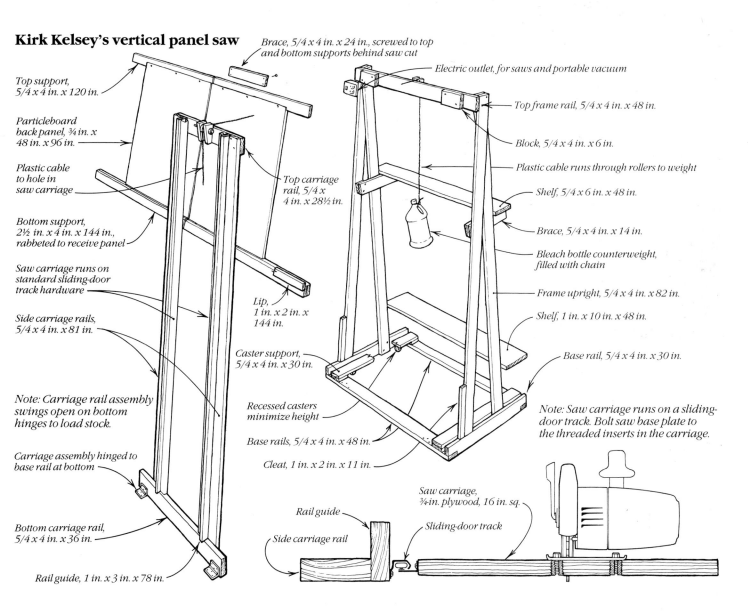

Brace, 5/4 x 4 in. x 24 in., screwed to top and bottom supports behind saw cut

Top support, 5/4 x 4 in. x 120 in.

Particleboard back panel, ¾ in. x 48 in. x 96 in.

Plastic cable to hole in saw carriage

Bottom support, 2½ in. x 4 in. x 144 in., rabbeted to receive panel

Saw carriage runs on standard sliding-door track hardware

Side carriage rails, 5/4 x 4 in. x 81 in.

Note: Carriage rail assembly swings open on bottom hinges to load stock.

Carriage assembly hinged to base rail at bottom

Bottom carriage rail, 5/4 x 4 in. x 36 in.

Rail guide, 1 in. x 3 in. x 78 in.

Top carriage rail, 5/4 x 4 in. x 28½ in.

Lip, 1 in. x 2 in. x 144 in.

Caster support, 5/4 x 4 in. x 30 in.

Recessed casters minimize height

Base rails, 5/4 x 4 in. x 48 in.

Cleat, 1 in. x 2 in. x 11 in.

Electric outlet, for saws and portable vacuum

Top frame rail, 5/4 x 4 in. x 48 in.

Block, 5/4 x 4 in. x 6 in.

Plastic cable runs through rollers to weight

Shelf, 5/4 x 6 in. x 48 in.

Brace, 5/4 x 4 in. x 14 in.

Bleach bottle counterweight, filled with chain

Frame upright, 5/4 x 4 in. x 82 in.

Shelf, 1 in. x 10 in. x 48 in.

Base rail, 5/4 x 4 in. x 30 in.

Note: Saw carriage runs on a sliding-door track. Bolt saw base plate to the threaded inserts in the carriage.

Saw carriage, ¾-in. plywood, 16 in. sq.

Rail guide

Side carriage rail

Sliding-door track

through the neck of a gallon bleach bottle and cut the extra links off when the weight was right. It is so well balanced that the saw remains in place on the track when unattended. The weight is attached to the carriage with plastic-coated cable, which runs through a pair of screen-door rollers at the top and is secured with a cable clamp at both ends. An outlet and a switch mounted on the frame enable Kelsey to turn on the saw and the vacuum at the same time. He used hot glue to attach the vacuum pickup to the saw's exhaust.

The saw is a great improvement, Kelsey reports, over the hand-held circular saw and sawhorses he used to use. He stores material on the upper shelf behind the saw and offcuts on the 10-in. wide bottom shelf. With its wide, stable base and recessed rollers to enable the frame to clear the garage ceiling, the saw can be moved around or pushed against the wall to make room for the car.

Stroke sander

A stroke sander can revolutionize the workshop by reducing tedious hand sanding. It takes skill to operate the machine, particularly when sanding thin veneers. But once mastered, it's a godsend.

John Nyquist has built several sanders over the years. Most are low-budget productions, made from scrap and salvaged machinery. The stroke sander (shown on p. 82) is an exception. "It's nothing new, just one man's interpretation," he says, "but that's what woodworking is all about."

Nyquist built the machine light so he could move it. He figures the 2-hp, 220-volt motor and the hardware weigh about as much as the fir frame, which is screwed to the floor for stability. With a 3½-in. pulley on the motor and a 2½-in. pulley on the drive drum, the sander runs a little fast, but does not bog down. Nyquist uses the machine with 120-grit (or finer) paper to smooth thin

John Nyquist's stroke sander

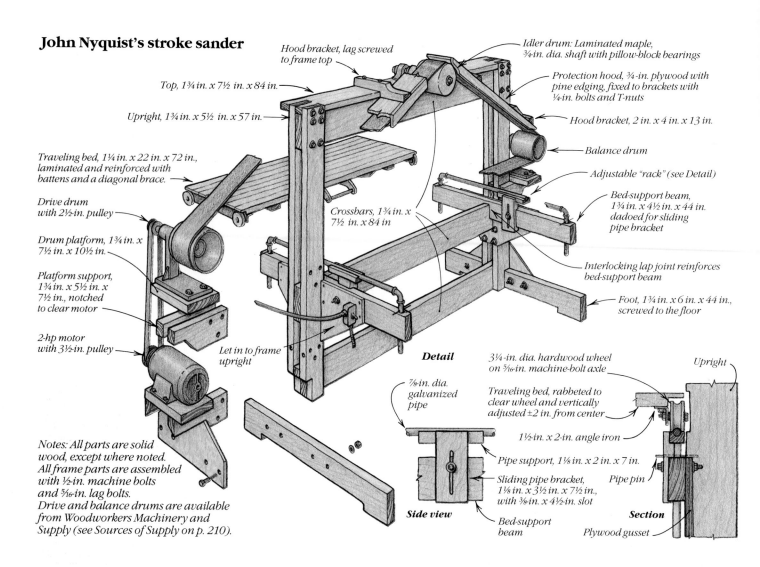

Hood bracket, lag screwed to frame top

Idler drum: Laminated maple, ¾-in. dia. shaft with pillow-block bearings

Top, 1¾ in. x 7½ in. x 84 in.

Protection hood, ¾-in. plywood with pine edging, fixed to brackets with ¼-in. bolts and T-nuts

Upright, 1¾ in. x 5½ in. x 57 in.

Hood bracket, 2 in. x 4 in. x 13 in.

Traveling bed, 1¼ in. x 22 in. x 72 in., laminated and reinforced with battens and a diagonal brace.

Balance drum

Adjustable "rack" (see Detail)

Crossbars, 1¾ in. x 7½ in. x 84 in

Drive drum with 2½-in. pulley

Bed-support beam, 1¾ in. x 4½ in. x 44 in. dadoed for sliding pipe bracket

Drum platform, 1¾ in. x 7½ in. x 10½ in.

Platform support, 1¾ in. x 5½ in. x 7½ in., notched to clear motor

Interlocking lap joint reinforces bed-support beam

2-hp motor with 3½-in. pulley

Foot, 1¾ in. x 6 in. x 44 in., screwed to the floor

Let in to frame upright

Detail

3¼-in. dia. hardwood wheel on ⁵⁄₁₆-in. machine-bolt axle

Upright

⅞-in. dia. galvanized pipe

Traveling bed, rabbeted to clear wheel and vertically adjusted ±2 in. from center

1½-in. x 2-in. angle iron

Pipe support, 1⅛ in. x 2 in. x 7 in.

Pipe pin

Sliding pipe bracket, 1⅛ in. x 3½ in. x 7½ in., with ⅜-in. x 4½-in. slot

Side view

Bed-support beam

Section

Plywood gusset

Notes: All parts are solid wood, except where noted. All frame parts are assembled with ½-in. machine bolts and ⁵⁄₁₆-in. lag bolts. Drive and balance drums are available from Woodworkers Machinery and Supply (see Sources of Supply on p. 210).

panels. Parts and ideas for the sander were collected over eight years. (The maple idler drum was inspired by a 1940s special issue of ***Popular Mechanics*** entitled "Shop Notes"; other ideas came from M. G. Rekoff, Jr.'s article, "Stroke Sander," in the Summer 1976 issue of ***Fine Woodworking*** magazine.) But once he got down to building, it took a long weekend and about $675 worth of material to complete. "It isn't complicated," Nyquist says. "It's more a matter of figuring out what you want to do and how to do it."

Nyquist worked from a series of sketches and notes — the plan shown above was developed after the fact. "It would have been a lot easier if I'd had it to begin with," he says, "but then I would've missed out on all the fun and mistakes I made while putting it together."

The frame of John Nyquist's stroke sander is made of quartersawn, kiln-dried fir bolted together like a trussed bridge. The imbuia wheels for the traveling bed ride on an adjustable rack of ⅞-in. galvanized water pipe. The only things he didn't make are the aluminum-alloy drive drum, shown at left, and a matching balance drum. The drums are adjusted on the platforms to suit the belt width and length and to align the rims.

carve a bunch of seats for a set of chairs. After inspecting a Sears duplicating carving machine, he figured "I could do that." Starting at the drawing board, he added and deleted features and eventually built some models out of welded coat hanger to test the strength of the trussed-arm design. The actual construction took an intense month to complete. "Using this thing is a challenge," Heitzman says, and after he built it, he didn't get around to doing chair seats for years. But it has plenty of applications in the scalloped, art-nouveau curve that Heitzman incorporates in much of his furniture.

The edge sander was the last machine to be added to the shop inventory, and it represents the state of Heitzman's art. "It works well," he says, "and also is one of the best looking." The sander is souped up beyond the realm of function, with aluminum, Delrin and bondo fillets that refine the joints in the welded frame. The body was painted with primer, then sanded and sprayed with a finish coat of "Pom-pom" yellow enamel, the color of choice in Heitzman's shop.

"Now that it's done," Heitzman says, "I don't regret any time that went into it," although he admits to having a moment of doubt in the midst of applying bondo to the welds. "One thing I've learned is that any amount of work on your adjustment mechanisms is worth it." If you can avoid having to reach for a separate wrench to change a belt or move a fence, you're that much more likely to make the adjustment when it is required and you'll save untold hours and hassles over the lifetime of the tool.

Attention to detail and a passion for order set Roger Heitzman's workshop apart. When I last spoke with him, he was thinking about a new boring machine—something, he said, "I could really tweak out on."

Pedal power

The main point of workshop machinery is saving sweat. Power from a wall plug replaces muscle power. The juice keeps flowing and the machines keep running as long as you pay the bills. A few workshops I visited tap alternative sources of energy to power some of their equipment. But in a small town in eastern Pennsylvania, I met one woodworker who comes close to being his own utility.

Fred Matlack runs most of his workshop machinery by hand or foot. He has four treadle-powered machines, as well as a hand-crank post drill and a pedal grinder. Matlack clearly prefers his human-powered tools, but he is no environmental purist; he also runs a small Craftsman table saw and a belt sander and has access to other power tools at work. As head of the Design Group at Rodale Press, he turns his hand to

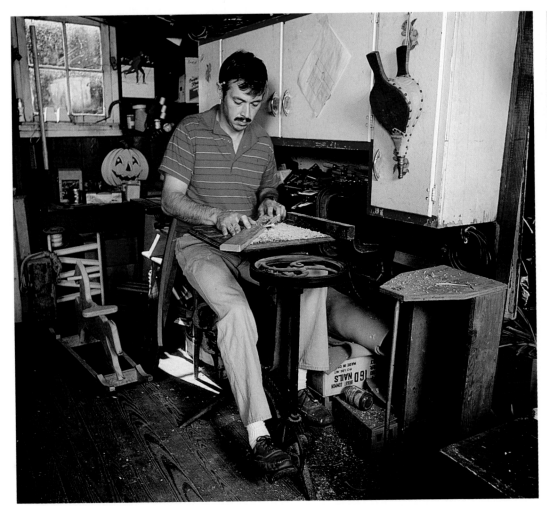

Fred Matlack powers his own machines. He once attached a motorized conversion kit from a Singer sewing machine to the small wood lathe (above), but returned to the treadle for greater power and control. The treadle shaper (at left) is surprisingly effective. Once he gets pedaling, the large, cast flywheel provides the momentum that keeps the cutters up to speed.

metalwork, silkscreening and all kinds of woodwork in the course of a day. When he gets home, the last thing he wants to listen to is a screaming saw.

"Basically," Matlack says, "I'm a scrounge." Rooting around an old chicken coop more than 20 years ago, he spotted two lumps of cast iron that belonged to a treadle-powered lathe and a "New Rogers" jigsaw. It took several cans of penetrating oil and three days of tapping to free the rusted parts, which had grown together over half a century. He added a flywheel to the jigsaw for momentum, picked up some leather sewing-machine belts and started cranking. The lathe was so small and quiet he brought it with him to college to turn chess sets and other small projects. "I was fascinated," Matlack recalls, "that you could do these things without a motor."

Most of the machinery in Matlack's shop had been tossed out or forgotten by others. "A lot of folks think I'm just cheap," he says, but Matlack has always been challenged by other people's cast-offs. He'd sooner fix something up and give it away than see it go to waste. Except for the post drill, which he bought for $35, he has salvaged or bartered for every other major tool in the shop.

I was familiar with treadle lathes, post drills and hand-crank grinders, but the Barnes pedal shaper was a novelty. Mounting the machine to demonstrate, Matlack explained that he used the shaper to run out all the moldings (from salvaged pine) for a third-floor addition to his house. "So it works," he says. He even turned a couple of cutter blanks on the machine lathe, and cut out the profiles with a hacksaw.

One of the advantages of treadle power, Matlack discovered, is that his two young sons can use the small lathe and scrollsaw without serious danger. They'd have to go out of their way to really hurt themselves, he explains, since the tools stop cutting almost as soon as the kids stop cranking. (The flywheel slows down with any resistance; a jammed chisel stops the lathe immediately.) Not only are the treadle tools less dangerous than high-powered machinery, but they are also excellent teachers. "You have to do your lathe work properly," he explains, "rather than using dull tools and making sawdust. The cutting tools have to be sharp and held at the proper angle or you just don't make it."

The treadle machines also provide good exercise, which Matlack especially enjoys in winter, when he's not riding his bicycle to work. "But it continually amazes me how little peddling it actually takes to get the work done," he says. Matlack figures only 15 or 20 minutes of every hour on the job is spent in the driver's seat. The rest is taken up in measurements, setup and other operations. "It's not what you'd call a production shop," he admits, "but it's fine for my purposes. I like dragging a job out. If you enjoy it, why rush it?"

Microchips in the workshop

Woodworking has always been slow to change. The Industrial Revolution shook things up, but a modern table saw, jointer, planer or shaper wouldn't shock 19th-century craftsmen. (Some of the machinery I've seen must have been used by those same craftsmen.) There's one modern tool, however, that would certainly widen their eyes—the computer. Employed to help run the business end of things, to assist with design or to tend a machine, computers are becoming an increasingly common fixture in woodworking shops. Here's a look at two shops where computers play a big part.

A computer-aided shop
I crossed the St. Croix River into Canada one rainy August night at a lonely border outpost in Vanceboro, Maine. As I headed north into rural New Brunswick, the countryside remained pretty much unchanged; the road was perhaps a bit straighter, but still flanked with dense bush. Legend inhabits the country on both sides of the border with lumberjacks and river drivers. Modern economics inhabits it hardly at all, and the area is notoriously poor.

About 45 miles north of the border, the workshop I visited was anything but hardscrabble. It is a compact, well-considered space, incorporating a wealth of practical ideas. It evolved gradually, on a modest budget, over the last 13 years. And its owner, Mac Campbell, is in it to make a living. Campbell builds a wide variety of furniture and cabinets in the basement shop. But the key to his flexibility (and to his living) is not the shop, but his living-room office. The office, Campbell is convinced, has "something to do with woodworking—and everything to do with staying alive in woodworking." If it takes up almost half of his living room, it comprises fully half of his business.

"You build a business like you build a piece of furniture," Campbell says. It goes together one piece at a time, and you make plenty of mistakes along the way. After several years in business—"working my tail off and not making any money"—he availed himself of a small-business consultant. The first two meetings produced no tangible results, and by the third he was desperate. "Can I afford to hire someone?" he asked. After studying Campbell's books, the consultant replied: "Not only can you not afford to hire somebody, you can't afford to stay in business past noon."

Campbell dates the birth of his business from that point. The consultant introduced planning, long-term goals, ongoing evaluation and focus, all the stuff that Campbell previously thought was reserved for "the big guys." Shortly thereafter, he went out to buy a typewriter and came home with a Kaypro computer. Many woodworkers choke on the price tag of a computer. Many more never get beyond the stigma of automation. But "in this day and age," Campbell says, "you can't afford not to have one. The computer absolutely will not lie." Campbell uses his as a project management tool, to plan and to forecast work and cash flow.

The computer taught him the "miracle of spreadsheets," and

Mac Campbell spends almost 50 hours a month at his office computer, one-third to one-half of his nonshop time. He relies on it for all kinds of functions, from bookkeeping and billing to writing articles and drafting. In the shop, Campbell uses computer printouts to guide his work at the lathe.

he began to play "What If?" What if I make ten of these? What if I take a week off? How much do I have to increase my hourly shop rate to buy a new jointer by December? In short, Campbell explains, "I started running the business."

In 1989, he upgraded his hardware with an APCO 286 computer (an IBM AT clone), a NEC color monitor (Multisync II), a Brother HR15 daisy-wheel printer and a Canon A65X dot-matrix printer, for which he traded a couple of tables. He uses the dot-matrix printer for all business and accounting functions and the daisy-wheel for presentations. Its clean, crisp type conveys the professional image that Campbell considers a necessity, since he's always selling something that doesn't exist. The new system cost $8,000 to $9,000, about four times the price of the Kaypro, which his son took to college last year. The recent addition of a Roland plotter and a Toshiba fax machine ups the ante by another few thousand dollars.

For software, Campbell uses five programs: WordStar 2000 for word processing, Lotus for spreadsheets, dBase IV to index photo negatives (it takes him less than a minute to locate any photo on file), Milestone for project management and shop scheduling, and Accounting Partner to keep the books. Campbell also does most of his design work on the tube, using a three-dimensional program called Cad Key, which allows the same sort of flexible manipulation of line as word-processing programs do for text. It provides six different standard views (top, front, back, bottom, right side, left side) and two three-dimensional representations (isometric and axonometric) plus any view he wants to create.

Lately, Campbell has begun to explore the interplay between the work he does on computer and the work that goes on in the shop with intriguing results. For example, Cad Key enables him to work the bugs out of a turning on the screen, then tack a printout above the lathe for reference, as shown in the lower right photo on p. 85. On the screen, he can enlarge or reduce the image and play with curves and details without ever making dust. "It's almost better than the lathe," Campbell says.

"I'm more productive downstairs if I've gotten as much design work as possible done up here."

A computer-driven shop

If Mac Campbell's shop is computer aided, Kochman Woodworking is computer driven. The heart of Bill and Jim Kochman's eight-man cabinet shop is the computer numerically controlled (CNC) seven-spindle, automated Alberti milling machine (shown below) linked to a network of Macintosh computers. A computer-aided-design-and-manufacturing (CAD/CAM) program generates the shop drawings (plans, elevations and details) and product lists for the European-style

cabinets they produce, as well as the parts lists that are fed to the machine. (The Kochmans have hundreds of cabinet designs in their CNC inventory.) "We thought this thing was like going to the moon," Bill says, "but it's still a fairly simple machine." The Alberti functions in only two dimensions, he points out, compared to a router they are looking at, which works in six axes.

For a small company, a CAD/CAM system is a gamble. But when Bill penciled it out, he came up with a simple equation: "For $1,000 a month, you can buy some really fancy equipment...and you're not going to get much of a helper for that." Within a

year of adding the Alberti, in 1985, they doubled their production without increasing labor. As Bill explains, "It's as though you had an employee who said 'look, in five years I'm going to keep working, but you won't have to pay me.'" The Kochmans consider themselves artisans—something between craftsman and factory. "But because we're so flexible," Bill adds, "we're able to bid against one-man and two-man shops."

Like the artisans of the Arts and Crafts movement who believed in the judicious application of machinery, the Kochmans use their CAD/CAM system to reduce mind-numbing calculations

While Bill Kochman works up a job on one of the office Macintosh computers (above), employee Dave McFadd and two attendant computers put the computer numerically controlled (CNC) Alberti milling machine through its paces in the shop (at left). 'Big Al' performs all routing and milling operations in a 2-ft. by 7-ft. work area.

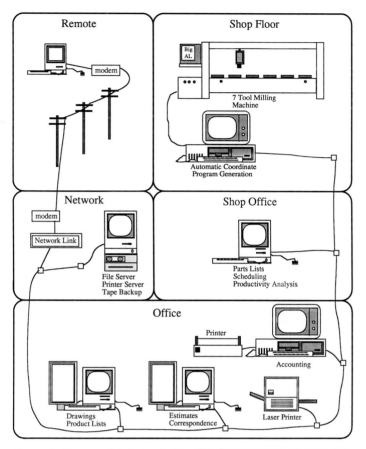

Remote

Shop Floor

Big AL

7 Tool Milling Machine

Automatic Coordinate Program Generation

Network

modem

Network Link

File Server
Printer Server
Tape Backup

Shop Office

Parts Lists
Scheduling
Productivity Analysis

Office

Printer

Accounting

Drawings
Product Lists

Estimates
Correspondence

Laser Printer

Generated by one of their computers, this diagram gives an overview of how the Kochman's CAD/CAM network links design and manufacturing processes. A cabinet plan generated in the office may be fine-tuned on the shop-office computer to conform to reality. The information is then relayed to the shop-floor computers, where it is broken down into a detailed list of machine operations performed by 'Big Al.' All the designs are housed in a central file storage (represented by 'Network' on the drawing), from which they can be retrieved at any time. The 'Remote' aspect of the network is used sporadically to transfer information from out-of-house sources (Bill Kochman's home computer or a consulting architect's office) to the shop. (Printout by Kochman Woodworking)

and costly mistakes. Parts lists that once consumed five to eight hours a week are spit out in seconds. "In the old days," Bill explains, "we used to cringe when we had to make a last-minute change." When a customer called recently to change the height of some upper cabinets by 1 in., it took only 20 minutes to make all the corrections on computer. Now, fully half of the time a job spends in the shop is devoted to finishing. "We have to have the product," Bill says. "People could care less how we do it."

Software is the key to the system's success, and Bill prefers to design his own. He spent six months writing in BASIC (a beginner's program), to "jig" the software he now uses. Its "interactive modules" make it possible to mix and match finishes and styles with abandon. Bill was not trained as a programmer, but he brought several years of computer experience to the business and naturally gravitated to design; Jim has a woodworking background and runs the shop.

Unlike Mac Campbell, who has begun to use three-dimensional design programs, Bill Kochman prefers a two-dimensional

graphic system. He considers the existing three-dimensional software either too clumsy to operate or of insufficient quality. And his customers respond better to the slick model kitchen in the showroom than to a computer printout. "We're not trying to force the computer to do something it's not good at," he explains. "We're where the automobile industry was at the beginning of this century," he adds. "The transportation system is dirt roads. It's not quite here yet, but it's coming...."

Workshop systems have come a long way since this welter of equipment was installed in the John Grass woodturning shop in Philadelphia.

Systems: The Workshop Envelope

God is in the details. —Mies van der Rohe

Chapter 5

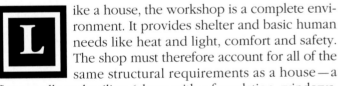ike a house, the workshop is a complete environment. It provides shelter and basic human needs like heat and light, comfort and safety. The shop must therefore account for all of the same structural requirements as a house—a floor, walls and ceiling (along with a foundation, windows, doors and a roof, if it is freestanding). Beyond that, the dedicated, functional nature of the workshop and the equipment that is used in it embrace a whole range of issues and specific requirements—electric power, dust collection, task lighting, solvent storage and vapor extraction—that are only peripheral in most houses.

Unfortunately, in too many workshops, these critical support systems are accorded scant consideration. After spending so much time, energy and money on the workshop structure and equipment, we're too often willing to put up with an inadequate, even unsafe or unhealthy, work environment. But, as Donald Williams, furniture conservator for the Conservation Analytical Laboratory (museum support center for the Smithsonian) told me, these systems should be non-negotiable. "They may seem extravagant to the person who's scraping by in the basement," he said, "but for me that's where it starts. You do without a table saw if you need to."

In this chapter I will outline the basic systems that are common to most shops. To attend to them all would require the diverse talents of a small corps of professionals—an architect, a builder, a mason, an electrician and a plumber, among others. You may have some of these skills yourself, or be able to crib enough information from the literature to undertake much of your own construction. If not, you may prefer to hire (or barter for) a professional to do the job. Electricity, in particular, can be dangerous — even deadly — so do not undertake any electrical operation about which you are at all uncertain.

In any case, entire books have been written about each aspect of the subject, covering everything from roofing and insulation to electrical wiring; and there are federal, state and local building codes that apply to just about any structural situation you can imagine. Refer to these sources (a few of which are listed in the Bibliography) or to a licensed professional for more detailed information. And contact your local fire marshal or insurance representative to make sure that what you are about to do is not only safe, but legal, and will not adversely affect your insurability.

Structure

Purpose-built workshop buildings come in every shape and size and in every conceivable type of construction, from poured concrete and rammed earth to log, timber-frame and standard balloon framing. Converted shops are at least as varied. In this book you'll find comfortable shops that are located in a pole shed, several old mill sites, the granite bowels of an industrial building, a Chevy bookmobile and hewn out of a chicken coop. I know of one Arizona sculptor who works in a hogan, the traditional earth and timber longhouse of the Navajos.

So many different types of buildings and construction methods are used to build shops successfully, that I won't attempt to discuss them all here. There are, however, several structural considerations worth mentioning, whether you're building from scratch or working in your basement.

Insulation   Insulation is as important for comfort and energy efficiency in a shop as it is in a home. What's more, insulation absorbs machine noise, making the shop a more pleasant place to work in and to live next to.

After roasting for much of six years in an uninsulated tin garage, Roger Heitzman took action before moving his California workshop into a corrugated-steel, light-industrial building. He attached a separate 2x3 stud wall to the inside of the steel frame with screwed-on brackets. Then he stuffed fiberglass insulation in the furred walls and ceiling and he sheathed the inside with ½-in. drywall. The effort paid off. Heitzman's half of the 2,400-sq. ft. building hovers around a pleasant 70°F during most of the summer, while it sizzles at 100°F in the uninsulated cabinet shop in the other half. During the three cool months of the year, auxiliary heat is supplied by two portable kerosene heaters (10,000 Btu).

Different construction situations and budgets call for different insulating materials. Fiberglass and polyurethane foam are two of the most popular, although Homasote panels and ceiling tiles are also used to advantage. A few timber-frame shops I visited were fitted with stress-skin panels, in which foam insulation forms an unbroken vapor barrier around the skeletal frame, effectively reducing drafts and heat transfer through the walls. Stress-skin panels are expensive but they are installed quickly (the interior wall covering and exterior sheathing are built into each panel), and reduced heating costs will make up for at least some of the initial investment.

Interior paneling contributes to the sound and thermal insulation of the workshop, and several shops I visited were either completely paneled or combined a wood-sheathed wainscoting on the lower portion of the wall with a dry-walled surface above. Wood paneling creates a warm, cozy atmosphere and provides a rugged, puncture-resistant surface to which tools and shelves may be easily attached. Drywall is relatively inexpensive, easy to install and is usually painted white for a bright working environment, but it is readily gored by an errant swing of a board, and fastenings must be driven into supporting studs or attached with special anchors. (I always feel more secure with a nail, screw or dowel in wood than with an anchored screw in drywall, particularly if the fastening must carry any amount of weight.)

In a large space, a dropped ceiling will aid significantly in retaining heat and absorbing sound and will reduce the risk of fire that comes with the accumulation of fine sawdust on studs, wiring and lighting fixtures. Of course, these advantages must be balanced against the loss of headroom.

Wood paneling has practical as well as aesthetic advantages. It is sturdier than drywall, it helps absorb sound and it provides some additional insulation.

Details like this lumber-camp door latch lend a practical, homespun character to Harold Payson's Maine boat shop. The latch is so simple people don't know how to use it. Payson nailed a ¾-in. by 1-in. by 2-ft. long stick of limber hardwood to the door, far enough from the rounded end to allow the stick to bend as it hits the notched catch, which is mortised into a hole in the casing. A slight pull or push opens or closes the door and, as Payson notes, 'a little oil in 36 years is all this simple door latch has asked for.'

A 14-ft. wide sliding door allows easy movement of wood and machinery in Joel Seaman's timber-frame shop (left), and opening it on nice days provides plenty of fresh air. The door is framed with 2x10s, 2x8s and vertical 2x4 stiles. Spaces between the frame and stiles are filled with 1-in. thick rigid foam, and a layer of Tyvek beneath the cedar clapboards prevents drafts. A door this large calls for heavy-duty hardware. Seaman used Richards-Wilcox sliding-door hardware and a cam-type lock at either end (shown above) to secure it snugly against the weatherstripped opening. (Photo at left by Joel Seaman.)

Doors It is important to remember that workshop doors frequently must accommodate more than just people. A standard 2-ft. 8-in. wide interior door is too small to comfortably allow movement of machinery and materials, much less a large piece of furniture or a small boat. Even a 3-ft. wide exterior door will prove too narrow for many workshops. The best access is provided by an insulated, custom-made door at least 4 ft. wide, or by a larger sliding door, such as the one shown in the photo above. In many garage workshops or freestanding structures, a standard overhead garage door makes it possible to open up an entire wall of the shop. This access to fresh air creates a pleasant work environment during mild weather and makes it easy to move equipment and materials in and out of the shop.

Garage doors and large sliders are difficult to insulate and seal, however, so they may create problems in cold weather. Since most heat loss in a building takes place around the windows and doors, good insulation is important not only in the construction of the door but in proper weatherstripping. A tightly sealed door will also help contain noise and dust, which is especially important if the shop is located inside the house.

By hanging two narrow doors within two larger doors, Martha Collins can create four different openings to accommodate movement of objects large or small.

Martha Collins's versatile door-within-a-door design (shown above) offers several different options for access. Daily entrance is provided by either of two 28-in. by 83½-in. double-glazed doors. Opening both doors creates a 56-in. wide opening, big enough for most large objects. These doors are, in turn, hung within a pair of larger doors. Though Collins rarely opens them now, the big doors proved useful when she moved in; the 94-in. by 94-in. opening was almost as large as the end of the 45-ft. trailer that delivered her shop equipment. Unlike most overhead garage doors or horizontal sliders I've seen, these doors are well insulated and sealed, and she only has to open as much door as she needs.

Floors Debate persists among woodworkers over the ideal workshop floor surface. Most shops have either a concrete or a wood-frame floor. The former is the rule for basements, garages and many small outbuildings. It has the obvious advantages of ease of construction, low maintenance and great strength, and its smooth, solid surface makes it easy to roll machinery or other carts and fixtures around the work space. What's more, the concrete stays cool in the summertime and it is one less combustible material in a shop full of dry tinder.

But concrete has some serious disadvantages over the more forgiving plywood or solid-wood surface. Concrete is often cold, damp and slippery, and it's hard on dropped

tools (and coffee cups) and harder still on feet, legs and back. Without a substructure of floor joists, there's no way to run wires or dust-collection pipes beneath the floor, unless they're installed in the slab, thus committing you to the original layout. And last but not least, because concrete is a poor insulator and a good conductor of electricity to ground—a much better conductor than wood—it increases the risk of electric shock if your machinery leaks power.

To cope with these realities, the people I visited who work on concrete have adopted several strategies, which vary greatly in their complexity and expense. Some simply cover the concrete with vinyl floor tiles or with rubber-mat runners in high-traffic areas, such as the bench/tool-chest corridor and in front of machinery and assembly tables. You can purchase hard rubber or cushioned mats, which are easier on the feet, but I know of at least one shop that does just fine with oversize truck mud flaps. Of course, any kind of floor mat will interfere with rolling carts and machinery, but this is a small price to pay for the greater comfort they provide.

If you are installing a new concrete floor, it can be made relatively warm and dry with proper site preparation and the addition beneath the slab of gravel, foam insulation and a good plastic vapor barrier. For the ultimate in thermal comfort, consider installing radiant-heat pipes in the concrete when you pour.

A number of woodworkers I visited covered their concrete floor with wood. Curtis Erpelding laid 2x2s on 16-in. centers, insulated between them with sheets of Styrofoam and covered it all with particleboard. (Plywood would make a more rugged, if more expensive, alternative.) He ran conduit between the 2x2s to service outlets on short posts located at each machine. Erpelding wanted to use flush-mounted electrical fixtures, but the Seattle fire department specified off-the-floor receptacles that would not be vulnerable to a splash of coffee. In practice, Erpelding figures they're also easier to keep clean and easier to reach.

This sort of in-floor wiring is rather permanent, but Erpelding explains: "I had a pretty good idea of how I wanted things laid out." Plywood ramps bridge the height difference between the wood platform and surrounding concrete floor and make it easy to roll his shop vacuum and production carts around. The built-up floor underlays the entire bench area and part of the machine space, thus retaining the practical advantages of concrete in the assembly and storage areas and around some of the machinery.

A wood floor makes a "friendlier" work surface than concrete, but it is not without drawbacks. When built above bare earth, it is also subject to moisture. Covering the earth with a good vapor barrier and perhaps a skim coat of concrete over gravel will improve drainage and reduce moisture infiltration. The insulation must not be exposed or it will eventually deteriorate, either as a result of moisture or nesting critters. Wood is obviously more susceptible to fire. Aware of this danger, Peter Axtell poured 2 in. of concrete atop the plywood floor in his spray booth.

Considering the weight of machinery and the activity that takes place in most workshops, a wood floor must be heavily built. Kelly Mehler's wood floor supports heavy industrial machinery with full-cut 2x12 floor joists on 12-in. centers, sheathed with three layers of tongue-and-groove oak flooring. The floor creaked a bit when Mehler installed his 2-ton planer with a forklift truck, but it never sagged. Mehler's shop was a car dealership in another life, and the floor is overbuilt for most workshops, but 2x10 joists on 12-in. centers (and more support posts and beams than you think you need) would probably not be excessive. Plywood floors should be protected with a good-quality epoxy paint or a porch-and-deck enamel. (Choose a light-color paint to keep the shop bright.) Solid-wood floors can be oiled, painted, varnished or left bare to develop a rich patina.

Whether the floor surface is wood or concrete, make sure that it is not slippery, especially around machinery. A smooth surface facilitates cleanup and rolling carts, but pushing a wide board across a jointer while standing on a slick, painted floor can be like pushing a car on ice—your feet may be more inclined to slide backward than the board will be to move forward. If necessary, attach traction strips to the floor in all work areas or, when you paint the floor, sprinkle sand on the wet paint to create a rough surface.

For safety and comfort, one of the best investments is also the simplest: good-quality footgear. It may seem excessive to pay more for shop boots than for fancy dress shoes, but when you spend all day on your feet, shoes that offer good cushioning and support are worthwhile in long-term health and comfort.

Electricity   After the structure of the building, electricity is probably the most basic system in the modern woodworking shop. If you work in the basement or a spare room in the house with a few small electric tools (drills, routers, sanders, etc.), you may only need to know how to find the outlets. But as soon as you add stationary machinery, lights, a dust collector or other major fixtures that require additional wiring, you'll need to know more about electricity. If you plan to build an entire workshop or overhaul an existing space, you should devise a comprehensive electrical plan.

It's easy to underestimate our reliance on electricity. All over my house and in many workshops I've visited are extension cords, power bars and multiple-outlet adapters that attest to our shortsightedness. In fact, I've never run into a woodworker who felt he or she had too much power or too many circuits and outlets in the shop. A major electrical installation can be expensive, but the initial investment is almost always repaid in greater safety, economy and convenience.

I feel about electricity as I do about color—I can *almost* see it. Although I am certifiably color-blind, I feel as though I would be able to see what the rest of the world sees if I had not somehow missed the kindergarten class in which crayons were first distributed. Electrical theory comes somewhat later in most schools, but I must have slept through or skipped that course, too.

"To wire a shop full of machinery," James Rickard assured me, "takes the intelligence of a snail and a lot of hard work pulling wire." Suitably humbled by having failed to match even that modest profile, I asked Rickard, himself a trained electrical and mechanical engineer and a consultant to D'Addario Strings, and Paul Silke, a retired electrical contractor and woodworker, for advice. With their help, I have pieced together the rudiments of workshop electricity, which are presented here.

When you finish reading this section, you (like me) will know just enough about electricity to be dangerous, but I hope you'll be able to ask the right questions about your

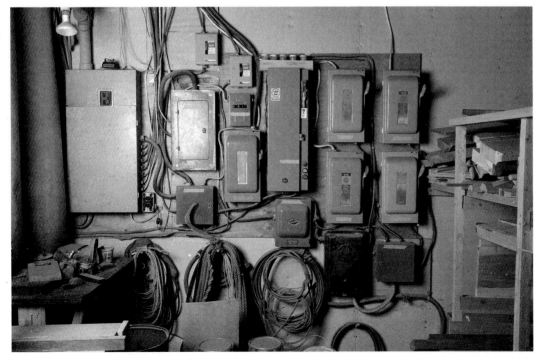

Wiring a shop can be a daunting endeavor for many woodworkers. The ganglion of wires and junction boxes that surrounds the main service entrance in Mac Campbell's basement shop delivers a combination of single-phase and three-phase (converted) power to his equipment.

shop's electrical needs. Then you should consult the local and national electrical codes (NEC) and an experienced electrician when you design and install your shop wiring. (For more detailed information, refer to the sources listed in the Bibliography.)

Circuits To plan an electrical system, follow the same procedure you used to develop a shop layout. Identify those machines and fixtures that require electricity, and distribute them (on paper) around the shop. These are supplied with electricity by circuits connected to the main service entrance of the house or shop. Just as you would distribute your machinery around the shop so that no single work area is overcrowded, the object in planning an electrical system is to divide the load as evenly as possible between circuits. As Martha Collins told me, "Pay special attention to the electrical

---

Power to the workshop

Most of us take electricity for granted. Our homes and shops either come with power, or we simply have it installed. The question is almost always how much juice we'll need and how much it will cost; never how to do without it. While the maverick in some of us yearns for self-sufficiency, for a few woodworkers I visited who live beyond the long arm of the power grid, the issue is decidedly more concrete. It affects not only the cost and speed of working wood, but the nature of the business itself.

Ever since he set up shop on a dirt road in western Massachusetts in the late 1970s, Peter Murkett has been wrestling with the demon of electricity. The nearest power line was a half mile (and ten poles) away when he arrived, so he settled down to hand tools, bench and shaving horse and dreamed of becoming his own utility. A maker of reproduction furniture, Murkett's early work was well suited to pre-industrial technology. He spent the first two years in a rustic 8-ft. by 14-ft. cabin shop, heating with wood, lighting with kerosene and making Windsor chairs, clocks and bentwood music stands entirely by hand. But as the business and workshop evolved, so did his need for power. As Murkett explains, "I gravitated to woodworking for romantic reasons. It's

For more than a decade, Peter Murkett has tried to find a comfortable level of appropriate technology in his two-story, 24-ft. by 32-ft. workshop. He built the place with a generator and worked the first year without electricity, before installing a small hydro plant to run a few DC motors and shop lights. Several years later, Murkett joined the grid, with a 40-amp AC circuit pulled from his home service entrance, soon to be replaced with a dedicated 200-amp service.

taken me a long time to realize that fact and then exorcise it."

With the completion of his two-story shop (shown above) in early 1981, Murkett's quest for power became more urgent. He monitored the flow of water from a spring behind his house to see if there was enough to justify a small hydroelectric installation. "I'm not sure there was," he now admits, "but I did it anyway." In the system he installed, water drops about 75 ft. through nearly a quarter mile of plastic pipe buried below the frostline to a small generating station beside the shop. It supplies slightly more than 75 watts of direct-current (DC) electricity year-round, or "a light bulb, more or less." Not

circuits. I had a professional electrician do mine—and it's not what I expected."

The service entrance, or the main electrical box, is the the source of power in any building. In a residence, it is usually attached to the basement wall or inside a ground-floor closet. A 100-amp to 200-amp service is typical of most modern homes. This is the total amount of "juice" you have to work with. A 200-amp service is better for a full-time work-shop, its lights blazing, stereo blasting and several people working on machines at once. If your shop will draw a lot of power, you can upgrade your service to 200 amps. This can be very involved and expensive or relatively straightforward, depending upon the available electricity and the way power has been delivered to your site. Discuss the requirements with the field representative of your local utility and have a licensed electrician perform the installation.

---

much power, he allows, but "enough to run a chairmaking shop."

To wring the most out of his small but steady supply of energy, Murkett stores the current in a bank of ten batteries (shown at right). When the batteries are fresh and fully charged, the system is capable of operating two or three small electric motors (a 1-hp lathe, ¾-hp bandsaw and ¼-hp grinder) and a few light bulbs. When the batteries are drained or cold, there is "brown-out" in the shop.

Due to the hand-tool nature the craft, it was, indeed, enough power to run a Windsor-chairmaking shop, even when Murkett was joined by two full-time apprentices. A shopmade lathe was the main energy consumer and for a while, Murkett conserved power by switching back and forth between the 1-hp motor and a treadle, using the motor to waste wood quickly and the treadle for finish cuts. Light bulbs were used judiciously to illuminate specific tasks and cast side-lit shadows, not merely to cheer up the shop. (A wall of south-facing windows and a bank of clerestory windows in the roof greatly reduce the need for artificial lighting during most days.)

A year after Murkett brought hydropower to the shop, new settlement down the road greatly reduced the distance to the power line, making it feasible to hook his house up to the grid. But since the house is 900 ft. away from the shop, Murkett worked for four more years with his homegrown system, cultivating the pleasant rhythm of hand tools, punctuated by an occasional spurt of water power. In a 1987 essay Murkett wrote for *Fine Woodworking* magazine, he noted, "When it's quiet in the shop, as it often is, I enjoy hearing the splash of water and the faint whine of the generator from the power house below."

But by 1987, Murkett was beginning to listen to other sirens, who demanded more from his business and, ultimately, the shop. "You get used to the old way," he explains, "and forget that with a possible expenditure of time and money you could be *a lot* better off." Dreams of table saws and long-bed jointers were becoming nagging ambitions. "It's not just the tools, it's the work you can do with them," he says. "Once the power is there, the equipment is there in unlimited ways."

Power came this time from the house, with a 40-amp, 220-volt alternating current (AC) circuit pulled from the main service entrance. He continues to use DC power for shop lights, but the introduction of AC power unleashed a minor

Murkett stores power from his spring-water-driven generator in a bank of ten deep-cycle batteries, wired in series. The batteries provide a reserve of roughly 125-volt power to run lights and small DC motors.

"industrial revolution" that is still in ferment. The treadle lathe was stored downstairs to make room for a growing assortment of machinery, including a small table saw, a chopsaw, four or five routers, three drills, a screwgun, a dust collector and, most recently, an 8-in. jointer. With the advent of each major piece of machinery, Murkett began tackling larger furniture and bigger jobs. It's hardly a high-tech shop—not yet, at least—but when we last spoke, Murkett told me that he was tired of blowing capacitors and was about to install a new 200-amp service that would deliver all the juice he would ever need, no matter how his shop and business grow.

In his essay, written on the verge of acquiring AC power, Murkett describes the philosophical transition that paved the way to his conversion. "I'm far less a zealot now than I was starting out," he explains, "and what keeps me in my 75-watt shop these days has less to do with ecological principle than the hands-on routine of working wood with a sort of one-man efficiency from log to finished product." But the days are long gone when he bent wood over the same bathtub he used to scald the pig. "At this stage," Murkett told me, "I'm more interested in mastering the business than in making a Queen Anne highboy. I wouldn't have said that five years ago...."

Approximate current draw (amps) for different motors

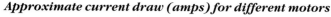

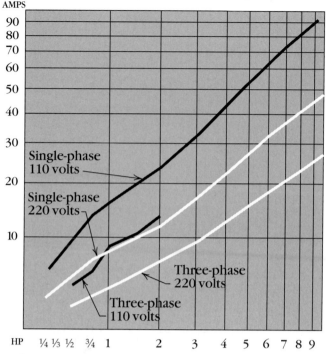

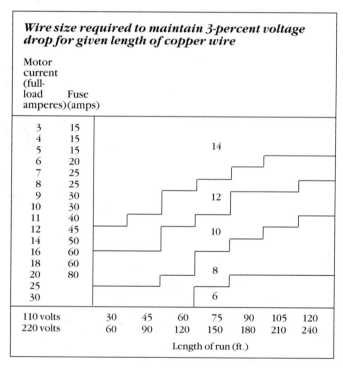

Wire size required to maintain 3-percent voltage drop for given length of copper wire

Motor current (full-load amperes)	Fuse (amps)							
3	15							
4	15							
5	15				14			
6	20							
7	25							
8	25							
9	30				12			
10	30							
11	40							
12	45				10			
14	50							
16	60							
18	60				8			
20	80							
25								
30					6			
110 volts		30	45	60	75	90	105	120
220 volts		60	90	120	150	180	210	240
					Length of run (ft.)			

Once you know a motor's horsepower, these tables allow you to plan wire and fuse sizes. Suppose your biggest motor puts out 1½-hp at 220 volts, single phase, and your shop is 200 ft. from the main electrical panel. The table at top tells you the motor will draw 10 amps under load. The table above tells you to protect the motor with a 30-amp fuse, and to run at least 10-gauge wire to carry the current from the main panel out to the shop. If the motor were three-phase, you would need only 12-gauge wire, saving expensive copper. In reality, main-panel-to-shop runs must be figured by adding the current draw of all motors and lights that might be on at one time, and to be safe, be generous.

If the shop is in a separate building or at some distance from the main service panel in your house, you should install a subpanel for added convenience and to provide plenty of room for shop circuits. (Make sure that any circuit you pull from the house panel is clearly marked and designated strictly for the workshop, and that the subpanel is connected by a separate wire to the earth ground at the main service panel.) The subpanel should have at least a 50-amp capacity. For a separate building, the service could be run from the house to the shop in an underground PVC conduit. (Codes differ, but Jim Rickard's town requires that underground conduit be metal and that it be covered with a board at the bottom of an 18-in. deep trench.)

In a full-time shop, each major machine should have its own circuit, so that you can operate more than one piece of equipment at a time without risk of overload or blown fuses and breakers. It's also a good idea to put the wall outlets and major lighting fixtures on their own separate circuits. That way, if you trip a breaker by overloading a wall outlet or one of the major machines, the shop won't be plunged into darkness. For convenience and economy, you could also wire banks of lights on separate switches. The banks will enable you to illuminate whatever part of the shop you're using without burning every light in the place.

The size of the circuit required by each machine is a function of the size and type of its motor, as indicated in the charts at left. The current required to start a motor is more than three times the amount of current required to operate the motor at its rated horsepower, so the circuit must be large enough to handle the start-up load. For example, a 1-hp, 220-volt, single-phase motor requires about 8 amps of current to operate at its rated horsepower, but would need about three times that much power, or a 25-amp circuit, to start safely. In a shop with an assortment of 1-hp, 1½-hp and 2-hp 220-volt motors, a combination of 25-amp, 30-amp and 40-amp circuits would do the job. All 220-volt motors draw less current than 110-volt appliances, so they can operate on lower-amperage circuits, with lighter wire and fuses. If other equipment (machinery, lights, outlets) is to share the same circuit, the circuit must be large enough to accommodate the cumulative current draw of all the equipment that is likely to be operating at the same time.

For 110-volt wall outlets, a standard configuration would provide 20-amp circuits and 12-gauge wire. Because the total load per circuit should not exceed 80 percent of the circuit rating at any one time, this circuit would comfortably handle a 16-amp continuous load, such as a 1-hp, 120-volt motor or a 2-hp motor at 240 volts. (A breaker or time-delay fuse in your subpanel will take care of the heavier start-up load of the largest motor on the circuit.)

To determine the number of lights you can run on one 20-amp circuit, simply multiply usable amps (16) by volts (120) to arrive at the total available wattage (1,920). In that case, ten 150-watt incandescent bulbs could be run comfortably on one 20-amp circuit, with power to spare for an electric drill or a few more lights. To calculate the current draw for fluorescent lamps, the load per circuit should be increased by about 20 percent to account for the additional ballast load. (For example, a two-lamp, 40-watt unit will have a wattage drain of 80 watts, plus an additional 16 watts for the lamp ballasts, for a total load of 96 watts.)

In wiring the 110-volt wall outlets for his shop, Jim Rickard ran two separate circuits to each box—one for each receptacle. This arrangement takes more wire, but the two circuits enable Rickard to run two tools (a grinder and lathe, for example) or a separate motor and lights at the same time in the same outlet without risk of an overload. If you find you often run a number of tools and accessories from one or two outlets, you might consider this approach.

Wiring All wires, fuses/breakers and switches should be rated to carry the maximum amount of current required for each circuit. Since wiring loses current to resistance, long runs require larger wire than short runs to deliver a given amount of electricity. (The chart at bottom on the facing page shows the appropriate wire and fuse for various combinations of current and run.)

Stick to copper wire for all workshop applications. It's more expensive than aluminum, but it's stronger and more flexible and a better conductor. Standard nonmetallic, sheathed Romex cable (designated NM in the trade) can be used in most dry residential and workshop locations. Use armored cable (BX) wherever there is a risk of mechanical damage or abrasion. If you need to run wires across a floor, where they could get stepped on or otherwise mangled, use rigid conduit or electrical metallic tubing (EMT). EMT is not necessary in most home workshops, but it is the workhorse of commercial wiring. Its advantage, if you can afford it, is that you can change circuits or wiring at any time, without tearing up the walls.

Wiremold is a surface-mounted metal molding that carries electrical wires. All sorts of Wiremold elbows, boxes and extensions are designed to connect to your existing system. As Paul Silke explained, Wiremold is ideal for "what you forgot to put in the walls or what you find you need after everything is sealed up."

Switches You have to be able to turn every motor on and off. Small, portable motors (⅓-hp or less) can simply be unplugged. Larger motors, however, must have separate switches. These can be mechanical or magnetic. Mechanical switches, such as common toggle light switches, are simple—throwing the switch moves the contacts and makes or breaks the electrical circuit.

Magnetic switches are more complicated. Pushing the start button sends power to a low-current relay. The relay energizes magnets that complete the circuit and deliver power to the machine. Magnetic switches have several advantages that make them preferable to mechanical switches for all major machinery. They start or stop machines at a touch. In the event of an overload or electrical fire, a thermal mechanism will disconnect the current to protect the motor. Magnetic switches with three-wire controls will automatically disengage if there is any interruption of power; when the power

resumes, you have to push the switch again to start the machine. These valuable safety mechanisms more than offset the higher cost of a magnetic starter. (National electrical codes require that motors over 2 hp controlled by magnetic switches be connected to an additional switch, or "disconnect," which must be accessible and clearly visible from the motor and machinery. A single disconnect can service several motors.)

Whether mechanical or magnetic, the on-off switch at each machine should be large, readily identifiable and accessible. In the event of a mishap, it's important to be able to hit this switch automatically, without fumbling. Kelly Mehler rigged up the simple contraption shown below, which makes it easy to shut the his table saw off with one hand (or even with a knee or hip), while maintaining a grip on the work with the other.

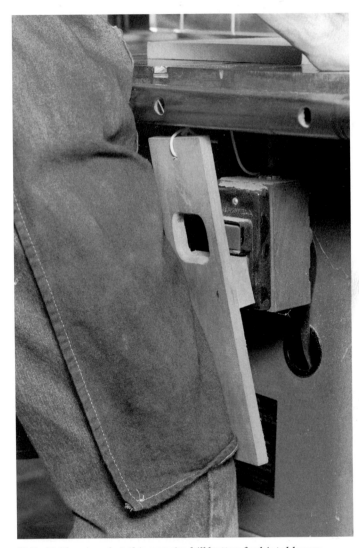

Kelly Mehler rigged up this oversize kill button for his table-saw switch. He made it of a scrap of ½-in. hardwood, 3½ in. wide by 12 in. long. A ¾-in. thick block glued to the back makes immediate contact with the off button, while the cut-out opening requires an intentional effort to reach the on button. A wire attached to the guide rail of the saw holds the kill button in place.

Grounds Your electrical system must be grounded at the main service entrance, either to a metal water pipe or a separate grounding electrode, as approved for your area. Any subpanels must likewise be grounded to the main service entrance with a separate wire, and all electrical outlets should be grounded in turn to the subpanel or main service entrance. All machines would normally be grounded through the motor and switch, but you can screw a separate braided-copper ground wire to the metal frame of the machine and any known ground to guarantee a good connection. With your machinery properly grounded, you can be assured that in the event of a short circuit the current won't make its way to ground through your body. (A grounded machine also will discharge accumulated static electricity from a PVC dust-collection system.)

The addition of a ground-fault circuit interrupter (GFCI or GFI) would provide the ultimate protection against short circuits. In the event of a short, it automatically shuts off the power before a potentially injurious amount of current is discharged. This device may be installed in the main service entrance, or portable GFCIs may be installed on individual machines or outlets. A GFCI should be used on any exterior shop outlet or wherever there is water nearby, such as around a workshop sink.

Outlets Dave Evenson of Cumberland, Wisconsin, spoke for most woodworkers when he told me, "You can't have too many electrical outlets." But where to place them is a more debatable question. Evenson is left-handed, so he located his wall-mounted outlets behind and to the left end of his bench,

immediately adjacent to his collection of drills and hand-held power tools.

But wall-mounted outlets behind the bench invite a snake-pit of cords across the most important work surface in the shop. Some woodworkers cope with this situation by installing short cords on their hand-held power tools, while others prefer to mount the electrical outlets on the base of the bench beneath the front edge of the top. Retractable cord reels are also popular; they can be hung from the ceiling anywhere in the shop and are out of the way when not in use.

To maintain flexibility, Paul Silke installed outlets every 4 ft. along the outside walls of his shop, with strips of Plugmold here and there around the workbench and wherever he is likely to use an assortment of portable tools, lights, battery charger, radio, etc. (Plugmold comes in varying lengths, with any number of outlet locations.) In addition, Silke put two overhead outlets above the sanding area at his radial-arm-saw table. To service each major machine, he installed a bronze floor receptacle with two single-phase outlets on the front and a three-phase outlet on the back.

Three-phase power Three-phase power has several well-known advantages over single-phase. The motors are smaller and simpler in their construction than single-phase motors, so they are less expensive, more efficient and less likely to need repair. Because they draw less current, they require smaller wires, fuses and switches. (In a current catalog, new single-phase motors cost more than twice as much as new three-phase motors of the same horsepower. Used three-phase motors and heavy-duty industrial machinery are often

Martha Collins uses a single-phase 'satellite' motor to start her 15-hp three-phase slave. The lever lifts the wooden platform and the satellite motor, making contact between the rubber drive wheel on the smaller motor and the shaft of the fractional-hp slave (the large motor at left in the photo). Collins houses her three-phase slave and an air compressor (at right) in a soundproofed compartment adjacent to her shop. The plywood door that covers the soundproofed compartment was removed for this photograph.

available at bargain prices.) Moreover, by installing a forward-reverse-stop switch on a three-phase motor, the direction of rotation can be instantly reversed. (You have to change the leads to reverse a single-phase motor.) This is an advantage on shapers and sanders, and provides greater flexibility if you build your own machinery. If you do commercial work or want to use large motors (5 hp and up), you'll need three-phase power.

There are two ways to get three-phase power. It can be provided directly by the power company, or you can use a converter to produce a facsimile of three-phase electricity from a single-phase source. Since three-phase power is usually restricted to industrial and agricultural locations, most woodworkers will have to use single-phase motors or rely on a converter. It is important to note, however, that shop-generated three-phase power is neither as powerful nor as efficient as that provided by the power company. Still, for many woodworkers, access to a whole world of inexpensive, but well-built industrial motors and machinery is enough to warrant conversion.

You can purchase a three-phase converter from an electrical-supply house or make your own, using a dedicated three-phase motor as a generator. This "slave" motor must be at least as big as the biggest three-phase motor you intend to operate. Here's how the system works: Single-phase power is supplied to the slave on two "hot" wires (with a separate ground). The slave is mechanically set in rotation, either with a starter-rope (wrapped around the bare shaft) or with a single-phase satellite motor, as shown in the drawing at right and the photo on the facing page.

Once in motion, the slave will continue to operate on single-phase current because it is under no load. The rotation of the slave generates a third "leg" of electricity, which is then directed to the other three-phase motors in the shop. The drawing at right explains the process schematically. (Sources of information on three-phase conversion are listed in the Bibliography.)

Alternative power Before leaving the subject of electricity, it is worth noting that there are other ways to obtain power in the workshop besides buying it from the local utility. For decades, the Amish have stored water in tall silos and used the vacuum created by draining the column to operate electric motors. Until 1982, all the major machinery—saws, planer, jointer, etc.—in Ben Thresher's Vermont mill (described in Chapter 1) was powered entirely by a water-driven turbine.

I visited several woodworkers who had developed their own, more modest power-generating capacity, more for reasons of economy and practicality than out of religious conviction or tradition. Without exception, these people take a justifiable pride in their accomplishment. They share the convenience of electricity, without suffering the brown-outs or rate increases of their neighbors. And most of them also enjoy their guilt-free independence of nuclear and coal-fired generating plants or large hydroelectric projects.

Faced with the prospect of a quarter-mile of power line and a 45-ft. wide swath through a beautiful stand of hard-

Converting single-phase power to three-phase power

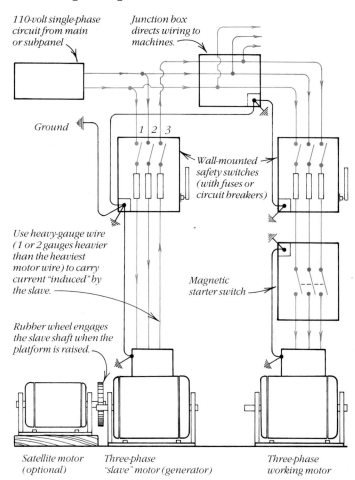

110-volt single-phase circuit from main or subpanel

Junction box directs wiring to machines.

Ground

1 2 3

Wall-mounted safety switches (with fuses or circuit breakers)

Use heavy-gauge wire (1 or 2 gauges heavier than the heaviest motor wire) to carry current "induced" by the slave.

Magnetic starter switch

Rubber wheel engages the slave shaft when the platform is raised.

Satellite motor (optional)

Three-phase "slave" motor (generator)

Three-phase working motor

Note: The slave must be larger than the largest working motor. It must be started mechanically, either by a single-phase satellite motor, as shown here, or with a starter rope.

wood, Jim Miller looked for an alternative. To power his house and shop, which are situated in a scenic mountain pass in northwest Tennessee, Miller turned to a combination of solar and generated power. He runs the house on solar and operates his hammered-dulcimer shop with a water-cooled Kohler generator, which he eventually plans to replace with two 45-watt photovoltaic panels. For now, the generator runs a 2-hp Inca table saw and a 1-hp dust collector, while Miller stores power in deep-cycle batteries and uses an inverter to run hand tools and lights.

With the steady increase in the cost of electricity and the recent advancements in photovoltaic technology, alternative sources of power have more than romantic appeal. If you live too far from the power grid to consider running a line to the shop, then wind, water and solar power, or perhaps a diesel or gas generator, may offer a viable alternative. In fact, depending on your site, one of these systems may provide the only practical source of electricity.

The Racal AGH1 Airstream Dust Helmet tackles airborne dust at its destination rather than its source. A battery pack powers a lightweight fan at the back of the helmet and can be clipped onto a belt or waistband.

Dust collection

When I started working wood about 20 years ago, dust came with the territory. The collection system in my earliest workshops amounted to a snow shovel and a gunny sack; my cheap filter mask gathered dust on the shelf during all but the most noxious operations. At the end of a day of heavy milling or sanding, I would blow the dust cake from my nose without concern. I must have figured that sawdust was "natural" and that untreated it was somehow safe to inhale. In any case, it had to be better than smoking cigarettes or breathing carbon monoxide.

Times have changed. The majority of woodworkers I visited have installed some kind of dust-collection system, many of them quite sophisticated. Those who haven't say it tops their list of priorities. One or two people I know have even quit working wood because of the dust.

Part of this conversion is due to a growing awareness of environmental pollution, which logically includes even relatively "clean" industries like woodworking. Part is due to the now well-established knowledge of the allergenic and carcinogenic properties of many woods and man-made composition materials. Exotic or resinous woods, or any materials treated with glue or preservative, are particularly dangerous. Also, the realities of insurance and fire protection have become more important as we have become more serious about our business or hobby. And, finally, we're just plain tired of eating our own dust.

Planning a system An effective dust-collection system need not be expensive or very elaborate. Several wood-workers I visited do the job with portable shop vacuums and window fans. Many, however, have installed some sort of blower-powered system that sucks sawdust and chips from each machine through ductwork to a central collector where fine dust is captured by filter bags and heavier particles drop into bins.

If your dust-collection needs outstrip the capacities of a shop vacuum, you'll have to do some homework to plan a system. You'll need to determine the appropriate diameter of the ductwork serving each machine or work station, as well as the type and size of the blower and the collector. To do so, you'll need to learn about air flow and system resistance and other aspects of dust collection. I can't walk you through the entire process, but the Bibliography lists several magazine articles that do. Or you can contact one of the equipment suppliers listed in Sources of Supply.

Though detailed technical information and calculations are essential for designing a specific system, there are a number of other considerations common to most dust-collection systems, and I'd like to discuss them here.

Ductwork Many of the shops I visited use plastic PVC pipe, despite the fact that galvanized metal is the recommended material for all industrial air-handling systems. According to one manufacturer I spoke with, PVC has several important drawbacks. It tends to accumulate static electricity, it is difficult to ground, and if a spark ignites a residue of sawdust inside the pipe the PVC could ignite or even explode. Its heavier weight also makes it impractical for large commercial installations.

That's serious stuff, and I'm told you can sometimes hear electricity pop as it is discharged inside a PVC pipe. Still, PVC remains popular because it costs much less than galvanized metal, and it is readily available and easy to install in small runs. What's more, the woodworkers I met who use PVC report little or no buildup of static electricity. This may result, in part, from the small diameter of their ducts and the relatively low volume of sawdust that is drawn through their systems. But the most important protection against static electricity is proper grounding. As long as every machine that is served by a PVC duct (including the dust collector) is properly grounded, there's little risk of accumulating a dangerous level of static electricity in the ductwork. (To err on the side of caution, several woodworkers have installed a solid-copper ground wire inside their PVC pipe. The wire runs the entire length of all PVC ducts and is attached to an electrical ground.)

One of the first decisions you'll have to make is where to locate the ductwork. If your machinery is arranged around the perimeter of the shop, the outside wall is the logical place to start. You can encircle the shop with pipe and drop a short branch line to each machine. Most shops have at least one major power tool (usually the table saw) in the middle of the room, which will require a separate branch line. This can be hung from the ceiling or run beneath the floor. I know of one shop where the ductwork is actually buried under a concrete slab, which puts it conveniently out of the way, but makes it almost impossible to clean, repair or modify. Any ductwork that sits on the floor is sure to interfere with shop traffic.

The ceiling is a common alternative, although the vertical branch line to your machinery may obstruct some operations. The concrete floor and high ceiling of many large, industrial spaces will make it necessary to hang a major duct from the ceiling, which is fed by a succession of vertical branch lines from each machine.

Straight runs of pipe, or gentle curves, are always preferable to right-angle bends and angular junctions, because they reduce pressure losses in the system and eliminate ridges and dead pockets that harbor dust. Where curved sections are required, smooth elbows and 45° T's should be used in place of square junction boxes or right-angle connectors that will accumulate dust. Flexible plastic hose is often used to connect machinery to major ducts, particularly where two or more machines share the same branch line. The ridges in the wall of the flex hose create dust traps that impede the air flow, but this should not present a major problem as long as it is used in short lengths (under 5 ft.). Flexible hose should never be used for major runs.

Many woodworkers prefer not to cement the joints in their PVC ductwork—mainly to provide easy access for cleaning—but leakage can be an important consideration. According to David Scott, president of Manufacturers' Service Company, a producer of dust-collection systems, "Ten percent leakage in a 50,000 cubic-feet-per-minute (cfm) system will lose enough air to add five to six machines." Duct tape is a common solution, since it is relatively cheap and can be readily removed if the system needs cleaning or ad-

justment, but Scott prefers a good-quality silicone sealant. Duct tape, he notes, is "unsightly, the fabric deteriorates and it doesn't have elasticity."

To fasten metal pipes together, Scott prefers rivets to screws or bolts. Rivets are more permanent, but their smooth inside surface won't restrict the flow of material inside the duct. Again, Scott points out that four screws protruding inside a 4-in. dia. pipe will reduce its efficiency considerably. Instead, he suggests three pop rivets at each joint—at 4 o'clock, 8 o'clock and 12 o'clock. Don't install any rivets near the bottom of the pipe (6 o'clock), where they can snag dust.

Bags, boxes and blowers Dust-collection bags and boxes take up space, and the blowers make a racket. Woodworkers in warmer climates can put them outside, which keeps the shop cleaner and much quieter. Those who are loathe to lose valuable warm air in the winter, or who don't want to offend the neighbors, often place them in a corner of the shop. Earl Magnuson built a separate enclosure room to house his collector. The noise is isolated from the work space and air is re-

The California climate allows Peter Axtell to put his cyclone collector outside his workshop, which saves space and cuts down on noise in the shop.

Matthew Burak's dust collection chamber perches like a barnacle on his second-floor machine room. A sliding door empties its contents into a cart or pickup truck below.

Walter Phelps needs a lot of dust collection to service his extensive machine room. Once collected by the cyclone blower, the dust is compressed and fused into tubular brickets, which can be burned like firewood. The compacted brickets consume about one-tenth the space of the original sawdust.

turned to the shop through a small furnace filter. The chamber, a 4-ft. by 4-ft. cubicle, is attached to Magnuson's partially excavated basement shop in Little Rock, Arkansas. It is insulated with fiberglass and ¾-in. thick, foil-faced foam panels, and an adjustable vent in the outside wall can be opened to add fresh air to the system, if necessary.

In his northern Vermont workshop, Matt Burak attached a cantilevered dust-collection bin (shown above) to the side of his second-story machine room. A squirrel-cage blower fills the approximately 380-cu. ft. appendage as often as once a week during periods of heavy millwork. A sliding trap door in the bottom of the bin empties the sawdust directly into a cart or the back of a truck.

The most elaborate system I saw was Walter Phelps's. In his southern Vermont sash shop, Phelps adapted a second-hand industrial "bricketer" to compress the dust

from his heavy-duty machinery. The system is fed by a high-efficiency cyclone blower and a 15-hp motor. (Centrifugal cyclone blowers are typically more expensive than standard squirrel-cage blowers, but they are more effective at separating the dust and shavings from the air.) The heavier particles are sucked into a rotary airlock, where they are fed and condensed by a slow-moving paddle and then pumped into a galvanized hopper. When the hopper is full, the German-made Spänex bricketer fuses the shavings into a 20-ft. long, tubular extrusion of compressed wood fiber, which breaks apart at the end of the line. The cooled brickets are deposited in a rolling hopper. (Phelps gives them to a friend who burns them in his stove.) This setup enables Phelps to keep heat in the shop without competing with sawdust for valuable floor space. It also mollifies his neighbors, who don't like to see big industrial cyclones outside.

Machine enclosures and pickups Apart from a good blower and collection bags, two things are required for an effective dust system. Machines must be enclosed and pickups must be installed near the source of dust. This is harder to do with some types of machinery than others, and the table saw is one of the shop's worst offenders. Most dust collectors access only the chamber below the table, which is marginally enclosed on many saws. And few woodworkers bother with a pickup for the blade, for fear of obstructing the saw's operation. (I'm aware of only one readily available commercial pickup for a table-saw blade, shown below.) As a result, perhaps as much of the dust escapes through the orifices in the base or is spewed from the top of the blade as is actually collected.

Many woodworkers give up on the table saw and focus their attention on other machinery that is easier to enclose, but I saw several good solutions to the table-saw problem. Charlie Mastro, of Seattle, designed the combination blade guard and collector shown in the lower-left photo and drawing below. Dust captured by a see-through plastic guard is drawn through a Plexiglas tube into a box beam that is connected to a branch line of the dust collector. The guard is screwed to the bottom of a 2-in. by 2-in. wooden shaft, which slides up and down inside a channel formed by the sides of the box beam; the shaft is locked in position with a quick-action clamp. The box beam is braced to the ceiling and the sliding shaft is counterweighted, enabling the guard to be lifted with one finger.

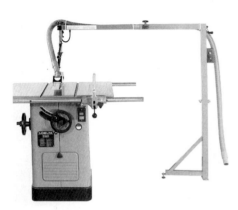

A dust-collection hose and pickup are optional equipment on the Biesemeyer BladeGuard. The guard can be adjusted sideways to permit a narrow fence setting or to cover a tilted blade; it can also move forward to cover the splitter blade on a panel saw. It includes a key-operated alarm system that is triggered when the guard is not in place.

Charlie Mastro's table-saw blade guard and dust pickup (above and at right) is suspended from the ceiling, leaving the table clear on all sides. A quick-action clamp locks the counterweighted I-beam at the desired height.

Charlie Mastro's table-saw blade guard and dust pickup

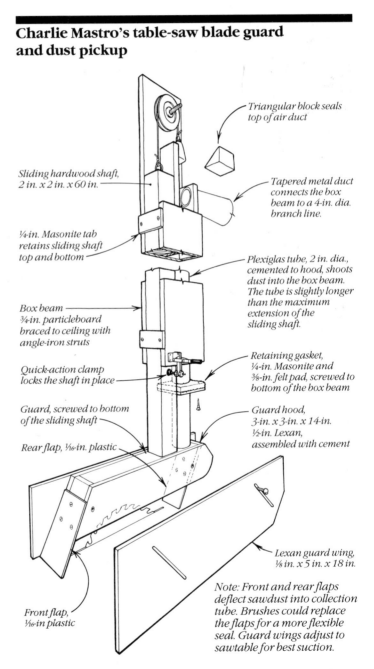

Sliding hardwood shaft, 2 in. x 2 in. x 60 in.

¼-in. Masonite tab retains sliding shaft top and bottom

Box beam ¾-in. particleboard braced to ceiling with angle-iron struts

Quick-action clamp locks the shaft in place

Guard, screwed to bottom of the sliding shaft

Rear flap, ¹⁄₁₆-in. plastic

Front flap, ¹⁄₁₆-in plastic

Triangular block seals top of air duct

Tapered metal duct connects the box beam to a 4-in. dia. branch line.

Plexiglas tube, 2 in. dia., cemented to hood, shoots dust into the box beam. The tube is slightly longer than the maximum extension of the sliding shaft.

Retaining gasket, ¼-in. Masonite and ³⁄₈-in. felt pad, screwed to bottom of the box beam

Guard hood, 3-in. x 3-in. x 14-in. ½-in. Lexan, assembled with cement

Lexan guard wing, ⅛ in. x 5 in. x 18 in.

Note: Front and rear flaps deflect sawdust into collection tube. Brushes could replace the flaps for a more flexible seal. Guard wings adjust to sawtable for best suction.

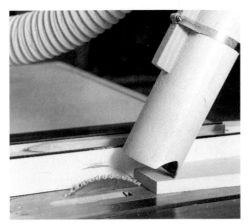

Matt Burak's table-saw collector is just a piece of 4-in. PVC pipe attached to a length of flexible hose. The pipe is fixed to a stick hinged to the ceiling. When the collector is swung up out of use, a cardboard disc hanging a few inches in front of the pipe is sucked against the opening when the system is turned on, thus forming a crude, but reasonably effective blast gate.

A sheet-metal hood directs most of the dust from the radial-arm saw to Norm Vandal's collector (above). Thomas Durney rigged the double pickup at left to suction dust in front of and behind the blade. (Photo at left by Thomas Durney.)

Mastro adapted the device from a pickup on a fancy German saw. It took him about a day to construct. In combination with his collector—a $400, 2-hp Jet machine, rated for 1,100 cfm—the homemade pickup makes a big dent in the ambient dust level in the shop. After about nine months of operation, Mastro suggested two changes to the design. He would move the plastic front flap on the guard forward to better deflect the dust from the front of the blade up the suction tube, and he would raise the height of the box beam to provide more than the current 21½-in. maximum clearance beneath the guard for certain operations. In addition, he noted that a narrower guard hood would permit closer placement of the fence, but it would further restrict the angle of the blade, which is currently limited to a 35° tilt.

A simpler, but effective, table-saw pickup (shown in the top photos), was designed by Matt Burak and uses a short

section of 4-in. PVC pipe attached to a length of flexible hose. The pipe is clamped to a piece of wood, which is hinged to the ceiling above the operator. When he's not using it, Burak swings the pipe up and fastens it to a hook on the ceiling. In operation, the pipe is simply unhooked and lowered onto the table. The height is self-adjusting—the pipe rides up onto the board as the board is pushed through. (The pipe is easily pushed sideways to accommodate narrow rip cuts.) "It's a little spooky at first," one of Burak's employees admitted, because the pipe obscures the blade. But he's gotten used to it.

Sawdust is easier to collect from a radial-arm saw than from a table saw, and effective pickups are therefore much more common on that machine. Two typical examples are shown in the photos above. Thomas Durney, of Laplata, Maryland, installed a double pickup, using a slotted PVC

Roger Heitzman made his planer dust cover of plywood and aluminum roof flashing. To determine the best angle for the interior baffles, Heitzman observed the direction of chips exiting the planer head. The lower compartment is filled with fiberglass insulation to help muffle the sound.

A plastic, fast-food beverage cup makes an ideal friction-fit connector for Warren May's dust collector. The large end is taped to the flexible hose of a portable collector, while the smaller, tapered end fits snugly into openings cut in various machine dust covers around the shop.

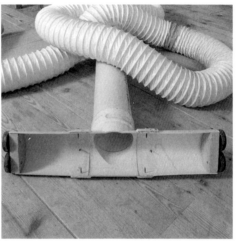

Two methods of clearing the floor of dust: Roger Heitzman sweeps it into a particleboard floor hood (above, left), which sits beneath the outfeed table of his jointer. Matt Burak made his own vacuum pickup from a length of PVC pipe, sawn in half (center and right). A T-section is installed in the middle and small wheels are mounted on the ends, which are blocked with wood.

rainspout behind the blade and a flexible aluminum 1¾-in. dia. carburetor preheater hose to suction sawdust from the front of the housing. Norm Vandal, of Roxbury, Vermont, built a sheet-metal box behind the blade to gather the bulk of the dust, which is projected backwards from the rotating blade.

The thickness planer is another major generator of sawdust, and few machines come equipped with an adequate hood. The photo at top left shows the dust cover Roger Heitzman designed for his Makita planer. Heitzman shaped and tacked aluminum roof flashing inside the plywood shell to keep shavings from accumulating in the corners of the box. He screwed four strips of Micarta to the top of the cover, which made it easy to slide boards back and forth between passes.

Warren May uses a portable dust collector to service several machines in his Kentucky workshop, and he's de-

vised a novel, friction-fit connector, shown at top right, for the end of the flexible hose. May cut the bottom out of an extra-large, fast-food beverage cup and used duct tape to attach the wide end of the plastic cup to the end of the hose. The tapered cup slips into a hole bored in the end of the dust cover and is easily transferred from one machine to another.

No matter how carefully you enclose your machinery or design your pickups, you'll have to deal with dust on the floor. You can sweep it up the old-fashioned way, or push it to a floor sweep-out, like Roger Heitzman's (photo above left), which is controlled by a blast gate. Or, you can vacuum it up with a rolling pickup like Matt Burak's (photos above center and right). "Sweeping is a disaster," Burak told me. It just redistributes the dust. He plugs the flexible hose into one of three wall pickups in his machine room and does the job more effectively than with a broom and dust pan.

Blast gates and remote switches Unless your collector is very large, or if you have more than two machines on the same system, you'll need to close off the ducts that are not in use to maintain sufficient suction at the operating machine. This is best accomplished with blast gates installed near the intake duct at each machine. You can purchase ready-made blast gates from a number of manufacturers, but they're not cheap. A 4-in. aluminum gate costs about $16; an 8-in. gate costs more than twice as much. Ten store-bought blast gates can cost as much as a small collector.

Many woodworkers make their own blast gates out of a variety of materials. Masonite, sheet metal or even cardboard can be fitted to the intake duct of the collector to close off the opening. Richard Schneider turns his blast gates out of wood, as shown in the photo at right, while Rick Stodola makes his out of small plywood discs, which rotate on a dowel in the same fashion as a stovepipe damper (see the drawing at right). Damper-style gates work fine for small shavings and dust, but long shavings from the planer or jointer tend to snag on the disc and clog the duct.

If you take the trouble to make your own, you might as well wire it to the dust-collector switch—open the gate and the system switches on, saving a walk to a switch across the shop (an obvious deterrent to using the system). In some shops, the dust collector is wired directly to the machine switches, so that it goes on automatically when any of the major machinery is started. But that doesn't mean you'll remember (or bother) to open and shut the gates every time you use a machine. If you wire the blast gates, you'll have to shut them when you're done with a machine or the collector will keep running.

Quite a few woodworkers have wired low-voltage microswitches into the blast gates to trigger the collector. A 12-volt or 24-volt transformer is required to operate the low-voltage system, and the collector must be fitted with a magnetic starter switch. Several different styles of microswitch are available at most electronic supply houses and usually cost a few dollars.

Thomas Durney built his blast gate (shown in the drawing at right) out of ½-in. plywood and ⅛-in. Masonite and routed the plywood to accept a microswitch. The hole in the

Richard Schneider's turned wooden plugs make effective blast gates for open-ended collection ducts.

Rick Stodola's "damper" blast gate and router-table pickup

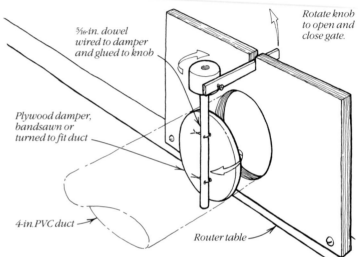

⁵⁄₁₆-in. dowel wired to damper and glued to knob

Rotate knob to open and close gate.

Plywood damper, bandsawn or turned to fit duct

4-in. PVC duct

Router table

Note: PVC duct fits into plywood housing bolted to router table. Tack duct to plywood and add cowling for effective dust collection.

Thomas Durney's microswitched gate

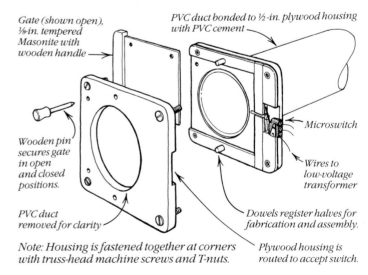

Gate (shown open), ⅛-in. tempered Masonite with wooden handle

PVC duct bonded to ½-in. plywood housing with PVC cement

Wooden pin secures gate in open and closed positions.

Microswitch

Wires to low-voltage transformer

PVC duct removed for clarity

Dowels register halves for fabrication and assembly.

Plywood housing is routed to accept switch.

Note: Housing is fastened together at corners with truss-head machine screws and T-nuts.

Wiring blast-gate switches

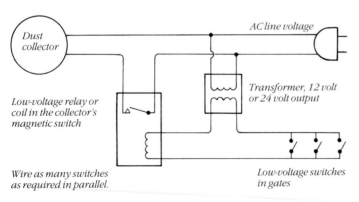

Dust collector

AC line voltage

Low-voltage relay or coil in the collector's magnetic switch

Transformer, 12 volt or 24 volt output

Wire as many switches as required in parallel.

Low-voltage switches in gates

Paul Silke's bullet-catch gate

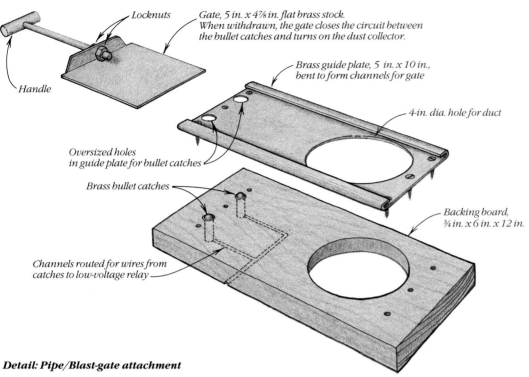

Handle

Locknuts

Gate, 5 in. x 4⅞ in. flat brass stock. When withdrawn, the gate closes the circuit between the bullet catches and turns on the dust collector.

Brass guide plate, 5 in. x 10 in., bent to form channels for gate

4-in. dia. hole for duct

Oversized holes in guide plate for bullet catches

Brass bullet catches

Backing board, ¾ in. x 6 in. x 12 in.

Channels routed for wires from catches to low-voltage relay

To pick up the dust from his Delta Unisaw, Paul Silke enclosed the bottom of the cabinet with plywood, in which he cut a 4-in. dia. hole for the duct. The gate is mounted on a board, drilled and routed to accommodate the PVC pipe, which rises through the floor beneath the machine.

Detail: Pipe/Blast-gate attachment

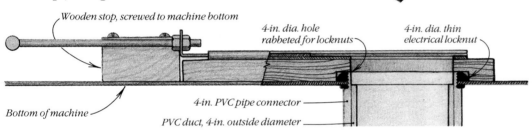

Wooden stop, screwed to machine bottom

4-in. dia. hole rabbeted for locknuts

4-in. dia. thin electrical locknut

Bottom of machine

4-in. PVC pipe connector

PVC duct, 4-in. outside diameter

---

gate is a close fit for Durney's PVC collection pipe, which is sealed with silicone adhesive. Pulling the Masonite slide activates the low-voltage circuit, which in turn energizes the dust-collector relay. To prevent slides in ceiling-mounted ducts from slipping out and activating the system while the shop is unattended, Durney secures them with small wooden pins. (Pins also hold the gates mounted in other positions open, to keep them from vibrating shut.)

Paul Silke, of Salem, Oregon, found that the microswitches he installed on his blast gates clogged with dust, so he replaced them with brass bullet catches, as shown above. A retired electrical contractor, Silke went to great lengths to design the ideal electrical and dust-collection system and, so far, the bullet catches have been foolproof.

Silke uses several variations on his gate assembly; the one shown in the drawing above is the most elegant of them all. The blast gate itself is a piece of 20-gauge brass, attached to a ¼-in. brass rod with a soldered T-handle. The gate slides in the channels of a 5-in. wide brass guide plate, which is screwed to the top of a board. (Galvanized steel would work as well as brass for all the metal parts, or you could do as

Silke did for the gate in his table saw and replace the brass guide plate with one made of wood.) Two spring-loaded brass bullet catches are installed in the board and soldered to the low-voltage bell wire that connects the gate to the relay in the collector's magnetic switch. Narrow channels are routed in the back of the mounting board for the wires. When the slide is withdrawn, the circuit between the two bullet catches is completed and the system barks to life.

If all you want is a convenient way to turn the dust-collection system on and off from the shop floor, there's an easier way. Curtis Erpelding uses a small radio-controlled (RC) transmitter to operate his dust collector from several central machine locations in the shop. Erpelding spent about $100 for three transmitters, a receiver and the relay, which is wired to the dust collector. (For complete portability, another woodworker I know carries an RC transmitter in the pocket of his shop apron, so he can control the collector from anywhere in the shop.) An RC setup is a good alternative for a very large shop where a lot of wiring or custom-made blast gates would be a nuisance, or if you already have store-bought blast gates.

Norm Vandal's dust collector

Norm Vandal's shop-made dust collector is a creative combination of salvaged and custom-made materials. A homemade bandclamp secures the plastic collector bags.

Junction-box detail
Sandwich bag between block, cap and lip.

— Filter bag

Cap, ½ in. x 1½ in.

Lip, ¾ in. x 1¾ in.

Block, 1 in. x 1½ in.

Top, ¾ in. x 3½ in.

Box side

Box bottom

Band clamp

Plastic bag

Filter bag, 26 in. x 38 in. x 52½ in., suspended from the ceiling

Junction box, 8¾ in. x 31½ in. x 58 in., screwed to wall in the corner

Hinged access door, sealed with a rubber gasket

Blower outlet

Leg, 4 in. x 4 in. x 47 in.

Section of 55-gal. drum

6-mil plastic bag, 36 in. x 60 in.

Sawdust

Band clamp (see detail below)

Pop rivets

Machine bolt and wing nut

Angle bracket

Metal banding, ¾ in. wide

Notes: Junction-box sides and bottom are ¾-in. plywood; cap, lip, block and top are pine. Plastic bags fit over short, cut-off sections of plastic drums screwed to the box bottom and sealed with silicone caulk. Band clamps secure the bags.

Two simple collectors You can spend a lot of money on a sophisticated collection system like Walter Phelps's (a new collector/bricketer like his would cost as much as a small house), but you can also suck up most of the dust without taking out a second mortgage. A perfectly acceptable in-shop collector can be fashioned from new and used materials at a fraction the cost. Norm Vandal's homemade collector (shown above) is a good example.

Vandal started out as a hand-tool woodworker, but over the years he has steadily added machinery to his 24-ft. by 30-ft. workshop, which he built in 1982 and now shares with one employee. To handle the dust, Vandal installed his collector in one corner of the shop and powered it with a 10-in. dia., radial-blade blower. (To prevent sparks, the blower has bronze blades.) The radial-arm saw, thickness planer, tenoner and shaper are all connected to the collector by 6-in. dia. galvanized stove pipe, with a blast gate at each machine. The system is controlled by a magnetic starter switch mounted on one of the central posts in the shop.

The dust is shot first into a plywood junction box, where the heavier shavings drop immediately into two collector bags. Vandal purchases 6-mil plastic bags from a mail-order packing-supply company and extends their life with duct-tape patches. The bags fit over two cut-off sections of plastic industrial drums, screwed to the bottom of the plywood box. They are secured to the drum flanges with ¾-in. metal banding. The air is returned to the shop through a custom-made cotton filter bag, suspended by six loops from the ceiling. (See Sources of Supply for distributors of the plastic and fabric bags.)

Periodically, Vandal beats the filter bag with a stick to release the dust. On occasion, he opens the door in the plywood junction box to redistribute the dust or lightly scrape the inside of the filter bag. (The dust cake on the inside of the bag helps trap some of the fine particles, so it's best not to scrape it too clean.) The system is strong enough to draw dust from two machines at once, but it would be enhanced by greater airflow around the outside of the filter bag. (In Toronto, Michael Fortune installed a movable baffle in a similar collector to divert the flow of dust to one or the other collection bag. He uses the hardware from a pair of old ski bindings to fasten his filter bags quickly and securely.)

Vandal estimates the total cost of his system at less than $500, including the plywood for the box, the relay switch ($5 from a salvage yard), blast gates (about $15 each), blower ($90) and the 2-hp, direct-drive Dayton motor ($200). The ductwork came free from local plumbing and heating contractors who had pulled it out of buildings they were converting from forced-air to hot-water heat. The system even earns him a little pocket change—he sells his maple and pine dust for animal bedding, at $1.50 per bag.

Apart from the bandsaw, which is connected to a portable shop vacuum, the only major power tools not hooked up to the system are the table saw and an old 20-in. jointer. The open jointer base, in particular, would have to be sealed with an elaborate box construction for effective collection. Instead, Vandal simply sweeps the shavings to a vacuum pickup located on the floor near both machines. To suck the fine dust out of the air after a major mahogany job, he opens all the blast gates and the shop door and turns on the collector.

For about $250, Rick Stodola, an amateur woodworker near St. Johnsbury, Vermont, put together the octopus collector shown at right to service six stationary machines and a sanding table. (Why are so many interesting dust-collection systems to be found in Vermont? Perhaps it's coincidence, or perhaps it's because New Englanders are constrained to the shop for a large portion of the year, when they dare not open the door without risk of frostbite.)

At the center of the system is a 1-hp, 1.75-cu. ft., two-bag dust collector, made by Central Machinery (see Sources of Supply on p. 210). On top of the blower, Stodola installed a 10-in. square by 6-in. high plywood junction box to accept the four main branch lines. Except for elbows and other

connectors, he used 4-in. dia. aluminum dryer ducts instead of PVC pipe to reduce the likelihood of static electricity. (The short run of pipe enables him to operate two machines at once.) The joints are assembled with duct tape for easy disassembly in the event of a clog, and cardboard cowlings at each machine help direct the flow of sawdust to the collection pipe.

Stodola's circular layout is a model of efficiency for a small basement shop. It's about 10 ft. in diameter, leaving about 4 ft. of clearance between the machines and the shelving along both walls. The tools are at different heights and positioned so that work is fed at a tangent to the circular layout, where it is least likely to be obstructed by other machinery or permanent shop fixtures.

Rick Stodola's octopus collector

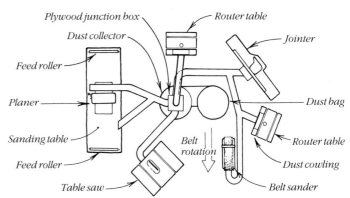

Note: Tools are at different heights so work can pass under or over them.

Rick Stodola's octopus extractor services six machines and a sanding table in his basement workshop.

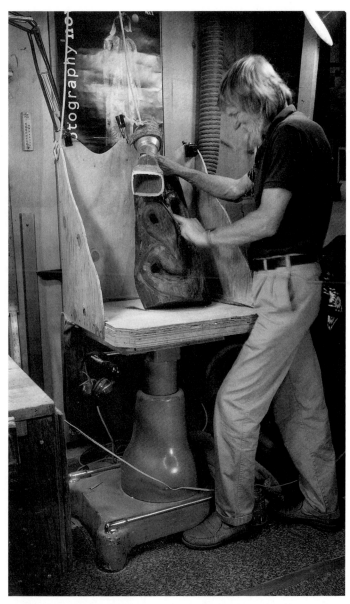

Sculptor Paul Perras maneuvers the sheet-metal nozzle of his carving-station dust-collector right where he needs it.

A plastic wastebasket with aluminum deflectors captures a lot of dust from Carl Hathaway's pneumatic sander. A hose connected to the basket through the stand leads to a collector.

Coping with fine dust For all their effectiveness, dust collectors, brooms and vacuums miss a lot of the most dangerous and irritating dust in the shop—the minute airborne particles churned up by a sander or thrown off of a table-saw blade. According to the Occupational Health and Safety Administration's (OSHA) Dr. Peter Infante, "There's no question...that wood dust is a carcinogen." And, obviously, it's not the long pine ribbons churned out by a planer that will kill you, but the almost invisible dust you inhale every day. Here are some of the methods woodworkers I visited employed to corral fine dust.

One of the simplest and most flexible methods was rigged up by Paul Perras for the carving station shown at left, which he installed atop the base of a surgical operating table. A sculptor who works with dense, resinous woods as well as stone, Perras needed a pickup he could position right next to the point of cut. He mounted a 45-gal. drum collector in the rafters above the carving station and attached a long length of 4-in. dia. hose, with a sheet-metal nozzle fashioned at the pickup end. Much of the time, the hose rests in one of the scalloped recesses in the top of the plywood station, but it can be raised or lowered with a rope cleated to the side of the station. (The rope passes through a small pulley that hangs from a swivel bracket above the station.) The plywood enclosure helps support the work and contains the dust in the immediate area.

Carl Hathaway, who works in Saranac Lake, New York, uses a pneumatic Sand-rite sander to smooth the ribs of his Adirondack guideboats and canoes (below, left). He attached a plastic wastebasket to the machine and added an aluminum shield to deflect the dust. A flexible hose connected to the waste basket draws the dust to Hathaway's Grizzly collector, which is located in an adjacent workroom.

Kelly Mehler (top photo, the facing page) found that his 5-hp collector was not worth starting for small operations. So at the lathe, pneumatic sander and workbench he opens a window nearby and relies on a simple combination of fans and dust masks to clear the air. (Forget this method in January, but the fan will help cool the shop all summer—whether or not you're making dust.)

The plywood sanding station (bottom photo, facing page) tackles one of the nagging problems of the workshop—how to collect sawdust from portable hand sanders. Most of us just wear a mask and let the dust fall where it may. In Michael Elkan's production box shop, dust is contained and funneled toward the pickup at the back by the sides and top of the box. The station was designed to handle a large volume of work and resembles the "elephant-trunk" system commonly found in major museum conservation labs, which typically employs flexible pickups at individual work stations for vapor and solvent extraction.

Up to this point, we've mainly examined the localized collection units that are designed to gather coarse dust at its source. But a growing number of woodworkers are beginning to pay attention to the fine particulate that hangs in the air long after a job is completed. I came across several effective "free-hanging" solutions, which vary greatly in cost and sophistication.

When working at his pneumatic sander, Kelly Mehler positions a household fan on one side of the machine and a large window fan on the other to draw off most of the offending dust.

At one end of the spectrum is the electrostatic precipitator Paul Potash installed in his southern California workshop. The unit (manufactured by Trion, Inc.) is roughly the size of a residential air conditioner and is suspended from the ceiling. A squirrel-cage fan (1,250 cfm) quietly draws the airborne particles through a standard mesh prefilter and past a high-intensity ionizing field. The negatively charged particles are then collected on a series of positively charged ground plates inside the unit. The expelled air is almost entirely free of suspended dust, smoke and fumes. Potash sweeps the floor regularly and, once a week, takes a few seconds to knock the accumulated dust off the plates.

Potash is fond of the system. But it doesn't come cheap. His Tepco model #1250 cost about $1,500, and even in his 420-sq. ft. shop, Potash admits that an additional unit would improve the circulation. In many applications, electrostatic precipitators are being replaced by less expensive, nonelectronic "media filter" units, which entrap the dust mechanically using a fine fiberglass filter.

The sanding station in Michael Elkan's box-making shop sucks up dust from portable sanders.

Below is a shop-built filtration box built by Ken Bishop, of Winston-Salem, North Carolina. Compared with most electrostatic or media-filter units I found, Bishop's box is a steal—it cost $60 in materials, including the purchase of a new fan. Mounted on casters, the 65-lb. box is easy to move to wherever he's working. Bishop built the box of plywood, Masonite and a 1,500-cfm attic-ventilator fan. It accommodates four standard furnace filters and works so well that during belt-sanding operations he has to vacuum or change filters every hour or two. "It never was intended to be a dust collector," Bishop says, "but it does a great job of sucking the particulate out of the air."

Dust masks Many of the woodworkers I visited wear dust masks when they work, either to augment an inadequate collection system or for added protection. If you do a lot of freestyle hand-sanding of odd-shaped pieces, a good mask is your last and best line of defense. (It doesn't hurt to wear a mask at other machines as well; all of them produce some fine dust.) Excellent respirators are available that will filter out mists and fumes as well as dust, or you can wear an inexpensive fiber filter mask if you're concerned only about dust. John Nyquist wears two 3M filter masks at once. The inner mask traps the moisture from his breath, while the outer mask stays dry and is less likely to clog. When it does eventually fill with dust, he blows it off with compressed air and uses it to replace the inner mask.

Perhaps the most impressive personal air-filtration system I found is provided by the Racal Airstream Dust Helmet (shown in the photo on p. 100). Air is drawn into the back of the helmet by a battery-powered fan and is propelled through a series of filters and expelled at the chin in a downward stream that passes across the front of the mask. Apart from the flip-up plastic visor, which deflects flying chips, the Airstream Helmet has some important advantages over less-expensive filter masks—a beard, moustache or glasses won't interfere with effective operation, and you won't have to suck air through a soggy bandanna or surgical-style face mask.

Racal makes several models of powered air-purifying respirators (PAPRs) to suit various filtration requirements,

Ken Bishop's shop-built filtration box effectively siphons off fine sanding dust. A small attic fan in the box circulates the air in his 2,560-cu. ft. workshop every two minutes. (Photo by Kenneth W. Bishop.)

Ken Bishop's air-filtration box

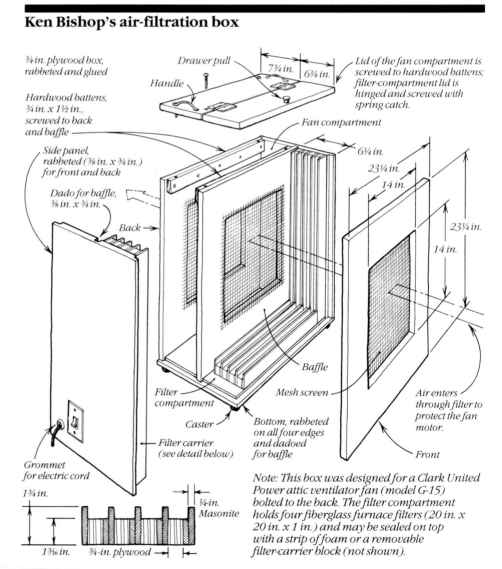

¾-in. plywood box, rabbeted and glued

Hardwood battens, ¾ in. x 1½ in., screwed to back and baffle

Side panel, rabbeted (⅜ in. x ¾ in.) for front and back

Dado for baffle, ⅜ in. x ¾ in.

Back

Drawer pull

Handle

7¾ in.   6¼ in.

Lid of the fan compartment is screwed to hardwood battens; filter-compartment lid is hinged and screwed with spring catch.

Fan compartment

6¼ in.

23¼ in.

14 in.

23¼ in.

14 in.

Baffle

Mesh screen

Air enters through filter to protect the fan motor.

Filter compartment

Caster

Bottom, rabbeted on all four edges and dadoed for baffle

Front

Grommet for electric cord

1¾ in.

Filter carrier (see detail below)

¼-in. Masonite

1¾₁₆ in.   ¾-in. plywood

Note: This box was designed for a Clark United Power attic ventilator fan (model G-15) bolted to the back. The filter compartment holds four fiberglass furnace filters (20 in. x 20 in. x 1 in.) and may be sealed on top with a strip of foam or a removable filter-carrier block (not shown).

but the AGH1, shown in the photo, is the one recommended for standard wood dust. (Racal's BreathEasy 1 incorporates the same helmet, but filters paint and solvent fumes through gas canisters.) Clean air doesn't come cheap—the simplest Airstream Helmet costs about $279—but it's worth a close look if you are particularly sensitive to wood dust, if you create a lot of it, or if you are interested in prolonging a healthy life in the shop.

In praise of the portable shop vacuum If you're feeling intimidated by all this equipment, there are some simpler options. Large central dust-collection units are usually more efficient than small, individual collectors, but a matrix of overhead ductwork takes up a lot of room and requires a large expenditure in pipe, reduction fittings and blast gates. Depending on the work you do and the size of your shop, a small portable unit, such as Tage Frid's Makita collector (shown below), may be more flexible and cost-effective.

Don't dismiss the humble Sears ShopVac. Many shops have two or three, either instead of or in addition to a large, central unit. Richard Schneider turned his 2½-hp ShopVac into a small central collector for his guitar shop. Most of the time, the ShopVac resides in a storage room adjacent to the shop. It is connected to the bandsaw and sander with PVC pipe, run through the crawl space beneath the floor. In her cabinet shop next door, Schneider's wife, Martha Collins, uses a large central collector and more than 100 ft. of pipe to handle the volume of sawdust from her industrial machinery.

Schneider's system is economical and quiet, and adequate for the relatively small volume of dust he creates. In fact, he discovered that even the ShopVac can be too strong for delicate operations like dusting the inside of a guitar. In that case, he just opens another blast gate to reduce the amount of suction. As Schneider explains, the ShopVac has the added advantage of portability: "You can clean your car with it or bring it inside to vacuum."

If you don't do a lot of heavy machine work, a portable dust-collection unit may be able to handle all your shop equipment. When there's no air or dust in the bag, the Makita #410 is easily toted around the shop.

Where natural light is in short supply, even a single bare bulb is better than nothing. North American woodworkers might take a dim view of the lighting in this Mexican guitar shop, but it does not seem to have hindered production.

Lighting

Near the close of the 18th century, Thomas Jefferson made the following observation:

Light. rule for the quantity requisite for a room. multiply the length, breadth & height together, in feet, & extract the square root of their product. this must be the sum of the areas of all the windows.

When I applied the Jeffersonian equation (believed to be derived from his contemporary, Robert Morris) to the living room and kitchen of the 200-year-old farmhouse in which I used to reside, my windows came up short by more than 30 percent. But Jefferson would have had more money to invest (or to burn) than the New England farmer who built my old place, and the Virginia winters are certainly milder than they are in Connecticut.

We don't know whether Jefferson, fond as he was of woodworking, applied the same formula to the design of the workshops at Monticello or, for that matter, to the other buildings around the estate. (Few such architectural details can be determined from the excavations of the carpenter's or joiner's shops there.) In any event, lighting plays a more pivotal role in the workshop than it does in most houses. Indeed, it may be the most fundamental shop system. We can

Cyndy Burton mixes guitar finishes in front of her bench-room window, using an auxiliary, incandescent task light. When the sun is out, the bench receives a strong raking side light from the large window.

work wood in the cold and without four walls or electricity, but we are helpless to work without light.

Inadequate light is not much better than none at all. Apart from its effect on our vision, poor lighting is known to have a negative impact on our psychological well-being. Precisely because light is so pervasive, it is often taken for granted. But try doing without it for a while and you'll start paying attention.

Natural light   When we think about light, we often think first of "natural" light. But in a lot of old workshops, natural light is just another way of saying darkness. Ben Thresher's Vermont mill (see pp. 17-21), which ran on water power until recently, is probably typical of many early workshops. Apart from the three bare bulbs that dangle precariously

from the shop ceiling, the place is substantially the same as it was a century ago. Step away from a window, even on the sunniest day, and you are plunged into deep shadow.

Many modern shops I visited use natural light to greater advantage. Large banks of double-glazed, south-facing windows in Richard Schneider's and Martha Collins's Washington workshops (see pp. 50-51) create a cheerful working atmosphere, even on cloudy days, which are common in the Pacific Northwest. Likewise, Cyndy Burton (shown above), relies on good natural light to mix the finishes she applies in her Oregon guitar shop.

Although its psychological benefits are manifest, natural light is a mixed blessing. Direct sunlight (and the shadows it casts) is hard on the eyes, and unfiltered ultraviolet rays can have a deleterious effect on wood finishes and colors. For soft, indirect illumination, windows should be placed high on the south wall or shaded by broad eaves. Awnings or window blinds and screens, covered with a translucent material like rice paper or Tyvek, also may be used to diffuse harsh sunlight. If your bench is placed directly against a south-facing window, consider its position carefully. Note, for example, that Schneider's and Burton's benches are perpendicular to the windows, rather than parallel to them. This takes advantage of good side light, while strong back light might tend to obliterate details or swallow them up in shadow.

Windows aren't the only source of natural light. In several shops I visited, skylights or clerestory windows bathe the interior workspace in diffused light, but cast a minimum of direct sun on the bench. At right is an interesting example of a low-budget skylight, which runs the length of Michael Elkan's 100-ft. long Oregon workshop. Elkan simply left his shop roof unplanked for 2 ft. on either side of the ridge and sheathed the outside with corrugated fiberglass panels. To keep the heat in, he "glazed" the bottom of the triangle with optically clear plastic. (For a good example of clerestory windows, see Peter Axtell's shop, shown on p. 167).

If your site permits, consider placing at least some of your workshop windows to receive a good northern exposure. This contradicts a basic tenet of energy-efficient architecture, but a soft, diffused north light is widely considered to provide the most comfortable, glare-free environment and natural color renditions. It is especially desirable at the bench or in a finishing area, where fine, detailed work and color matching take place.

Artificial light   Most woodworkers I know prefer natural sunlight, but in the oldest workshops I visited, the reconstructed Anthony Hay shop at Colonial Williamsburg (18th century) and the Dominy workshop, now housed at the Winterthur Museum (19th century), it was the *only* source of illumination. Not even candles or oil lamps appear in the Hay or Dominy inventories and account books. This may be explained, in part, by the inherent danger of an open flame in the woodshop and by the marginal efficacy of these early artificial light sources. But it probably has at least as much to do with the organization of the shop routine around the daylight hours and the seasonal nature of many woodworking businesses. I am unaware of any study on the subject, but I suspect that artificial light did not become a permanent fixture in most workshops until the second half of the 19th century.

Few craftspeople I know toil from sunrise to sunset, as was probably typical in many pre-industrial workshops. (Summer would have meant long hours in the shop, while winter must have involved more "downtime" and outside activity around dusk.) Instead, we accommodate our shop routine to standard business hours or squeeze it into whatever free time we can steal. Evening shop work may have been unheard of in the 18th century, but it's certainly not uncommon now. At night or in the winter, the importance of good artificial lighting cannot be underestimated. In a basement workshop, or in any space with an inadequate supply of natural light, it is crucial at all times.

Fluorescent lamps are at the heart of many modern artificial lighting systems for the workshop. The fixtures are relatively inexpensive (second-hand industrial hardware is often available), they are the most efficient and long-lived of all forms of standard lighting and they are capable of uniformly illuminating a large area. In addition, a wide variety of fluorescent lamps are available, which produce light of vastly different qualities. (See the sidebar on pp. 116-117 for an introduction to fluorescents and other basic sources of artificial light.)

So why do so many people hate them? In the first place, despite the selection of fluorescent lamps on the market, most of us are familiar with only "cool-white" or "warm-white" bulbs. These are the cheapest and least "natural" of all artificial light sources, and they offer poor color rendition. What's more, fluorescent fixtures emit an annoying hum, and their rapid pulses can result in the notoriously dangerous "strobe effect," which can make a rotating sawblade appear to be stationary. (If you use only fluorescent lamps, machine

This skylight runs 100 ft. along the roof ridge of Michael Elkan's Oregon shop. Corrugated fiberglass panels outside and clear plastic inside keep the rain out and the heat in.

areas should be lit by at least two tubes to minimize this effect.) The lamps also tend to flicker incessantly at temperatures below about 50°F, which is a real nuisance in part-time workshops, and more so in cold climates.

Still, most woodworkers tolerate at least some fluorescents in the shop, not only because of their price, but because of their well-diffused illumination. A combination of warm-white and cool-white bulbs or the so-called "full-spectrum" fluorescents is generally preferred. Full-spectrum lamps are more expensive than conventional warm-white or cool-white tubes, but they provide a color temperature that more closely approximates that of sunlight, or about 5,500 Kelvins (K). Martha Collins replaced all of her standard fluorescent tubes with Duro Test Vita Lites (a brand of full-spectrum fluorescents) and relocated them over specific task areas in the shop. This resulted in about 20 percent more light and true color rendition. "A mere $300," she told me, "but what a difference!"

Shedding (artificial) light

There is a good deal of confusion about the relative merits of various forms of artificial light. In my search for information, I came across the Real Goods Trading Company's Alternative Energy Sourcebook 1990. *The following excerpt helps shed some light on the most important distinctions.*

There are four basic types of electric lamps, or "light bulbs," which are most suitable for use around the home: 1) incandescent, 2) tungsten-halogen, 3) compact fluorescent and 4) standard fluorescent.

Incandescent
The "all-American" incandescent light bulb is, in reality, an electric space heater which produces a little light. Approximately 90 percent of the electricity that passes through a standard incandescent lamp is converted to heat, and only 10 percent into visible light. An inert gas fill, such as nitrogen or argon, is used inside the glass bulb to slow the oxidation of the filament which, over its lifetime, slowly evaporates to blacken the inside of the lamp envelope and typically reduces light output by plus or minus 20 percent.
The simple construction of incandescent lamps

The conventional incandescent bulb sheds more heat than light.

minimizes their initial cost, but...they represent the most energy *inefficient* and *shortest* lived of all lighting sources. Lamp *efficacy* (light output divided by power input) ranges from 8 to 20 lumens per watt and lamp service from 750 to 2,000 hours. While longer lamp life is possible with extended service, rough-duty, and long-life lamps, these operate the least efficiently of all incandescents, producing fewer lumens per watt, because their filaments run at lower temperatures. Note, the more red/orange an incandescent lamp appears, the lower its operating efficiency.

From an energy-efficiency standpoint, incandescent lamps should ideally only be used where 1) no more energy efficient alternative is available, 2) they will be operated for short periods, relatively infrequently, and energy consumption is not an issue, 3) the light source must turn on instantly and operate at full light output regardless of temperature or 4) full range dimming is desired. Where incandescents are used, it is most efficient to use smaller numbers of higher wattage lamps than greater numbers of lower wattage ones.

Tungsten-halogen
Tungsten-halogen (or quartz) lamps are turbocharged incandescents. Compared to standard incandescents, these produce a brighter, whiter light and are more energy-efficient by operating their tungsten filaments at higher temperatures. In addition, unlike the standard incandescent light bulb that loses approximately 25 percent of its light output before it burns out, the halogen lights' output depreciates very little over their life, typically less than 10 percent. Tungsten-halogen lamps produce about 10 percent more light per watt input than standard incandescents and last longer, having useful service

lives ranging from 2,000 to 3,500 hours, depending on the model.

The higher operating temperatures used in halogen lamps produce a whiter light, which eliminates the yellow-reddish tinge associated with standard incandescents. This makes them an excellent light source for applications where good color rendition is important or fine-detail work is performed. Because tungsten-halogen lamps are relatively expensive compared to standard incandescents, they are best suited for applications where the optical precision possible with the compact reflector models can be effectively utilized.

Compact and standard fluorescents
There are several types of fluorescent lamps. The two best for residential application are single-ended compact fluorescents (commonly called "PL" lamps) and double-ended standard fluorescents. Both are low-pressure mercury-vapor gas-discharge light sources. When an arc is struck between the lamp's electrodes, the electrons collide with mercury atoms which emit ultraviolet radiation. This radiation in turn excites the phosphors

Even in a shop full of overhead fluorescents, you'll need focused task lighting for many operations that require close scrutiny. At the bench and for certain machine operations, your own body or the work itself may create a shadow from ceiling-mounted fluorescents. Other operations, such as carving or inlay work, may require strong directional light, casting shadows that help define detail. For these situations, smaller, directional incandescent fixtures are ideal, and the ubiquitous articulated "student" desk lamp is the most common solution. Many shops have a half dozen or more of them scattered about, with holes bored in convenient working locations in benchtops and brackets to receive the mounting shaft.

Student lamps are likely to overheat with anything larger than a 60-watt or 75-watt bulb, but you can get by with even less power (and heat) if you are able to position the lamp close to your work. Clip-on lamps with large reflectors are a popular and versatile alternative, although they often come

---

(the white powder coating the inside of fluorescent tubes) to fluoresce, or emit light at visible wavelengths. The quality of the light fluorescents produce depends largely on the blend of chemical ingredients used in making the phosphors; there are dozens of different phosphor blends available. The most common and least expensive are 'cool white' and 'warm white.' These, however, provide a light of relatively poor color rendering capabilities, making colors appear washed out, lacking luster and richness. On a color rendering index scale (CRI) of 1 to 100 they rate 69 and 52 respectively. The higher the number, the more accurately a light source renders colors.

Phosphor blends are available that not only render colors better, but also produce light more efficiently. These incorporate relatively expensive phosphors that peak out in the blue, green, and red portions of the visible spectrum and produce about 15 percent more visible light than standard phosphors. Wherever people spend much time around fluorescent lighting, specify lamps with higher (80+ CRI) color rendering ratings.

Fluorescent lamps are also available in several different color temperatures, which relates to how warm or cool the light produced by the lamp appears. The lower the color temperature, the warmer or more orange/red/yellow the light appears. The higher the color temperature, the cooler or more violet/blue/green the light appears. Color temperature is rated in degrees Kelvin (K). For reference, a candle has a color temperature of around 1,800 K and incandescent lamps range from 2,500K for standard lamps to 3,000K for halogens. Sunlight varies with the time of day and weather conditions; on a clear summer day, the sky's color temperature is about 5,500K at noon, while it may be between 6,500K and 7,500K on an overcast day. Fluorescent lamps are available with color temperatures between 3,500K and 5,500K.

For residential applications, most people will prefer a 3,000K lamp. Where a space is illuminated primarily with daylight, a cooler temperature lamp such as a 3,500K lamp would be more complementary, or 4,000 K or 5,000-plus K lamps where northern-exposure light is received.

The rated service life of fluorescents varies greatly. Most compact-fluorescents have an average rated life of 9,000-10,000 hours, depending on the model. The rated life for standard double-ended fluorescents ranges from 7,500 hours for standard 15-watt models to 20,000 hours for 40-watt models. These are based on the lamps being operated on a 3-hour duty cycle, on for 3 hours, off for 20 minutes. Though turning fluorescents off and on more frequently will shorten their life, the cost for lamp replacements is far less than that for the electricity used to operate them when they are not needed. It is more cost-effective to turn off fluorescents when they will not be needed for five minutes or more.

The temperature at which any given fluorescent system will effectively work varies greatly, depending on the specific lamp and ballast combination. The optimum operating temperature for most fluorescents is between 60°F and 70°F, though most standard double-ended types will operate satisfactorily between 50°F and 120°F. Special lamps and ballasts must be specified for applications outside of these temperature ranges.

In general, fluorescent lighting operates far more efficiently than incandescents—four to six times more efficiently than 120v incandescents—and is much longer lived. Because fluorescent lamps are linear-light sources, versus a point source, they produce a relatively diffuse light which can be effectively used to provide direct or indirect lighting with minimal shadowing.

Choosing a lamp
The important thing is to choose the right lamp for the application. Energy-efficient fluorescent lamps, for example, are a good choice for a general background illumination. Standard incandescent lamps are an obvious choice in areas where light is needed only intermittently. The intense, tightly-focused white light produced by quartz halogen lamps is ideal for task lighting.

Choosing the proper lamp, however, is only half the battle. The other half is in selecting—or, in some cases, devising—a light fixture that will efficiently put the light produced where it will do the most good.

The raking light of Roger Heitzman's portable incandescent fixture creates shadows that define the details on shaped and carved work. Heitzman made the fixture from a cheap quartz floodlight mounted on an old camera tripod.

adherence to an ideal source of light. If, for example, Williams is restoring a piece that will ultimately be lit by incandescent bulbs or cool-white fluorescents, he tries to simulate the same color temperature when he is color matching or finishing.

Williams's ideal shop would therefore contain several different lighting sources, including full-spectrum fluorescents and two or three different kinds of incandescent lamps to reproduce various lighting situations. Hand-held ultraviolet lights are also one of the first tools for a restoration workshop. They're a lot cheaper than a microscope, but can reveal almost as much information about previous touch-up work or the presence of residual finishing materials. As Williams says, "Light bulbs are cheap, work that comes back to you is not."

Most of us are familiar with the three most common types of household electric lamps: fluorescents, incandescents and tungsten/halogens. But there have been some interesting recent developments in lighting technology. New, state-of-the-art compact, fluorescent bulbs produce the same amount of light as a standard incandescent light bulb, yet they last ten times as long and consume far less energy. While they are similar in temperature sensitivity to standard fluorescents, the compact bulbs are quiet and cool in operation. In color temperature, they more closely approximate household incandescents (warm) than standard fluorescents (cool). As you might expect, such lamps are much more expensive, but their advantages make them attractive.

Planning a lighting system Once you've determined the mix of natural and artificial light you prefer, you'll have to figure out how many fixtures you'll need to illuminate the shop, of what power and where to put them. A lighting engineer might arrive at an adequate formula, but it's an imperfect and highly subjective science. The effectiveness of your lighting system has more to do with the placement of fixtures and the way you use the workspace than with sheer wattage or footcandles. As with the Jeffersonian equation for window area that I mentioned at the beginning of this discussion, the variables defy a formulaic approach.

It's a good idea to develop your lighting plan in the same fashion as your floor plan, since the placement of lighting fixtures should take into account the position of major machinery and work areas. Begin by blocking out all primary lighting fixtures and sources of natural light on paper, perhaps on a separate overlay. (Maurice Gordon, whose shop plan is shown on p. 59, developed his lighting layout on the computer, using the special overlay function of a computer-assisted design program.)

The basic overall lighting layout for many shops can be simple. Paul Silke, for example, lights his 960-sq. ft. shop with three rows of four 8-ft. long fluorescent fixtures, each fixture containing two high-output lamps. The rows are spaced 8 ft. apart, and the outside rows are 4 ft. from the walls. These are augmented with only one or two small incandescents that Silke uses for carving or finishing, and a few other fluorescent task lamps.

undone when you least expect it. If you can afford it, track lighting provides an excellent, flexible system for incandescent illumination.

With a little imagination, you can rig an effective task light out of cast-off parts, like Roger Heitzman's carving lamp (shown above). For portability, Heitzman mounted a cheap outdoor quartz floodlight on an old camera tripod and wired it with a retractable cord reel from an Electrolux vacuum cleaner. He uses it at the bench to throw a raking side light or back light across the work.

The incandescent bulb is notoriously inefficient—it produces lots of heat and not much light—but it is more appropriate than fluorescents for narrowly focused activities, or situations where the lamp is turned on and off a lot, or if it must function in cool temperatures. There are a wide variety of shapes, sizes and types of incandescent bulbs, from the small 50-watt Halo lamps made by McGraw Edison, which provide a reasonable color temperature (about 3,750 K) and very little heat, to the small, but intense tungsten-halogens, which provide bright white light and lots of heat.

Specialized work can dictate particular lighting requirements. For example, the reliance on fluorescent lights amounts to what furniture conservator Donald Williams calls "conservation by braille." When it comes to lighting, Williams underlines the importance of location—not shop location, but the location in which your work will eventually reside. This usually involves compromise, rather than rote

Silke's lighting plan works well for his rectangular shop layout, with machinery distributed more or less evenly across the middle of the shop. Obviously, a more complex layout or specialized circumstances will require adjustment. But if you begin with good overall illumination, you can add whatever fixtures you want to accommodate designated task areas. A model, like John Monteleone's (shown on p. 40), will enable you to simulate the effects of natural light, thus drawing your attention to areas that may require more illumination at certain times of the day.

In addition to planning for natural and artificial light, there are several other things you can do to help illuminate your workspace. Paint as much of the shop as possible in a light color. The walls and ceiling are particularly important reflective surfaces, but a light-color enamel paint or vinyl tile will also make a big difference on the floor. If you use wood paneling or flooring, choose a light-colored wood such as pine or maple instead of a dark or stained species. In a very small shop, you might also consider the use of mirrors to reflect light and create the impression of a larger space.

Heat and humidity

Heating (and cooling) the workshop is of great importance to your working comfort and the proper maintenance of tools and materials. In addition, specific operations, such as gluing and finishing, require a reliable heat source. Most standard home heating systems are applicable to the workshop and they should be evaluated according to their efficiency, safety, cost and personal preference. Oil, electric-baseboard and wood heat are among the most common workshop heating systems, followed by self-contained gas burners, radiant electric heat panels, and even in-slab radiant floor heat (the Cadillac of home-heating systems). Make sure to consider your shop routine when you evaluate heating systems, and choose the one that will best address your own circumstances. Remember, too, that an efficient heating system relies upon good insulation, proper site location and sound construction methods.

Each system has advantages and drawbacks. For example, wood heat is practical and attractive to many woodworkers—it warms a space quickly and consumes mountains of shop scrap—but the shop will cool off quickly, too, if you forget to feed the stove. What's more, wood heat requires regular chimney cleaning and plenty of room for fuel storage. Though wood heat can be less expensive than other types, make sure your insurance company doesn't make up the difference in higher premiums.

Electric baseboard units may be safer, more convenient and less obtrusive, but they are expensive to operate and must be kept free of dust. In many workshops, two systems are combined for versatility, such as a woodstove and a backup oilburner or electric heater. Open-coil electric heaters are not advisable in a woodworking shop, and portable kerosene and propane burners should be avoided in tight spaces since they operate with an open flame and their exhaust is toxic. Whatever heating system(s) you select,

keep the area around it free of dust and shavings, and situate the burner safely away from any chemical storage, spray booth or your wood supply.

During mild weather (or in warm climates) you might want to glue or finish without heating the whole shop. If so, you could isolate one part of the shop for a more efficient, localized application of heat. Roger Heitzman, for example, installed a fully enclosed, 3-ft. by 9-ft. glue-curing room in one corner of his California workshop. The space is heated with an electric baseboard fixture and reaches 90° in less than 30 minutes, while the rest of the shop remains considerably cooler. (Heitzman used to park his glue jobs in a van outside the shop, along with a kerosene heater—an unsafe practice that he was glad to abandon.)

In some parts of the country, and at certain times of the year, cooling the shop is of paramount importance. All of the conventional household cooling systems, from an open window and shutters to air conditioning, can be applied to the workshop. But Mac Campbell went a step further when he wired a clock-timer switch to the window fan in his New Brunswick workshop. During the dog days of summer, he simply leaves a window open at the far end of the shop and sets the timer to run the fan between 2 a.m. and 4 a.m., filling the shop with fresh air during the coolest part of the night.

Wood stoves are a popular and practical source of workshop heat. A certain romantic quality helps woodworkers overlook their occasional inefficiency and the pollution they spew.

In many workshops, humidity is of greater concern than heat. Too much moisture in the air is a common problem in basement shops, making dehumidifiers standard equipment throughout much of the country. One Massachusetts woodworker I know empties a 5-gallon pail of water every day in the summer from his shop dehumidifier. Shops in arid climates may have the opposite problem, and humidifiers may be required there.

The biggest difficulties, however, are faced by woodworkers in areas where the humidity is capricious. Drying wood and keeping it dry without degrade is a delicate process anywhere, but in areas of fluctuating humidity, such as southern California, it is almost an art. As Long Beach woodworker John Nyquist said to me, "Wood is a blotter," and it is capable of absorbing and releasing surface moisture almost as quickly as a paper towel.

The climate in Nyquist's shop is tempered somewhat by the Pacific Ocean, which is only a half mile away, but by most standards, it is capricious indeed. "This is desert," Nyquist explained. Daytime temperatures of 92°F are common from May to September, but the humidity is a lot less predictable. Nyquist has watched it plummet from a comfortable 65 percent to a lip-cracking 25 percent in a few hours, as desert winds blast down the Santa Ana mountains from the interior. Every woodworker in the Southwest has a wood-drying nightmare to relate, and Nyquist told me about several hundred feet of 8/4 rosewood that he had to plane to less than an inch to remove the surface checks that developed during one parched weekend.

To mitigate the effects of such drastic fluctuations, Nyquist humidifies his shop with a swamp cooler, a kind of primitive air conditioner common throughout the Southwest. A squirrel-cage fan in the cooler pumps the air through a series of damp, absorbent wicks and back into the shop. In the wintertime, he uses a forced-air, natural-gas furnace to take the chill off. (To remove airborne dust, he activates the furnace fan without firing the heater.)

Compressed air and finishing rooms

Compressed air is one of the most versatile shop systems. It will power a dazzling array of hand tools, presses, pumps and holding devices. And it does so with great efficiency—air tools are stronger, faster, quieter and less likely to wear out (they have fewer moving parts) than their electric counterparts. Compressed air is unexcelled at spraying finishes and blowing off dust, which are its two most popular functions.

Not every woodworker wants or needs a powerful air compressor and an extensive finishing room in the shop. Several I've met prefer a rubbed-on oil finish precisely because they don't like to spray. Others leave the finishing to someone else. But for those who do their own spray finishing or run a lot of pneumatic equipment, these subjects will require special study.

Compressed air What amazes me most about air compressors is that I have lived so long without one. I recently bought my first compressor, a tiny ¼-hp unit with a suitably minuscule tank. It's not much good for spraying paint or running major shop equipment, but it's just fine for blowing off dust, cleaning machinery and pumping tires, about the only tasks I need it for right now.

Compressors come in all sizes, from ones smaller than mine to 5-hp and 10-hp units (and up) that can operate a range of heavy-duty pneumatic tools and spray equipment. Portable models in the 2-hp to 5-hp range can be rolled around the shop to drive machinery or spray a piece of furniture. The larger the storage tank, the more air you'll have on

Compressed air opens a world of possibilities for finishing and for powering shop tools.

Roger Heitzman's air-compressor cover/muffler cuts the noise without obstructing airflow, and it's counterweighted to provide easy access to the motor.

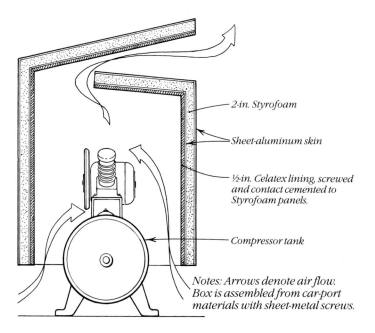

2-in. Styrofoam

Sheet-aluminum skin

½-in. Celatex lining, screwed and contact cemented to Styrofoam panels.

Compressor tank

Notes: Arrows denote air flow. Box is assembled from car-port materials with sheet-metal screws.

hand and the less frequently the compressor will kick in to keep it full. In a permanent installation, the pipe in the system provides additional storage. Your choice of a compressor and tank will depend upon the air-pressure and volume required by the various tools and devices you plan to operate. Refer to the Bibliography (p. 208) for sources of detailed information for calculating your needs and setting up a system.

Like electricity, compressed air loses pressure the farther it has to travel, so it's a good idea to locate your compressor as close as possible to the largest end user. (Only an explosion-proof model should be located near the finishing area.) But before you bolt the compressor beneath your bench, consider these factors: compressors make a lot of noise, they require good air circulation and the pump does not like dust.

To cope with these problems, many woodworkers keep their compressor in an insulated room or a custom-built ventilated box. Like a dust collector, an air compressor can be kept outside in mild climates. Roger Heitzman installed both outside his workshop. To protect his neighbors (and his reputation), Heitzman built the insulated cover/muffler shown above. Built of materials salvaged from an old carport, the box is insulated and baffled to cut down the noise.

Condensation is another perennial problem in any compressed-air system, since the air is heated when it is compressed, then cooled in the tank and delivery lines. Filters, petcocks and sometimes U-shaped traps are typically installed in the delivery line, which also should be angled to permit moisture to drain.

As a safety precaution, be sure to pull the plug on your air compressor or disconnect it with a switch if you plan to be away from the workshop for any length of time. If the machine is permanently left "on," a ruptured hose or a slow

leak could cause the motor to operate continuously and possibly overheat.

A cautionary note about pipe. There's considerable controversy about the use of PVC pipe as a delivery system for compressed air. I've seen it in lots of workshops; it's cheap, readily available and easy to install. However, PVC pipe is liable to degrade from abrasion or vibration, and compressed air is not nearly as innocuous as it seems. I've heard enough horror stories about exploding pipes and plastic shrapnel to make the alternatives look much more attractive. Either threaded iron pipe or soldered copper tubing will provide a safer air-delivery system. Iron is cheaper, but copper might be easier to install, particularly in a complicated layout with a lot of corners and elbow joints.

Finishing rooms A sprayed finish goes hand in hand with the air compressor that propels it. You can spend a lifetime in the workshop without ever spraying a finish, or if you only spray occasionally, you may get by for years spraying outdoors or in a corner of the shop. But if you're serious about spraying, you'll want a separate finishing room to protect your work from dust and to isolate the rest of the shop from volatile fumes and flammable overspray.

Exhaust and safety are the two most important aspects of a successful finishing room, and they are closely related since effective removal of fumes contributes to a safe working environment. In several shops I visited, standard commercial spray booths have been installed, with all the attendant hardware. But more often, woodworkers adapt a room in the shop for finishing. If you're cramped for space, you could take a tip from Scott Jenkins of Francestown, New Hampshire, who built removable walls for his basement spray booth, so he can use the space for other purposes.

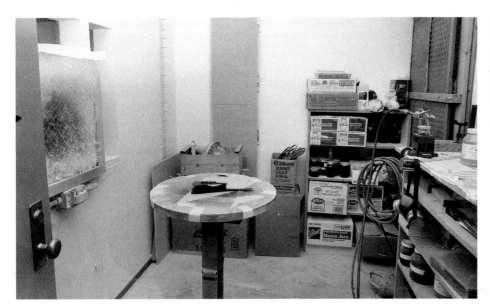

The same essential requirements should be observed for any spray area, permanent or portable. In addition to the delivery system (compressor, spray gun and assorted floor pots or hand-held canisters), a spray room or booth should be equipped with explosion-proof switches and lights and an explosion-proof exhaust fan. Many woodworkers have a cavalier attitude toward these precautions, but you are courting disaster if you use standard household window fans and lighting fixtures.

In two shops I visited, the finishing room was carefully designed to provide an isolated, dust-free environment. Mac Campbell enclosed an 8-ft. by 16-ft. finishing area adjacent to his basement workshop. It is separated from the rest of the shop by a stud-wall partition and a 4-ft. wide door, in which he's installed a standard, removable furnace filter. (Other shops I visited use two filters for greater effect.) A two-speed, 18-in. sparkproof furnace fan mounted in a finishing room window draws air into the room through the filtered door. When he's running the fan, Campbell has to open a window in the shop or the exterior shop door to replace the air drawn into the finishing room and avoid creating a downdraft in the shop stove. This can cool the place in a hurry, especially in winter, so he runs the fan and keeps the windows and door open only while spraying.

Air flow speeds the solvent-release process, though, so Campbell installed a second small fan on the shop ceiling, which he uses after the spraying is done and until the finish dries. It circulates air between the shop and the finishing room through a duct that Campbell made by enclosing the area between two ceiling joists with ⅛-in. plywood. The air passes through an old filter bag attached to the finishing-room end of the duct and returns to the shop via the furnace filters in the finishing-room door.

Convinced that the single-thickness furnace filters in the finishing-room door were passing a lot of dust, Campbell recently covered them with a fabric filter bag that he cut open. This dramatically reduced the amount of dust passing through the door, but highlighted several other leaks in the system. Campbell tackled each in turn. He installed a better seal around the door to keep dust from coming through the cracks and noticed that wind howled through the electric wall outlets. After he replaced the outlets, the system was so air tight he could barely open the door to the finishing room when the fan was running. And when he did, a small hurricane rushed in from the shop, defeating the purpose of the whole exercise. He finally installed a two-way switch for the fan, allowing him to shut it off from either the finishing room or the shop, before opening the door.

Ever since his last shop burnt down (due to vandalism, not accident), Richard Schneider has been sensitive about fire. He lost $20,000 in one night and spent almost a year stripping and painting equipment and getting the shop up and running again. So he exercised great caution when he built the finishing room in his new shop (shown above). The walls have two layers of ½-in. drywall, with overlapping seams, and solid-core doors separate the room from the rest of the shop. For maximum air flow, one door opening is entirely sheathed with furnace filters (as shown in the photo above). When the filtered door is open and the other door is closed, air is drawn through the filters, across the revolving spray table in the center of the room and is pumped out through the explosion-proof fan, which is mounted in a window on the opposite wall. (The fan intake is also covered with a filter to protect it from overspray.) All lights and switches are of industrial, explosion-proof quality, and an overhead skylight on the north slope of the roof provides diffuse, daytime illumination.

The setup is designed so that, in the event of a fire, the skylight will melt (or blow out) and function like a chimney, burning up instead of spreading out. With the double-wall construction, Schneider figures a fire could burn for up to 45 minutes inside the finishing room before it threatens the rest of the building.

Fire and shop security

Mercifully, few of us learn firsthand how serious a threat fire is to a woodworking shop. To keep it that way, consider the possibility of fire when you plan a new shop or change an existing one. I find it useful to think of workshop fire in four ways: prevention, detection, control and recovery.

As usual, prevention is the best protection. This includes proper electrical work and effective dust collection, isolating your heat source from combustible materials, airtight disposal of oily rags, and storage of flammable solvents in secure metal cabinets and/or containers. As I've mentioned before, the greatest risk of fire is in the finishing area, and it should be well ventilated and structurally isolated, with fully insulated electrical fixtures. If you follow these precautions and observe a few common-sense shop habits, like cleanliness and no smoking, you may never have to worry about fire control or recovery.

If a fire begins, some type of detector may alert you in time to prevent major destruction. Household smoke alarms and automatic sprinkler systems are the two most common methods of detection I've found in workshops. If a fire gets going, the sprinkler system will obviously help to control it, as will running water from a workshop sink and portable extinguishers—if you're there to use them.

In fact, running water may be the best (and simplest) protection against the most basic type of shop fire, which can be ignited in the woodpile by a spark from the stove or from a motor switch arcing in sawdust. It would extinguish most "Class A" fires, which involve ordinary combustible materials such as paper, wood, cloth and some rubber and plastic materials. Class B, C and D fires involve combustible liquids, flammable greases, or energized electrical equipment and combustible metals; these require extinguishers approved for such applications. (An A:B:C extinguisher, which is designed to handle fires in those classes, will cover most workshop needs.) There are specific regulations that pertain to the selection and placement of fire extinguishers, but, in general, they must be located close to the hazardous area (stove, spray booth, etc.). If you keep an extinguisher by the door you can grab it on your way out and use it to fight your way back in, without having to cross through the flames.

Certain construction methods can also help control fires. The double-drywall walls and overlapping seams in Richard Schneider's finishing room, for example, make it more difficult for the fire to spread to other parts of the building. If all else fails, recovery is your last refuge. I think the Amish have the best insurance policy—family and friends pitch in and rebuild the burnt-out structures. Most of us, however, need to think seriously about purchasing insurance. It won't save your favorite tools or a torched labor of love, but it just might get you going again.

Security is an oft-neglected aspect of fire prevention, but since many fires are ignited by vandals, a sensible security system may protect you from fire as well as theft. Depending on where you live, security may or may not be of much concern. Several urban woodworkers I visited have adopted security measures that would seem excessive to country woodworkers who still leave their shops (and houses) unlocked. John Nyquist's Long Beach, California, workshop is a veritable fortress—surrounded by high walls, iron gates, deadbolts and coils of razor wire. There are no windows in the shop and, after he lost some equipment through the skylight in the roof, he covered that too. (Inscribing an ID number on each tool can help the police track it if the worst occurs.) Roger Heitzman's shop has an alarm system that rings the police department. In the end, reasonable security and a low profile—not paranoia—are your best protection against theft and vandalism.

Plumbing

I would be remiss if I failed to comment on the state of the workshop water closet and the fate of the cheesecake calendar. Workshops are not known for their tasteful powder rooms, and I've sampled a few that were decidedly execrable, including one boatyard outhouse in Maine that was situated at the end of a long pier. It flushed automatically, two times a day.

I trust that tidal privy has been shut down by the Environmental Protection Agency, but many shop bathrooms continue to be pretty grubby. Sawdust accumulates in the sink and toilet bowl, as it does everywhere else, and unless you anticipate surprise visits from well-heeled clients, there's little incentive to clean it. It may be no more than coincidence, but one of the tidiest bathrooms I saw in my travels was at the Wood Studio in Toronto, a group shop comprised of six men and four women.

As I mentioned earlier, there is a more serious aspect to workshop plumbing. In addition to fire prevention, running water is invaluable for flushing eyes of foreign particles, cleaning small wounds and scrubbing hands, tools and brushes of oil and assorted chemicals. I know a few woodworkers who have gone to the expense of installing a complete bathroom, including a heater, fan and shower stall, where they can wash up and change clothes before retiring to the house. This helps keep peace at home and may improve the resale value of the shop, since it can be more readily converted to other purposes.

In every shop I've worked in, and in most of those I visited, brushes were washed in a sink or can and the waste solvent flushed down the drain, chucked out the back door or burned. None of these practices is particularly safe or environmentally responsible, and you would be better off disposing of hazardous solvents at a local recycling center. My own town offers a periodic collection of hazardous household waste, which would accommodate the needs of most small shops. (To dispose of larger quantities of hazardous waste, contact a treatment, storage and disposal facility.)

Oh yes, about the calendars. They still exist, of course, as does a popular breed of screw-gun posters. They're a little more discreetly deployed than in earlier days, but they remain tucked away in bathrooms and behind cabinet doors. I'm afraid that some habits will linger in the workshop, no matter how mature the trade has become.

Owen Dean was among the last of a breed of itinerant chair bodgers in the High Wycombe district of England. His 'machinery' consisted of a pole lathe and an assortment of rude brakes and shaving horses, which could be easily assembled on the spot or carted from place to place, along with the shop. (Photo c. 1940 by Ronald Goodearl.)

Specialty Workshops

Evolution makes many starts. — R. Buckminster Fuller

Chapter 6

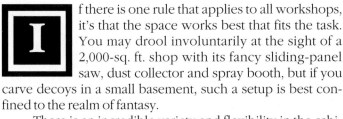 f there is one rule that applies to all workshops, it's that the space works best that fits the task. You may drool involuntarily at the sight of a 2,000-sq. ft. shop with its fancy sliding-panel saw, dust collector and spray booth, but if you carve decoys in a small basement, such a setup is best confined to the realm of fantasy.

There is an incredible variety and flexibility in the cabinet and furniture shops I've visited, but they merely hint at the wealth of possibilities that can be found among the allied woodworking trades of boatbuilding, chairmaking and woodturning. These crafts have specific needs for tools and space that are tangibly reflected in the workshop. Moreover, in each of these "specialty" shops, the nature of the work, the

materials and the machinery have a profound effect on the working environment.

It's not that you couldn't turn bowls in a chair shop or build chairs in most boat shops—such versatility is common. It's more a matter of efficiency and habit. Since most of the shops in this book were designed primarily to build furniture or cabinets, it seems appropriate to set aside one chapter for a visit to a few specialty workshops. These shops have evolved over time, as their owners' needs and resources have changed. But, like the evolution of a species, the dedicated function of these specialty workshops has caused them to develop their own distinctive characteristics.

At the end of this chapter are two different kinds of specialty workshop: those designed for travel and those designed for kids. In these particular shops, it's not so much the type of work that's unusual as the place where it's done or the age of the people who do it. In either case, there are intriguing issues to consider that you might not encounter in ordinary workshops.

A guideboat shop

Many of my favorite boat shops resemble archaeological excavations. They are fascinating middens of material culture, eddies for all sorts of jetsam that has yet to find its way to the dump. Encrusted coffee cans and grease fittings claim bench space alongside plan drawings and yesterday's lunch. Somewhere there must be an example of an elegant or manicured boat shop, but I have yet to find it. This is all the more incongruous in that the watercraft that emerge from many of the same boat shops often exhibit the most painstaking and impeccable craftsmanship.

I have a simple theory about this apparent anomaly. It's that the boatbuilder who is not busy building boats is probably out sailing one. No other occupation, including overhauling the table saw, cleaning the bench or filing tax forms, is half so absorbing as a close tack across the bay. (I should note that you could draw a similar connection between instrument makers and their music, but this theory fails to explain why their shops tend to be immaculate.) It's also true that the collateral paraphernalia of the boatbuilding trade—outboard motors, sails, rigging and such—requires a host of specialized accessories that would threaten the order of any workspace.

When we think about boats, we naturally look to salt water, and places like Maine, Nova Scotia and Puget Sound come immediately to mind. But one of the richest traditions of wooden watercraft flourished hundreds of miles from the nearest lobster. For more than a century, the canoes and elegant pulling boats that were designed to navigate the freshwater lakes and rocky creeks of New York's Adirondack mountains have set a standard for discriminating boaters.

Last winter, I visited Carl Hathaway's landlocked boat shop on the outskirts of Saranac Lake, New York. Hathaway is one of a handful of craftsmen who build and repair traditional Adirondack watercraft, like the guideboat shown in the photo below, and Saranac Lake is one of the dowager capitals of the industry. Once "the pickup truck of the Adirondacks," the elegant double-ended guideboat reached the apex of its development around the turn of the century, when an emergent leisure class of Americans sought to experience the wilderness in comfort and style. The craft is now in revival, having suffered a decline brought about by the country's recent romance with the outboard motor and

The Adirondack guideboat set the standard for strong and stable lightweight design. With its sawn ribs, smooth-skin (carvel) construction and bevel-lapped planking, the traditional guideboat is descended from the European pulling boat, not the North American canoe. It cut an elegant figure on the water, and a painted guideboat was described in one 19th-century catalog as 'the black snake of the wilderness.' In this photo, Willard Hanmer, former owner of Carl Hathaway's shop, installs a seat in a nearly finished guideboat.

Carl Hathaway's Saranac Lake boat shop was built in the 1920s by Willard Hanmer. The photo at left shows the shop as it was in Hanmer's time. Hanmer moved boats in and out through the French doors. (He used the below-grade entrance beneath the doors to store his car.) The photo below shows the opposite side of the building and the shed-roofed structure that Hathaway added after a fire in the 1970s.

the plastic hull. At the time of my visit, when the water nearest the shop was buried beneath a foot of ice and about as much snow, Hathaway was beginning his busiest boatbuilding season.

The Hathaway Boat Shop reflects the unselfconscious attention to business that is typical of boatbuilding shops everywhere. Like most boatbuilders I've visited, Hathaway is hardly a compulsive housekeeper. Work surfaces are covered with sawdust and a seemingly hopeless tangle of tools, while systems for dust collection, finishing, lighting and the like are either straightforward or nonexistent. "When we start having to hunt for the tools," he says, "it's about time to clean the bench off and start again."

The principal layout consideration of the workspace is the relationship of the boats to the 29-ft. long bench that lines one entire wall of the building. Boats in progress (there's room for two alongside the bench) are situated only 2 ft. away from the bench and parallel to it, providing ready access to hand tools and clamps. Hathaway works comfortably in the alley between the two, planing planks on the bench and installing them on the boat with economy of motion. He works on one side of the boat at a time, turning it around to plank the other side, and he uses a rolling steel cart (the kind used to serve food) to bring miscellaneous tools and materials right to the job.

To compensate for the low height of his built-in bench (33 in.), Hathaway planes the strakes on a 7-in. high platform on top of the bench, which raises the planking to about the same height as the hull, eliminating a lot of tiresome stooping and stretching during the lengthy fitting process. I wondered why, in his 30-year occupancy of the shop, Hathaway never bothered to raise the bench. The reason may have something to do with inertia and something to do with the height of the windows behind the bench, which are all but obscured already by the overflow of tools on sills, shelves and walls. But Hathaway points to the fact that the narrow planing surface remains above the benchtop clutter, and it is easily replaceable. "When you set up a shop, you set it up for yourself," he explains.

Hathaway bought the shop from Willard Hanmer, a native of Saranac Lake who was born to the tradition. Hanmer began work in his father's boat shop around 1910, when he was only 9 or 10 years old. He began sticking tacks (the average guideboat uses more than 2,000 of them), then learned to cane seats and eventually graduated to sanding. In an interview I found in the archives of the Adirondack Museum in Blue Mountain Lake, New York, Hanmer explained that a hand sanding "couldn't hurt anything and it would take a long time to rub a hole through a boat." In the 1920s, he built his own shop, which Hathaway bought in 1962 after Hanmer's death. Hathaway worked with the elder craftsman for only two winters but has been at it ever since. (Less than a year after my visit, Hathaway decided to sell the shop to his assistant, Chris Woodward, allowing it to serve a third generation of Adirondack boatbuilders. But he is retaining the right to work there for as long as he likes. "I won't give it up entirely until I'm dead," Hathaway told me.)

Hathaway made few changes or additions to the original workshop. His only major alteration was of necessity, following a 3 a.m. lightning strike about 15 years ago. By midmorning, flames were leaping 30 ft. above the roof and had gutted one end of the shop. Pitch boiled out of the downstairs ceiling beams. Amazingly, not a single boat or power tool was lost, although here and there a chunk of charred timber remains as a grisly reminder of the shop's near demise. "The only thing that saved it," Hathaway concludes, "was the plastic on the windows—the fire was starved for air."

Before the fire, heavy boats were hoisted on a rolling dolly suspended from a steel I-beam above double French doors that opened onto the ground floor of the shop. This enabled Hathaway (and Hanmer) to back a trailer into the

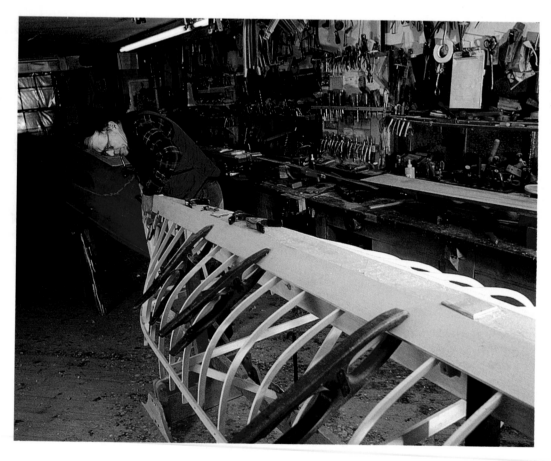

Carl Hathaway positions himself between the bench and the boat for most of his planking operations. He alternates between planing strakes on the bench and fitting them on the guideboat.

Carl Hathaway's boat shop

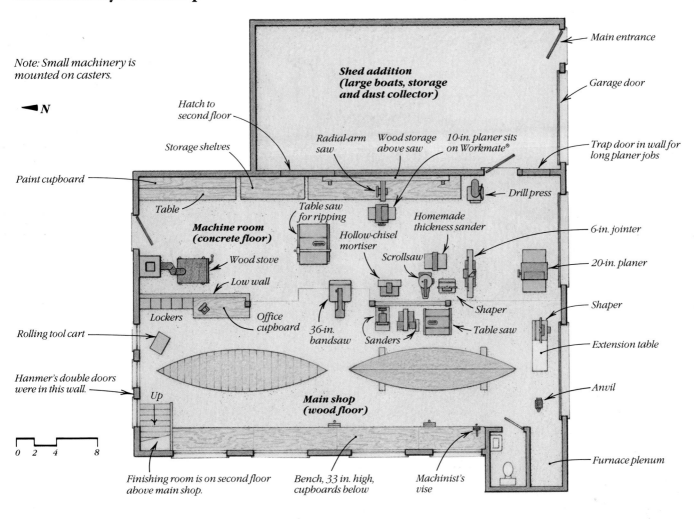

Note: Small machinery is mounted on casters.

N

Main entrance

Garage door

Shed addition (large boats, storage and dust collector)

Trap door in wall for long planer jobs

Hatch to second floor

Radial-arm saw

Wood storage above saw

10-in. planer sits on Workmate®

Storage shelves

Paint cupboard

Table

Table saw for ripping

Drill press

Homemade thickness sander

6-in. jointer

Machine room (concrete floor)

Hollow-chisel mortiser

20-in. planer

Wood stove

Scrollsaw

Low wall

Shaper

Lockers

Office cupboard

36-in. bandsaw

Sanders

Shaper

Table saw

Extension table

Rolling tool cart

Hanmer's double doors were in this wall.

Up

Anvil

Main shop (wood floor)

0 2 4 8

Finishing room is on second floor above main shop.

Bench, 33 in. high, cupboards below

Machinist's vise

Furnace plenum

---

drive, hoist a boat on the dolly and roll it right into the shop. Boats were fed to the second floor for finishing through a 4-ft. by 5-ft. hatch in the outside wall of the shop.

After the fire, Hathaway replaced the burnt-out double doors with a wood-framed wall and a few smaller windows, and he built a shed addition on the side of the shop to house larger boats. (Woodward told me that the original shop floor could not be trusted to hold much more.) An overhead garage door provides convenient access to the addition, but smaller boats must be wrestled in and out of the shop through a 42-in. wide door linking the addition and the main shop. The shop ceiling is only 7 ft. high, which doesn't make it any easier to move things around, "but boy, do we need it for heat!" Hathaway says.

Like Hanmer, Hathaway does all of his finishing upstairs, hauling boats up through the original 4-ft. by 5-ft. hatch, which now opens into the shed addition. (In cold weather, he clears out a space for finishing in the main shop.) Dust presents a perennial problem and he has been unable to keep the upstairs clean, especially with a forced-air furnace riling up the dust. According to Hathaway, Hanmer's wife finished all his boats while he was out digging stumps

for the next season's supply of curved stems. Every spring, she'd sweep and dust the finishing room and wet-mop it clean, then lock Hanmer out of the shop. Hathaway doesn't have the luxury of a dedicated finisher, nor has he been able to organize his schedule so efficiently, but he now uses a Grizzly dust collector, located in the addition.

The earliest guideboat shops had no power tools, but with the advent of water-powered turbines in the second half of the last century, the larger establishments began to streamline production with jointers, planers and saws. There will always be a certain amount of hand fitting in wooden boatbuilding, but Hathaway is introducing all the power he can. Where he once planed and sanded almost entirely by hand, he has recently adopted Hanmer's pattern-shaping methods to prepare his bottom board, stem and ribs, and he relies on a Sand-Rite pneumatic sander to smooth the strakes.

Except for his bandsaw and a vintage 20-in. Williamsport planer, most of the other shop machinery is either lightweight or on wheels. "If they weren't mobile, they'd be inoperable," Hathaway says. "You'd need a shop three or four times this size to have stationary tools." Instead, Hathaway simply carries or rolls a tool out when he needs it

Carl Hathaway's tilting boat rack

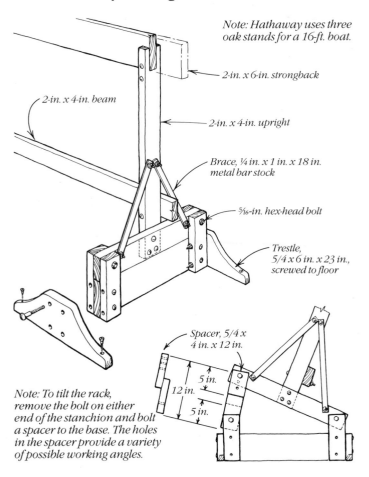

Note: Hathaway uses three oak stands for a 16-ft. boat.

2-in. x 6-in. strongback

2-in. x 4-in. beam

2-in. x 4-in. upright

Brace, ¼ in. x 1 in. x 18 in. metal bar stock

⁵⁄₁₆-in. hex-head bolt

Trestle, 5/4 x 6 in. x 23 in., screwed to floor

Spacer, 5/4 x 4 in. x 12 in.

5 in.

12 in.

5 in.

Note: To tilt the rack, remove the bolt on either end of the stanchion and bolt a spacer to the base. The holes in the spacer provide a variety of possible working angles.

Hathaway's tilting boat rack allows him to position a boat at a variety of angles for easy planking and sanding.

and moves it out of the way when he needs the space for something else. The largest tools are separated from the main shop by a low wall. (Diagonal wood planking underlays the bench and main shop area, while the heavy machinery sits on concrete.)

One of Hathaway's favorite machines is always used outside the shop. He saws his own boat planking with a Wood Mizer bandsaw mill, and he appreciates its portability. It may not cut as quickly as a circular saw, but it is safer and cheaper to operate, and the thinner blade chews up less wood in the kerf. Hathaway notes that the bandsaw blade is roughly one-quarter the thickness of a circular sawblade, so "every fourth cut you've got a free board."

With more than 300 hours of labor in each boat, small conveniences like the tilting boat rack (shown in the photo and drawing at left) make a big difference. Hathaway built his racks according to Hanmer's design. Used to level and plumb the boat for planking, they can be tilted in either direction to present the work in the most comfortable position for planking and sanding. Hanmer once said the racks took "about a week to map out and build, but it paid off."

Two chairmaking shops

Chairs are everywhere, and we naturally take them for granted. But it would be hard to find an artifact of furniture whose history and construction carry greater significance. Chairmaking is an ancient craft, but until the 17th century access to the chair itself was a luxury of class. In Europe, the rise in popularity of the chair more or less paralleled the emergence of democracy, which was accompanied by a diversified economy and a bona fide middle class. Our language retains allusions to the chair's aristocratic origins, in expressions like the "seat of power" and the "chairman of the board."

In its strength and grace, the Windsor chair could be considered the archetype of seating furniture. Its construction represents the masterful wedding of several distinct families of woodworking. Legs and stretchers are turned from close-grained hardwood such as maple or birch; the seat is carved from clear softwood such as white pine; and the back is rived, shaved and bent from supple hardwood such as oak or hickory. Such diversity is not only a marvel of technology, but it also made the Windsor chair a natural prototype for experiments in mass production and interchangeable parts. Long before Henry Ford and the automobile, chairmakers were farming out components of their operation to specialist "bodgers."

In the 19th and early 20th centuries, the High Wycombe district of England was one of the most famous crucibles for this cottage industry. Bodgers took their craft to the area's woodlands, where they manufactured split-and-turned chair parts in itinerant tent camps to supply workshops in the city that assembled the chairs. According to Ronald Goodearl, who photographed bodgers Alec and Owen Dean in the late 1940s (see p. 124), "Each man would turn out 144 parts per day (one gross) including legs and stretchers. This would include cutting up the green timber

Dave Sawyer builds Windsor chairs in a timber-frame building in downtown South Woodbury, Vermont. The 200-sq. ft. shop contains all that a chairmaker needs: workbench, shaving horse, lathe, steam box and bandsaw.

and rough shaping. The time for each part in the lathe was only a minute or two and it was amazing to see them work...."

At the time of Goodearl's visit, the Dean brothers were thought to be the last of several generations of green-wood chairmakers in the Chiltern Beechwoods. Only a decade or two before, timber rights were dispensed at annual estate auctions and turning shacks dotted the wooded landscape. Bodgers worked for about a year or so in one spot, felling and splitting the timber and turning the green billets on pole lathes. At the height of the industry, as many as 200 different patterns of chair parts were produced in the woods and carted to nearby towns, where seats were carved and the chairs were assembled and finished.

The Windsor chair, in its North American incarnation, and the ladder-back chair, a more rustic design with European origins, continue to support a number of North American chairmakers. These craftsmen may be less mobile than their forbears, but their workshops are similarly down-to-earth. Many could be mistaken for a country outhouse or a chicken coop, and they are equipped with little more than a

lathe, a bandsaw and the ubiquitous shaving horse. What's more, a significant portion of the work is still done outside, using riving brakes, splitting stumps and green wood.

Dave Sawyer is one of the new breed of revivalist chairmakers, a laconic New Englander whose speech is as deliberate and compact as the growth rings of a high-ground oak. Sawyer began his woodworking career in a boatyard, where he grew familiar with steam bending and working curved parts. Later, he gravitated to hand-hewn hay forks, ladder-back chairs and other items of "green woodworking." When I first visited Sawyer several years ago, he was building Windsor chairs in a room sandwiched between the kitchen and the porch of his Vermont farmhouse. The room was built as a woodshed but had been converted to a living room by the time Sawyer's family arrived. The shop was inundated by kids' toys and household belongings. Since Sawyer is an easygoing fellow, I guessed that his equanimity would override the proximity of house and family. To myself, I wondered if a more tightly wound or less focused person would go nuts.

"Maybe I'm half crazy already," Sawyer told me, but after about seven years in his home shop, he decided to make a break. He moved into the heart of South Woodbury, only a few miles from home and directly across from the old general store, which pumped its last gas around 1962. His post-and-beam building was built as a blacksmith shop and at various times housed a gristmill, a sawmill and a creamery. (More recently, it had served as a garage and as a mandolin shop.) The stream that descends from the six-acre mill pond tumbles directly beneath the window behind his bench.

Sawyer's "new" shop is only 13 ft. by 16 ft., quite a bit smaller than the 350-sq. ft. shop in the house (although much of the old space was used as a playroom by the kids). Still, it's big enough for his Ulmia bench, a work table made of 2x4s and 2x6s, his shaving horse and the only two workshop machines he owns, a small lathe and a 14-in. bandsaw, which takes up half the doorway. "If I wanted a table saw, I couldn't fit it," he says, "but then I haven't wanted one, so I'm all set."

Laying out the shop was straightforward. "When I moved in," Sawyer explains, "there was only one place to put the workbench and one place for the lathe." They sit on adjacent walls beneath the only two windows in the shop, which face southeast and southwest and overlook the road and stream. The ample double doors are covered with translucent plastic panels (designed for solar heat collectors) that resemble *shoji* screens and make the shop appear to be much larger than it is. The space is easily heated by an Atlanta wood stove; firewood is stored outside and in the corner. A steam box hangs on the wall behind the stove where he can pull it down and rest one end on a chair, while water heats in a 5-in. dia. capped iron pipe, which fits right inside the stove through a special lid with an elliptical hole.

With the exception of the seat, Windsor chairs are made with green wood. An adjoining room (used for finishing by the mandolin maker) serves as a "cooler," in which other chair parts are kept to prevent them from drying out during construction. Most of his turning and bending wood is stored in a garage that was built on top of a swamp. Moisture percolates through the holes in the concrete floor, which, Sawyer explains, "is just what you need for keeping green wood." He totes his chair rungs home to dry over the kitchen stove before assembly.

Some Windsor chairmakers split wood for parts with axes and froes and do most of the shaping on a shaving horse. Others rip their stock with a bandsaw and do most of their shaping at a bench. Sawyer does both, using those aspects of each technology that are most appropriate for the fabrication of each component. He does most of his major riving outside, using a knock-down brake (bottom photo, facing page), and splits the stock as small as he dares before turning to the bandsaw. "Where I'd get two pieces by splitting, I might get three or four by sawing," he explains. (Every now and then he borrows a neighbor's Hitachi resaw to rip turning squares.) He uses the horse for all drawknife and spokeshave work and the Ulmia workbench for fine shaping, carving and sawing. He clamps the seat between dogs on the bench and shapes it while the outside is still rough, then works the edges by clamping the seat in the tail vise.

When Sawyer rides his dumbhead shaving horse, it lurches and creaks like a wooden ship straining under a heavy swell. Many of the parts are loose and appear to move in concert. "I've been waiting for the head to work loose, but it must've been made green and shrunk on the tenon," he says. Perched on the horse, his knees tucked in close to the

Dave Sawyer's Windsor-chair shop

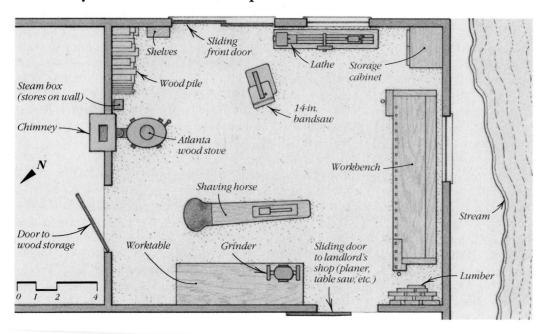

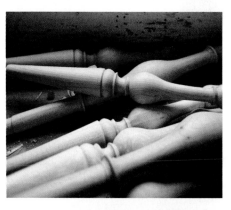

At the bench, Sawyer's work is illuminated in part by light from a southwest-facing window (at left). Above, he prepares the spindles for a comb on one of his Windsors.

Sawyer's workshop extends outdoors, where he rives chair parts with a knock-down brake and a froe.

seat, Sawyer uses a spokeshave to remove wisplike shavings from each spindle. As it approaches its finished dimension, he slips the slender neck of the spindle in its respective hole in the back rail of the chair and rotates it to determine where it is out of round. Then he leans it in a notched jig clamped in the tail vise of the bench to trim the high spots.

The sign above the door of Sawyer's shop is handsome but, considering the size of South Woodbury, I couldn't help wondering if it pulled any business. Sawyer seemed unfazed: "I think I got one serious customer from the sign." The rest of his business, like his chairs, was built slowly and made to last. "My customers keep coming up with interesting projects," he said, and the biggest problem isn't getting the work, it's getting it out. "Anyway," he added, "I haven't learned everything about Windsor chairs yet...when I do...I'll get into boatbuilding, or something like that."

Brian Boggs's workshop addition to his house doesn't look out of place in his suburban neighborhood. Six windows along the south wall do a good job of lighting Boggs's shop. The eaves project about 2 ft., which protects the interior from the harsh summer sun. Boggs had fluorescent lamps in his old shop, but he banished them from the new space. 'I'd rather work in dim light,' he says, 'than have something buzzing all the time.'

Brian Boggs added a workshop onto his home in Berea, Kentucky, not long after Sawyer moved his shop "downtown." Having spent four years building ladder-back chairs in a converted church, Boggs applied for a zoning variance to move the business to his residential neighborhood. While keeping one eye on his real-estate investment and the other on the skeptical local authorities ("My old shop looked like a sawmill," Boggs notes), he designed the new shop to complement his bungalow-style house (shown on the facing page). Except for the metal tubs and the tidy woodpile outside, it could easily pass for a family room, and it can be readily converted to a garage by a future owner.

"I've saved a *lot* of money working at home," Boggs says. Apart from the low-cost commute, the workshop annex shares heat and power with the house, requires less material to build than a comparable free-standing structure, and it effectively buffers one side of the building. But Boggs points out that it was an option only because he is a green woodworker. "They never would've given me a variance," he explains, "if I used a router and table saw."

With careful planning, you can design a shop that will satisfy local building codes, and with a little discretion, your neighbors may never be the wiser. But a healthy balance between a home workshop and a happy household is easier to achieve on paper than in reality. Both Boggs and his wife, Pat, were anxious about the possible invasion of their lives by the business and the impact of the family on Boggs's routine. So far, at least, the convenience has outweighed any drawbacks.

"I like everything about working at home," Boggs says. He weaves chair seats in the living room (where the carpet won't bruise the wood) and uses the kitchen stove for a makeshift steam box. And he enjoys having his two young sons visit him in the shop, where he can keep an eye on them if his wife needs to run an errand. (When one of the boys was only 18 months old, he was eager to work with his father.) To catch up on orders, Boggs often spends a few evenings a week in the shop, a habit that could easily get out of hand. The secret, Boggs explains, "is discipline...you've got to be a good manager of your time."

There is no sign above the front door, and almost a year after moving in, there is no doorknob either. Customers visit by appointment only, and it seems to Boggs that they are more sensitive to his privacy than they would be in a public space. "I like the fact that they know where they are," he says.

Ladder-back chairs are often considered rustic country cousins to the sophisticated Windsor. They are split and shaved entirely from green wood and are finished without power tools. Boggs uses mainly red oak and hickory for chair frames and usually weaves the seats of strips of pounded black ash or hickory bark. But his chairs achieve an elegance rarely found in much more expensive, "high-style" furniture. "The more you specialize, the greater your chance of success," he explains, "if you can stand the repetition."

Repetition breeds monotony in some; in Brian Boggs, it fosters invention. Years at the shaving horse inspired the design of a unique ratchet mechanism that saves time and helps grip stock securely. In another invention, Boggs used the

Brian Boggs makes elegant ladder-back chairs. This arrow-back arm rocker is his interpretation of an ageless design. (Photo by Albert R. Mooney.)

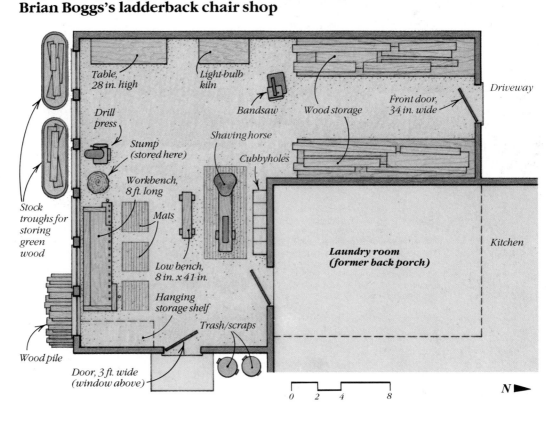

Brian Boggs's ladderback chair shop

Table, 28 in. high

Light-bulb kiln

Driveway

Drill press

Bandsaw

Wood storage

Front door, 34 in. wide

Shaving horse

Stump (stored here)

Cubbyholes

Workbench, 8 ft. long

Stock troughs for storing green wood

Mats

Low bench, 8 in. x 41 in.

Laundry room (former back porch)

Kitchen

Hanging storage shelf

Trash/scraps

Wood pile

Door, 3 ft. wide (window above)

0 2 4 8

N ▶

Heated with only a 100-watt light bulb, Boggs's chair-rung kiln hovers between 120°F and 130°F. It is 23 in. wide by 51 in. long by 48 in. high and is made of plywood and ½-in. thick, foil-faced foam insulation.

Boggs shifts from shaving horse to low-beam bench frequently to shape parts and chop mortises. When he's working on one, the other serves as a platform for tools.

guts of an old wringer washing machine to build a bark-slicer that prepares the considerable volume of seating material he needed for his chairs. He's calculated that he's woven more than 15 miles of bark. "Enough to get you thinking about alternatives," he says. As of this writing, he is fine-tuning a newly designed chairmaker's spokeshave, which he plans to have cast in stainless steel.

One local woodworker described Boggs's shop as "minimalist," but I found it to be thoughtfully designed and well suited to the specialized demands of his craft. In less than a year, he has changed his floor plan several times, in search of the most efficient layout. The L-shaped footprint (shown on p. 135) wraps around the former back porch (now the laundry room) of the house, providing comfortable floor space in a compact layout. "As it turns out, the shape is real handy," Brian says. He stores lumber along both walls in the long branch and uses the 15-ft. by 24-ft. south-facing portion of the shop for work. Because the space is small, it's easy to keep clean. "You *have* to keep it clean," he says.

Like Dave Sawyer, Boggs spends much of his life at the shaving horse, and seven years in the saddle has given him a proficiency with the drawknife and spokeshave that few can match. From his position on the horse, materials are kept within easy reach on the left, and the sturdy 4-in. by 8-in. by 41-in. low-beam bench shown above is on the right. Boggs works back and forth between the horse and the low bench, using the squat hickory beam for mortising operations and as a handy platform for tools when he's on the horse. Only 1 ft. off the floor, the beam is easy to step over. "It's almost like it's not there," he says.

The horses are located directly in front of the door for easy access to the material stored in the backyard, as well as a good view and plenty of sunlight in warm weather. To reduce stock quickly, he pulls out a hewing stump, which stows between the drill press and the workbench along the south wall of the shop. Boggs concedes that the concrete

floor is not as comfortable as a wooden work surface, but he prefers the shock-absorbent quality of concrete for splitting wood and chopping mortises on the low bench. He's also allergic to dust and finds the concrete easy to keep clean.

Ladder-back chairmakers are more particular about their materials than you might imagine, given the rural origins of the craft. But while cabinetmakers fret about wet wood and go to great lengths to obtain well-seasoned material, Boggs stores most of his under water. He installed a pair of 180-gal. stock-watering troughs behind the shop at a cost of only $75 each. Hickory can check in less than 20 minutes, so Boggs cuts the logs into 4-ft. lengths, splits them into eighths as soon as he gets them and covers them with plastic until he can submerge them. The galvanized troughs carry a lot of material that would otherwise choke the shop. On the other hand, chair rungs must be thoroughly dried before assembly, and this is accomplished with the low-tech kiln shown in the photo above. At the other end of the process, Boggs uses his shavings to polish wood and stuff seats; the rest goes to mulch. "I turn my shavings into berries," he says.

Unlike many woodworkers who are busy rationalizing the next machine purchase or paying off the last one, Boggs would rather reduce his dependency on machinery than acquire more. He built his first 70 chairs without any power tools and still prefers hand tools to machinery in almost every situation. One of the appealing features of a ladder-back chair is that it can be built with even less equipment than a Windsor, which requires a lathe to turn the legs and stretchers. Boggs used to do a lot of resawing on the bandsaw, but now uses it mainly to cut firewood. Likewise, he has trained himself to use a hatchet to shape rockers and contoured arms. "It's not power you need from machines," he says. "It's control and accuracy." And that only comes with time and repetition. "You can't compare machine work to unskilled hand work."

One of Boggs's goals—besides making a living—is to master hand-tool technology. "There are two ways to be efficient," he explains. "One is to mechanize, the other is to streamline." He's tried both and has determined that "streamlining is quieter." The purpose of highly evolved hand tools, like his new spokeshave or the tenon cutter, is only partly to save time. "I really like risk. Not like a mountain climber who loves the fear of dying, but more like a musician.... Someday I'd like to be able to do this with an ax," he says, pointing to the chamfer on the front of a leg post. "Just having it in my power to control that!"

Turning on the farm

Woodturners inhabit a world all their own. Unlike other woodworking specialists, they are capable of transforming a lump of unseasoned, unprocessed timber—wet firewood to anyone else—into a functional bowl or a piece of sculpture in a matter of moments. As Richard Raffan wrote in his essay on turning in *Design Book Four* (The Taunton Press, 1987), "The joy of turning wood is that I can create an object with greater speed and fewer hassles than is possible in almost any other medium...."

One of the appealing features of the turner's craft is that it does not require extensive initiation. The process of turning wood is so immediate that it is readily understood, even by an inexperienced observer. The lathe spins the work and the tool cuts it; it's about that simple. There's no wood to joint and plane, no dovetails or mortises to chop and, often, no plans to follow. Complicated issues of grain direction, wood shrinkage and gluing are not critical for most novice turners. Not everyone who picks up a gouge is an artist, but with very little practice or training you can at least make

something, which is the reason most of us start woodworking in the first place.

The heart of the process and the key to the turner's workshop is, of course, the lathe. It is the turner's equivalent to the potter's wheel or the blacksmith's forge, the one tool without which a turner could not turn. It has been around for thousands of years and has developed independently all over the world. Workbenches and other equipment, such as the bandsaw, the drill press or the grinder, are useful accessories, but they are of secondary importance to most turners. Consequently, a visit to the turner's workshop usually begins, and sometimes ends, with the lathe.

There is no shortage of commercial lathes on the market, but for several woodturners I visited, the prospect of making their own proved too hard to resist. Like the craft itself, the lathe is one of the most straightforward and accessible pieces of woodturning machinery. Since it spins the work instead of a sharpened cutter, the lathe does not rely on the kind of tolerances that are typical of the table saw, shaper or jointer. It also needn't achieve great speeds of rotation for effective operation. The great advantage of making your own lathe is that you can tailor it to suit yourself.

Vernon Leibrant is a natural tinkerer and a self-tutored turner. He began making wooden tops in the late 1940s on a little Sears and Roebuck lathe in his father's shop. (One of his early accomplishments was a top that could spin for nine minutes on a pull.) A one-time logger and sawmiller, Leibrant now farms apples at the foot of the Cascade Mountains in northwest Washington State, surrounded by country roads that bear the names of his family relations.

Vernon Leibrant, apple farmer and woodturner, works in an old chicken coop in the shadow of the Cascade Mountains.

Leibrant turns big bowls on a big lathe. When he wants to turn between centers, he enlists the aid of an equally outsized tailstock (above).

To finish his bowls, Leibrant rests them on this rotating table and sands by hand or with a drill-mounted grinding wheel.

I've seen lots of shops in which people turn wood, but Leibrant's seemed to reflect the primal nature of the craft itself. In the back of a converted chicken coop behind his house, he turns overgrown bowls from local woods for fun and a little profit. Until four years ago, he had never seen another person turn. When he did, he was surprised to discover that "everything I thought I'd invented, everybody's doing."

Leibrant's lathe (shown in the photos above) is unique. It is sculpture in its own right, fabricated from abandoned milling machinery. "Everything I have is from an auction sale or my own collection," he explains. Vibration is the bane of the turner's craft, but the massive weight of Leibrant's lathe spins his hefty bowls with the reassuring rumble of a small streetcar. The 250-lb. headstock pedestal is made from a cast-iron shingle mill "knee bolter" built for a 40-in. sawblade. Its babbitt-bearing stanchions are bolted to a concrete pad, 30 in. by 48 in. by 20 in. thick. The lathe can spin a 6-ft. dia. bowl in its present location (Leibrant's largest is about 4 ft. in diameter), but with a higher ceiling and a hole in the floor, he probably could turn the world.

"The same with the tailstock," Leibrant adds, "you could move it out there a half mile." The tailstock is made from an old drill press, and the rotating shaft provides a "live" turning center. It is bolted to a cast-iron feedmill pelletizer, which weighs about 600 lb. and slides on parallel railroad tracks. To secure stock between centers, Leibrant cranks the shaft (it has a 4-in. throw) and removes the handle before he turns.

The tool rest consists of a car axle mounted upright on the balance wheel from a shingle mill. An car scissor jack is mounted on top of the axle to maintain pressure against the shop ceiling. (The jack is wrapped in plastic to keep it from dripping grease.) "I don't tie the tool rest down at all," he says. Between the weight of the balance wheel and the pressure of the car jack, the axle can be easily secured wherever it's needed around a large bowl. Leibrant has ten different tool rests, which bolt to the angle bracket mounted on the vertical shaft. For faceplate turning, he uses a ½-in. thick by 10-in. dia. steel faceplate, riddled with holes for attachment screws.

The whole business is powered by a 2-hp Belsaw thickness planer, with a jackshaft and a step pulley for changing speeds. Leibrant turns between 90 rpm and 1,000 rpm, depending on the size of the stock and how balanced it is on the lathe. "I turn faster than a lot of people," he says. "You get into a lighter lathe and you have to turn slower [to minimize vibration]." The lathe runs off a flat leather belt, covered with a plywood guard. To maintain tension on the belt, the planer is anchored to the wall with a come-along.

Leibrant built the rotating sander table (shown at bottom, facing page) to finish his bowls. The metal base is made from a large fan frame and the table is powered by a ⅓-hp washing-machine motor, which is so tired he has to kick-start it to get it going. (This enables him to spin it in either direction.) With an assortment of thick foam pads on the table, he can sand a bowl right-side up or upside down, and either by hand or using a drill-mounted grinding wheel, as shown.

Rolling workshops

We are a nation of nomads. In 1988, almost one out of every five Americans changed residence. And our society's legendary love affair with the automobile, the symbol and vehicle of modern mobility, is more firmly entrenched than our marriage vows. There are now more than 170 million cars and trucks on the road, or roughly one for every American of driving age.

It was only a matter of time, I suppose, before the great American tradition that spawned the teepee, Conestoga wagon and Winnebago would invent the rolling workshop. In my own perambulations about the continent, I have come across portable workshops in every conceivable shape and size, from compact backpack tool kits and bumper lathes to customized pickup trucks and purpose-built trailers. (Two such examples are shown in the photos below.)

About five years ago, while scouring the country for workbenches, I came across the Cadillac of rolling workshops. Following a corkscrew trail along a rocky creek in the parched foothills of Sonoma County, California, I arrived at J. Baldwin's converted workshop van, which was parked alongside his vintage Airstream trailer. I stretched out my sleeping bag on Baldwin's workbench, with my nose barely 2 ft. from the shop ceiling, and drifted off to sleep amid the grunts of wild pigs rooting around the underbrush. When I visited Baldwin again recently, he had moved to the other side of the mountain and was no longer living in the trailer. The shop, however, was still in operation.

Two plywood cabinets flank the box of Lester Walker's Datsun pickup truck. Walker, of Woodstock, New York, built one cabinet for woodworking tools and supplies and the other for camping equipment. On the road, the space between the two cabinets is covered with waterproof canvas and serves as a tent.

When he's on the road, turner S. Gary Roberts of Austin, Texas, sets up shop behind his Jamboree recreational vehicle. Roberts shortened the bed of a Craftsman lathe and bolted it to a metal frame, which he welded to the RV bumper. A locked plywood cover protects the lathe from the elements and provides storage for tools. (Photo by S. Gary Roberts.)

J. Baldwin resurrected his shop from the fire-gutted shell of a 2½-ton, 1958 Chevy van. Originally an insulated meat truck, the van had become a municipal bookmobile before Baldwin bought it in 1977 for about $3,000. He spent another $1,000 and countless hours over the next seven years transforming it into a nomadic community workshop. The bulk of his equipment is shoehorned into the 7-ft. by 12-ft. body of the truck; a 6-ft. wide extension doubles the space for assembly and benchwork. As Baldwin says: "I built it because I got tired of fixing up barns to be workshops. I can just drive this thing up to a house site and go to work."

At the time of my last visit, Baldwin had just finished making a float valve for a water tank and was building a roof rack for his car, but the shop's main purpose is "prototyping ideas." It is, as Baldwin likes to point out, "a three-dimensional sketch pad," and works as well for fiberglass and aluminum as for wood. In temporary quarters across the country, the shop has been used to produce everything from geodesic domes (37 at last count) and wind generators to a batch of 300 looms. Baldwin built the looms in two days, passing ma-

terial through the window behind the drill press, across the benches and out the other side. Finished parts were hung outside to dry in a tree.

"Everything works well," he says, "and I wouldn't change a thing," except perhaps for the radial-arm saw (shown at bottom right, facing page), which he considers replacing with a chopsaw. What drawbacks the shop has, such as its tight space and its inherently unlevel condition, are the predictable consequences of its mobility. After decades of trailer life, Baldwin has developed the body language of a hard-rock miner. "You get used to walking around with your arms folded in," he says. Still, I was surprised to find it more comfortable than many shops several times as large.

Baldwin traces the origins of his "highly evolved toolbox" to the Buster Brown lunch box of his childhood, which was home to a few rusty screwdrivers and a battered adjustable wrench. Over the years, his tool kit has grown by accretion, but his attitude has remained functional and down-to-earth. Almost every tool in the shop was bought used or "blemished," or is what Baldwin calls a "road kill," adding

J. Baldwin's mobile workshop

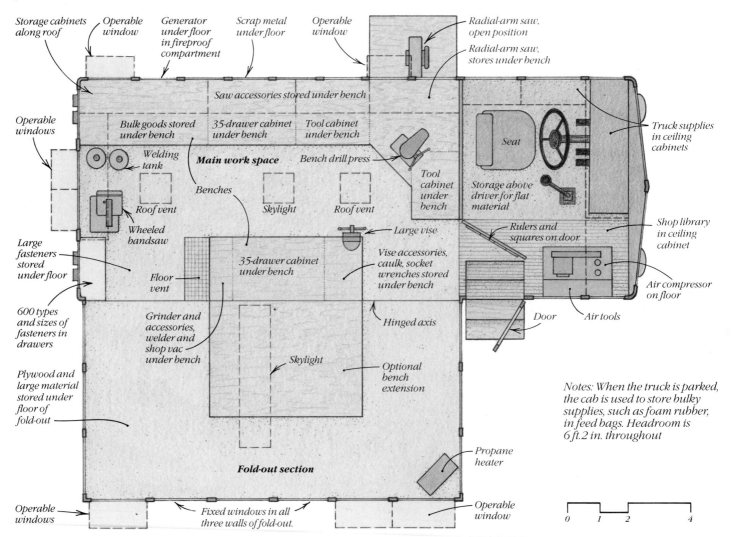

Storage cabinets along roof
Operable window
Generator under floor in fireproof compartment
Scrap metal under floor
Operable window
Radial-arm saw, open position
Radial-arm saw, stores under bench
Saw accessories stored under bench
Operable windows
Bulk goods stored under bench
35-drawer cabinet under bench
Tool cabinet under bench
Seat
Truck supplies in ceiling cabinets
Welding tank
Main work space
Bench drill press
Tool cabinet under bench
Storage above driver for flat material
Benches
Roof vent
Skylight
Roof vent
Large vise
Rulers and squares on door
Shop library in ceiling cabinet
Wheeled bandsaw
35-drawer cabinet under bench
Vise accessories, caulk, socket wrenches stored under bench
Air compressor on floor
Large fasteners stored under floor
Floor vent
Hinged axis
Door
Air tools
600 types and sizes of fasteners in drawers
Grinder and accessories, welder and shop vac under bench
Skylight
Optional bench extension
Plywood and large material stored under floor of fold-out
Notes: When the truck is parked, the cab is used to store bulky supplies, such as foam rubber, in feed bags. Headroom is 6 ft. 2 in. throughout
Propane heater
Fold-out section
Operable windows
Fixed windows in all three walls of fold-out.
Operable window
0 1 2 4

J. Baldwin's mobile shop is a marvel of compression. The 1958 Chevy van contains sufficient tools, materials and bench space to work metal, fiberglass and wood. The fully enclosed extension can be set up by two people in about 20 minutes. The roof, floor and outer wall of the extension ride together on the side of the van. The shed roof is hoisted first. Then Baldwin uses a boat-trailer winch to lower the remaining two panels. The bottom one becomes the extension floor, the other flips up to support the roof. (The three panels are joined with special 3-in. wide piano hinges designed for RV doors.) Finally, two trapezoidal end panels, which are stored upside down between the tail lights to permit access to the ball hitch, are bolted in position. (Photos at left by Kevin Kelly.)

The radial-arm saw stores in an exterior compartment and is lowered on a hinged panel for action. When operating the saw, Baldwin installs a panel behind it to keep the noise and dust outside. A Workmate® supports the end of long stock.

that "we use the shop to fix it up." (He straightened out two cockeyed Sears cabinets, which cost $45 instead of $269, by wheeling them right off the loading dock.) Once a year, he sets up a bench grinder on a Workmate® outside and holds a "sharpfest," putting a fresh edge on every tool in the shop.

"To a lot of woodworkers," he says, "the ritual is more important than the work. I can't imagine using a beautiful Stanley plane if I can do the same job in half the time with a router. My chisel will be used to chop mortises," he says, brandishing the tool. "It will not shave hair off my arm...but I rarely do that."

"The key to this place is versatility," Baldwin notes. Electrical outlets are everywhere, supplied by a 4,000-watt, slow-speed Onan RV generator, which also runs the shop's radial-arm saw, bandsaw, table saw and drill press. The shop is stocked with 600 different sizes of fasteners, many of them stored in the hardware cabinet shown in the photo at far right on the facing page, and equipped with more than a ton of hand tools. "Everything in here has a purpose," he explains. And every purpose has a place. "If you don't know where everything is," he continues, "it's as useless as a library without a card catalog." All the tools are color coded with a strip of blue tape, which identifies them as Baldwin's. Different colored tapes on each cabinet make it easy to direct people to the right bunch of drawers. The 6-ft. 2-in. high ceiling is also flagged with red tape as a warning to tall visitors.

Baldwin laid out the shop with full-scale cardboard mock-ups of each major tool and cabinet, which he pushed around the empty space on the floor plan. ("You can lie with drawings, but you can't lie with a full-scale model," he says.) He installed a 2-ft. wide workbench along one wall and placed a shorter bench near the center of the opposite wall; it becomes part of an island when the extension is erected. Along the front edges of the benches are 12 possible work stations, drilled to accept a pair of Columbia Versa Vises. Baldwin usually keeps a larger Wilton vise mounted on the corner of the island bench, but with a vise on either side of the aisle, he can clamp work between benches and work from any position.

The space is packed like a solo sailboat. The wall above the long bench is home to assorted tools and other paraphernalia, all securely hung for the road. Tin cans attached to the wall, for example, carry small containers of oil and other frequently used items. Nine overhead compartments carry everything from tape and extension cords to "solvents, brews, carcinogens." (The latter compartment is under the watchful eye of a photograph of R. Buckminster Fuller, patron saint of Baldwin's shop.) Beneath the benches are a pair of Sears tool cabinets and an assortment of drawers and apple crates. There's more storage beneath the island bench and, when the truck is parked, the cab is used to stow bulky supplies, such as foam rubber. Additional material fits in compartments beneath the floor and lumber is stacked below the open extension.

Baldwin's benches are sturdy and functional. They are both 38 in. high (hip-high on Baldwin) so large pieces can be easily slid from one to another. The bases are bed-frame an-

gle iron and Dexion, a perforated steel angle that Baldwin salvaged from old beagle cages. (The high carbon content of the bed-frame steel makes it stronger than hardware-store angle iron.) Bench frames are triangulated and bolted to the floor to prevent them from wiggling. The wall bench is surfaced with 2-in. thick Douglas-fir floorboards rescued from a 100-year-old almond warehouse. Most of the benchtop overhangs the tool chests by at least 1 in. to provide a handy edge for clamping, and it's sealed with caulk where it meets the wall to prevent small parts from wandering into the crevices. The island benchtop is 1⅛-in. thick underlayment plywood glued and bolted on top of some more 2-in. thick fir. "I'm not above nailing or even bolting work to the bench," Baldwin says. If the top gets too riddled, he simply packs the holes with bondo, sands the top down and refinishes it with three coats of satin varnish.

In a mobile workshop, layout has ramifications beyond the efficient function of the workspace. For road safety and efficient wear of brakes, shocks and springs, the weight must be carefully distributed side to side and end to end. The weight of the Onan generator, which resides beneath the floor near the rear of the van, is balanced by the heavy compartment of fasteners on the other side. The radial-arm saw, and the drill press are offset by the 1-hp air compressor in the cab and the grinder and welder, which ride beneath the island bench.

Compartment doors are secured with a spring-loaded, sheet-metal latch, and bolt drawers are held shut on the road with a locking bar that fits in the floor and is bolted to a ceiling stud. All of the major power tools are bolted in place, except for the table saw, which is packed tightly inside the truck when it's on the road, but is stashed beneath when the shop is encamped. The bandsaw is also on wheels, so that it can be unbolted and removed easily at a job site. The truck is packed so tightly that nothing moves when it's in transit; only the motor-mechanic tools are accessible. Windows can be opened to handle long stock. Even the side panels of the extension can be removed, since they're not structural, to work on large objects.

To keep the shop cool in the summer and warm in the winter, Baldwin framed the walls with 1-in. by 2-in. studs, infilled with 2-in. thick blue foam (glued in for structural strength) and covered with an RV-aluminum skin. This construction weighs about 1¼ lb. per square foot and is extremely stiff. The van is finished with a high-gloss white enamel paint inside and out, which reflects light and makes the shop feel much larger than it really is. The truck came with a roof-top air-conditioner, which Baldwin removed to make room for canoes, but the color scheme and insulation (R-11) keeps it comfortable even in the California sun. (He heats with propane in winter.) Except for the skylight, which is caulked with silicone and is the only thing that leaks, all waterproofing is accomplished with overlapping seams in the aluminum.

The extension can be set up by two people in about 20 minutes, and can be fully operational in about an hour. (One person can do the job alone, and the shop is fully functional even without the extension.) The extension sits on 1-in. dia. aluminum legs, made from schedule-40 water pipe. "People always remark on these spindly legs," Baldwin says, "but they're in direct compression and they do fine." The heaviest panel is the roof, which weighs 92 lb. Altogether, the extension adds only 250 lb. to the weight of the truck. When packed away on the side of the truck, it is balanced by the generator and radial-arm saw on the other side.

The whole business (including the shop and extension) is held together with more than 2,000 pop rivets, and when folded for travel, it is narrower and shorter than a Cadillac Eldorado. "It drives like a fat car," Baldwin says, with a gross vehicle weight of 10,000 lb. and a maximum cruising speed of 55 miles per hour. It averages seven miles per gallon with the Airstream trailer in tow, eight to nine miles per gallon without it.

Baldwin's color-coded tool identification system is useful for directing visiting gofers, e.g., 'The wrench is in the red cabinet.' Drawers are lined with indoor/outdoor carpeting, which protects the tools and keeps them quiet on the road. (Old chair springs keep the files from filing each other.) After repeated soakings with WD-40, the carpet lining helps prevent rust.

J. Baldwin's simple storage drawers

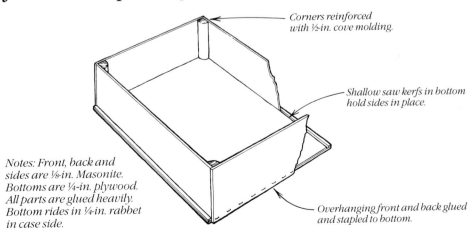

Corners reinforced with ½-in. cove molding.

Shallow saw kerfs in bottom hold sides in place.

Notes: Front, back and sides are ⅛-in. Masonite. Bottoms are ¼-in. plywood. All parts are glued heavily. Bottom rides in ¼-in. rabbet in case side.

Overhanging front and back glued and stapled to bottom.

Baldwin made all the drawers for this compact hardware cabinet in an hour. 'They're an affront to cabinetmakers,' he says, but they hold about 600 baby-food jars crammed with nuts and bolts, as well as film cans full of smaller stuff. The drawers can be pulled out of the chest and carted right to the job.

Always cognizant of local authorities, Baldwin is careful to tidy up the truck when he takes it for a cruise. With a fresh wash, two canoes on top and the Airstream trailing behind, it resembles any other recreational vehicle. (A few leaping-trout decals complete the effect.) Technically, it's a motor home, but as Baldwin points out, in this case, the basement shop pulls the house. "The last duty of the shop will be when it builds our house," he says. "We'll empty the truck into the house and sell it as a mobile stage."

Kids in the shop

Woodworking, like making music and cooking, has a universal attraction for kids. Two-year-olds as well as teenagers delight in transforming a chunk of wood into a fanciful or functional object. In the process of working this magic, the child also learns about responsibility, safety and planning, not to mention design and proportion, all of which help prepare him or her for other endeavors in life. But as important as these educational benefits are, we adults shouldn't forget that the process itself ought to be fun.

I'm convinced that the best thing an adult can do to help a child in this process is to provide the physical tools, the know-how and the emotional support, then get out of the way to let things happen. The adult becomes a facilitator, rather than a teacher or director. The projects that children initiate and, as much as possible, carry out will provide the greatest satisfaction. What they make is much less important than the fact that they made it.

Many kids love to work wood as much as adults do. Sheila Dawson, shown here lending a helping hand to Arielle Morrison in her school-bus workshop, has introduced woodworking to San Diego children with her innovative program, 'I Can Build It Myself.'

Kids enjoy working anywhere, but giving them a sound, well-designed workspace is like providing a good home. It's a secure environment that encourages them to take the risks that foster growth. Good lighting and layout and all the other issues that apply to adult workshops hold true for children's workshops, only more so. For safety reasons, most children work almost exclusively with hand tools. All children should certainly begin there, and graduate to the safest power tools only when they have proven their ability to manage them responsibly under careful supervision.

The workbench is even more central to a hand-tool shop than one in which machinery plays a major role. A flimsy bench can be frustrating for an adult, but it can make woodworking impossible for a child and may turn the youngster away from woodworking for good. You may be willing and able to work on a sawhorse or the kitchen table holding the stock with one hand and the tool with the other, but your 5-year-old deserves better. A toy workbench won't do the trick, either. A child's bench must be sturdy and flat, no less so than an adult's, and provide a reliable means of holding the work at a comfortable height. This frees the child to control the tool with both hands, with the confidence that the work won't squirt across the room.

Real tools are as important as a real bench. Cute little tool kits with plastic saws that won't cut and hammers with rubber handles lose their attraction very quickly. Children soon realize that only a real plane will make shavings and a real vise is needed to hold work securely, and they resent being given imaginary tools. Far better to provide small but authentic tools and help the child learn to use them properly.

The high-school woodshop is a fixture of North American education, but there are few formal woodworking programs designed for young children. The workshops discussed below have been assembled specifically to teach these kids. They are more ambitious than what most parents might undertake at home, but the teachers who put them together have incorporated lots of thoughtful features that can be applied to any home or school shop.

Sheila Dawson has been introducing grade-school kids to the basics of woodworking for over 15 years. She even teaches preschoolers that many adults would scarcely trust with crayons. "I can teach any kid who can talk with me," Dawson says. She travels all over San Diego, California, in the converted city transit bus shown on the facing page, instructing private groups of youngsters and public-school elective classes during and after school hours. In the summer, Dawson logs about 60 miles a day between teaching sites. (Dawson describes her shop and her teaching philosophy in her self-published book, *I Can Build It Myself.* See the Bibliography on p. 208).

"This really *does* work," Dawson says, proudly, as she shows me around the bus. She works with a maximum of ten kids at a time and has a compact, adjustable work center for seach one along opposite walls of the bus. Despite the apparently cramped quarters—there's slightly more than 12 in. between benches and only about 3 ft. of floor space between

Sheila Dawson's workbus for children

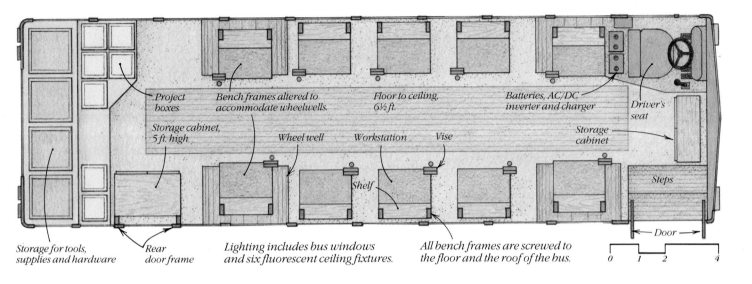

Project boxes

Bench frames altered to accommodate wheelwells.

Floor to ceiling, 6½ ft.

Batteries, AC/DC inverter and charger

Driver's seat

Storage cabinet, 5 ft. high

Wheel well

Workstation

Vise

Storage cabinet

Shelf

Steps

Storage for tools, supplies and hardware

Rear door frame

Lighting includes bus windows and six fluorescent ceiling fixtures.

All bench frames are screwed to the floor and the roof of the bus.

Door

0   1   2   4

Sheila Dawson's converted city transit bus provides ten workstations, and she provides encouragement, instruction and a watchful eye.

the rows—Dawson explains that it's a very safe place. As she tells the parents of prospective students, "This is safer than any playground. It's totally supervised and it's a *purposeful* activity." She admits that there's always a risk when you work with an unknown group of people—kids or adults—but she tries to identify uncoordinated or undisciplined children at the outset and restricts their activity if necessary.

Dawson began woodworking with her own son in her husband's shop. Frustrated in her efforts to find a school program that would nurture her son's interest, she set up her first experimental woodworking program on the patio of her son's private school. By the end of the first summer, she had established a few practical safety rules and had a basic set of child-tested project models.

About six months later she put her program on the road, offering private lessons and elective public-school classes in a 24-ft. bakery truck that she and her husband converted to a shop. (Dawson operates under a city business license and carries premises liability insurance as a vocational/trade school in addition to insurance on the vehicle and con-

tents.) She eventually outgrew the first truck and a second 35-ft. school bus, finally setting up a ten-bench shop in the 1972 Twin Coach diesel bus she now operates.

The current bus was a long-awaited luxury. Its diesel engine is practically indestructible, and the automatic transmission is a treat. "I could do my nails while driving," she says jokingly. All class work is done with hand tools, so, unless she's using all the fans on a hot day (there's one above the window behind each bench), Dawson can usually power the overhead fluorescent lights with two deep-cycle marine batteries and a step-up inverter. If she needs more power, Dawson will run an extension cord to the sponsoring home or school.

The self-contained workstations (shown above) are the heart of the shop layout. Each consists of a plywood bench-top, 2 ft. wide by 20 in. deep, with a small Stanley or Sears vise at the left corner. The corner-mounted vise is convenient for clamping both vertical and horizontal work and is easy for the kids to manage. Its jaws are lined with tempered Masonite pads, which protrude by about ¼ in. to protect tools and the vise. At the back of the bench, an 18-in. high pegboard panel and shelves hold the rest of the tool kit. The shelves are angled slightly and lipped to retain their contents when the bus is in transit.

By turning a screw-and-gear drive mechanism at the base of the bench with a power drill, Dawson can position the benchtops from 18 in. to 34 in. off the floor to accommodate children of all sizes. The screw and gears tend to get clogged with sawdust, so she's thinking of replacing them with a counterweighted bench design. (She has also built simpler freestanding adjustable benches, shown below.) Her rule of thumb for bench height is simple: "The belly button has to be three fingers over the benchtop." This positions the child's elbow at an approximate right angle for effective sawing or hammering.

Dawson began with eight benches, but eventually added two more as her program picked up steam and she got better at her work. "I'd never go over ten," she says. The 16 in. to 18 in. between benches is fine, although she wouldn't mind an extra foot of width in the center aisle. "If they got much farther apart," she says, "I'd lose a kid down there." As it is, she can keep a watchful eye over the entire shop from either end of the bus. "An open classroom makes me nervous," she explains. After years of teaching, she amazes the kids by recognizing sounds of improper tool use behind her back. "I can hear when they're turning the drill backwards," she says, and her trained ear will also warn her when a clamp isn't tight or a nail is too big. "I do believe that I could teach this class blind," she says.

Dawson is careful to select good-quality tools, which last longer and are more effective than cheap ones. Children also respond well to being entrusted with "adult" tools. Hanging from the pegboard and on the shelves behind each bench are the following tools: a 7-oz. curved-claw hammer (with about 3 in. cut off the handle), an eggbeater drill (with a directional arrow painted on the gear) and twist bits, a try square, a stubby slot screwdriver, a scratch awl, Surform rasps, hard-rubber sanding blocks and plenty of sandpaper, a 3/8-in. centerpunch, a nail set and a ruler. The pencil is the most important tool at the bench—"Think first with the pencil," she instructs her students—and its location is marked with the number 1.

Also at each station are a pair of eye goggles, a dust brush, a dustpan and a waste bin, along with assorted scraps of wood (for leveling work on the bench or padding it in the vise), and 4-in. aluminum C-clamps, which are frequently used to secure the material while it is being worked. (The children often call them "sea clamps.") Glue and most hardware is stored in a cabinet at the back of the bus, along with other tools and materials that are used less frequently or only with Dawson's permission or supervision, such as a brace and auger bits, a coping saw, a small hacksaw, rasps, files and wood putty.

At the back of each bench is a small wooden miter box, the companion to the handsaw that lives in a scabbard beneath the bench. Small children appear to be dwarfed by the 16-in. or 20-in. Disston crosscut saw, but it is easier for them to control than a backsaw, with its awkwardly angled handle,

Dawson built simpler, adjustable benches like this for her stationary workshop at the Mission Hills Arts and Crafts Center. Their height can be adjusted from 24 in. to 32 in. by pulling the pins in each 1-in. thick plywood leg and raising or lowering the bench. If a child is still too short, Dawson has him or her stand on a shallow platform.

Dawson provides plans and models for dozens of projects—children, like the rest of us, often need a nudge to spur creativity.

and more durable than a coping saw's thin blade, which is likely to heat up and break under pressure. In Dawson's shop, the handsaw must be used with the miter box, although more experienced children may use a coping saw or a hacksaw to cut off material clamped in the vise.

All projects are built with birch or fir dowels and #2 (shelving) pine supplied by Dawson. In her garage, she cuts away any knots on a radial-arm saw and rips the stock to width on a table saw, leaving the marking, crosscutting, gluing and assembly to the children. In a stack of plastic boxes at the back of the bus are plans and models for dozens of projects, from rolling and flying toys to walkie-talkies, rubber-band banjos and back scratchers. Skilled fourth or fifth graders may tackle advanced games and coping-saw puzzles. To minimize frustration, Dawson encourages kids to undertake projects that can be completed in about an hour, or the time allotted for a school period. She has only two restrictions on projects: They must never be large and never look like weapons. "We don't do guns, knives, swords, rubber-band shooters, slingshots, arrows, throwing stars, skateboards or furniture," she says.

Apart from the rules for specific tools (for example, kids aren't allowed to talk when they saw), Dawson has very few formal safety rules in the shop. Safety glasses or goggles are used mainly during hot weather, when the window fans churn up the sawdust. The bottom line, she tells the kids, is "When you make me nervous, the shop stops."

"I consider myself a facilitator, a problem solver," Dawson says, and she allows the kids to struggle just long enough to learn something from the effort, but not long enough to get frustrated. "The kids think I'm teaching woodworking, but I'm not. I'm teaching life skills," she says. And the education goes both ways. As Dawson explains, "I learned everything I know from children."

To sample shop life within the public school system, I spent a day in Richard Starr's Richmond School classroom in Hanover, New Hampshire. Although the children are older than Dawson's students (grades six through eight) and the shop is larger, I found Starr's and Dawson's philosophy of education and many of their workshop practices to be strikingly similar. (Starr, like Dawson, has written a book about his methods, *Woodworking with Your Kids.* See the Bibliography on p. 208.)

According to Starr, "It's more of a crafts program than an industrial-arts program. I don't care about teaching content or curriculum, and I have no minimum expectations." His main priority is that the kids learn to have fun with the tools. Like Dawson, he accepts a maximum of ten kids in each elective period. The only power tools in the shop are a bandsaw and radial-arm saw, which Starr uses to prepare stock and keep the shop running. He walks the same delicate tightrope, doing just enough to keep the kids from bogging down but not so much that they feel like they don't own the work. For those students who will graduate to a high-school industrial-arts program, Starr's classroom may be their first and last exposure to self-directed, supervised woodworking in a hand-tool environment. By the ninth grade, they will be plugged into a full range of motorized power tools and a conventional course structure.

The school day begins at 8:05 a.m. "I give up trying to keep this place clean," Starr says apologetically as we enter the shop, sweeping off a workbench with his hand to make room for my camera. "There are all kinds of inefficiencies here," he says, "but most of them have to do with my inability to clean up in three minutes." Devoid of children, the place has a look of ordered chaos, with remnants of incomplete projects encroaching on the workspace. There's a north-facing wall of windows, which augment the overhead fluo-

Richard Starr teaches woodworking to junior high-school students in Hanover, New Hampshire. A teacher for more than 20 years, Starr still imparts his own enthusiasm for woodworking to his students.

Starr keeps all his classroom hand tools in three large chests. Stout wooden hinges support the heavy storage-compartment doors.

rescents with a soft, even light. The linoleum floor cushions the feet and helps protect dropped tools, but with a little oil or wax it can become a skating rink. (Starr sprinkles Speedy Dry, a compound used by auto mechanics, on the floor when it gets slick.)

"I'll be back in a few minutes," Starr says, "with kids." About ten minutes later, he returns with four boys and two girls. He swings open the three ponderous wall-mounted tool chests, shown above, and the kids start organizing their work. They deploy themselves at one of four simple benches

Starr built for the shop. The benches are all roughly 29 in. high, with a 42-in. wide by 66-in. long laminated-maple top and two or three vises mounted on the corners. The vises, mostly Records, are faced with ¾-in. thick oak pads. The various vise configurations (shown in the drawing on p. 150) provide a variety of clamping options. The bench height works well for most of his students, but Starr encourages smaller kids to climb on top if they need extra purchase on a tool. Benches are often pulled together for additional clamping support or if a larger work surface is required.

Vise positions for children's workbenches

Note: Any of these configurations will allow one or more children to do a variety of work at the bench.

The most important feature of the benches is the overhang; each top extends about 8 in. beyond the base, providing plenty of room for clamping. For bench stops, Starr uses "disposable" wooden dogs, 1 in. square, which fit snugly (after some initial persuasion) in ⅞-in. dia. holes bored at an angle in the benchtops. "We used to turn the dogs," he explains, "but these are great." They can be ripped on the bandsaw in seconds. "I let things go to the minimal functional standards, and it doesn't seem to make a difference."

Starr chooses tools for the shop with care. "It's important to identify those tools that will add to the shop and the kids' abilities and those that will be abused or misused," he explains. (Compressed air, for example, could make cleanup a lot easier, but it will almost certainly be abused.) The shop is generously supplied with the usual hand tools, but as in

Modifying plans from a magazine article, Starr combined a ratchet and a standard ten-speed bicycle sprocket to make an efficient treadle lathe (shown above). The heavy wooden flywheel to the left of the sprocket enables the kids to stop pumping for a while to concentrate on cutting. Starr removed the motor fan from the small scrollsaw (at left) and installed a hand crank on the end of the shaft, as demonstrated by seventh-grader Jennifer Jones.

almost every shop, clamps are in perpetual short supply. "One of the best workshop fixtures I know," Starr announces to me and the class, "is a person with another pair of hands."

Although the bandsaw and radial-arm saw are off-limits to the students, two human-powered tools, the treadle-powered lathe and the hand-crank scrollsaw (shown on the facing page), are among the most popular tools in the shop. In terms of both safety and technology, they are appropriate "starter" power tools in any hand-tool shop. (The kids use a heavier iron-bed treadle lathe on a wooden stand to turn bowls.) The power supply comes from the kid who's using the tool and, unlike most motorized machinery, the tool won't work unless it's used properly.

Starr also keeps a shaving horse in the shop, but the kids prefer to shave wood at the bench, with the work clamped in a vise. "Maybe it's the weight of the bench, or maybe the shaving horse isn't that good," he notes. When shaving at the bench, children quickly discover that the bench is less likely to slide if the work is clamped in a side vise, rather than an end vise.

At the end of each period, the kids replace the tools on the shelf beneath the tool chests and Starr puts them away. The end of the class day comes at 2 p.m., but after six 45-minute periods supervising nearly 50 youngsters in the human exercise of Brownian motion, Starr is visibly tired. "One of the keys to getting kids to be more responsible," he says, "is to get them to ask the magic question before they can leave: 'Anything else I can do, Rich?' They don't have to mean it," he adds, "they just have to say it."

*Paul Silke's Oregon workshop
reflects a lifetime of dreams.
Silke spared no effort, either in
the machinery or in the
electrical and dust-collection
systems that support it.*

Dream
Workshops

Each one of us has, somewhere in his heart, the dream to make a living world, a universe.
—Christopher Alexander, *The Timeless Way of Building.*

Chapter 7

Not long ago, I received a phone call from a doctor in Oregon who wanted some advice. Facing the prospect of building the workshop of his dreams, he was intimidated by the details. With all the decisions he knew he'd have to make along the way, he was frankly scared that he would make a mistake. "Rest assured," I told him, "You will. You will undoubtedly discover, probably long before you move in, that there are some things you might have done better, and there will be many things you could have done differently."

The dream shop is an elusive commodity. For some people, I suppose, dreaming is best done at night, far away from their workshop and their checkbook. But many of the craftspeople in this book have been chasing the dream shop

all their lives and, like the green light at the end of Daisy's dock in Fitzgerald's *The Great Gatsby,* year by year it seems to recede before them. In fact, the more we know about our craft, the more difficult it can be to satisfy our expectations.

In selecting a few special workshops to include in this chapter, I was faced with a dilemma. No shop is perfect, and no place I've visited could possibly appeal to every reader. But there are a few shops—a handful, really—that stand apart from the crowd. These are distinguished by several qualities, which, like art and pornography, are easier to identify than to describe. In the first place, they represent an effort to dedicate a wholly new space, or to overhaul an existing one, to woodworking. In each case, the owner has conceived of his shop as a complete environment, ideally suited to his particular needs, rather than as a workbench here and some machinery there that just happened to fit in the garage. They also address the notion that function and comfort are not mutually exclusive in a workshop. Finally, each of these workshops reflects the ingenuity of its occupant, if not in the building itself, then in some aspect of its design or organization.

In the main portion of this chapter, I have presented three of the most impressive workshops I found, followed by a gallery of photos of two other inspired (and inspiring) examples. None of the shops are mortgage nightmares, although they all represent major investments of energy and planning and may be worth a lot of money. It is important to note that the less extravagant places are no less functional or delightful, only less costly, and that all of the creators are still fine-tuning their dreams.

Paul Silke's compleat workshop

Most people slow down in retirement, but when Paul Silke quit the electrical-contracting business in 1980, he dropped out of his regular golf game as well to make time for the workshop. When one of his foursome inquired, rather sarcastically, "What do you build in your shop?" Paul answered simply, "I build workshops."

After nearly 50 years of woodworking, Silke finally built a workshop (shown below, on the facing page and on p. 152) in 1975 "just exactly the way I wanted it." It is his fourth major workshop, each one an improvement on the last, but this one was built to outlast its owner. He took pains to design a building that would not only provide an efficient workspace, but one that would be pleasing to look at, too. Keeping an eye on the resale value, he wanted to be able to convert the shop to a comfortable home with a minimum of effort. "I wanted something that wouldn't cheapen the neighborhood," he says.

The shop is dug into the side of a hill at the end of a quiet residential crescent in Salem, Oregon. It is only a few paces away from his home and is landscaped with dogwood trees in the yard, flower boxes on the windowsills, grapevines on the arbor and a handsome wrought-iron gate at the end of the paved drive. "To this day," he says, "people think somebody lives here."

"For a hobby shop," Silke explains, "the main thing is to have a pleasant place to work." His is laid out in a roomy rectangle, 24 ft. wide by 40 ft. long, with a bench area at one end and a concrete slab at the other for wood storage. (The overhead garage door makes it easy to unload equipment right into the shop or to pile wood directly on the lumber

Silke's shop building is landscaped and built like a house to blend into the neighborhood and provide future resale opportunities. (Photo by Paul Silke.)

Paul Silke's retirement shop

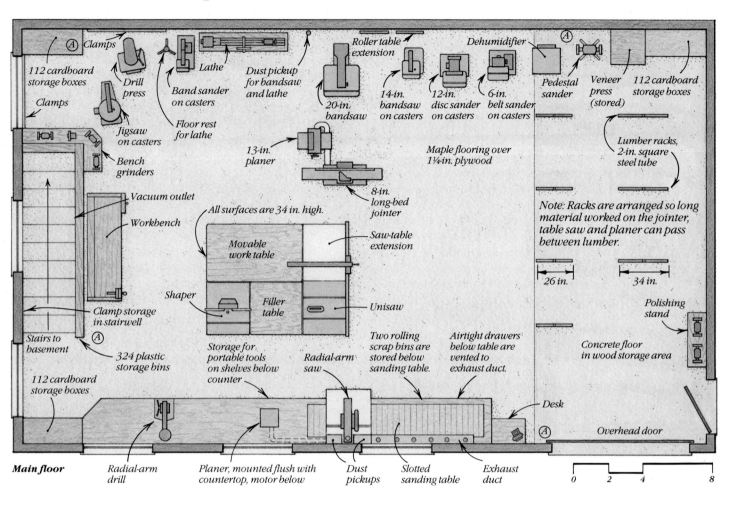

Main floor

- (A) Clamps
- 112 cardboard storage boxes
- Clamps
- Drill press
- Band sander on casters
- Lathe
- Jigsaw on casters
- Floor rest for lathe
- Bench grinders
- Vacuum outlet
- Workbench
- Dust pickup for bandsaw and lathe
- Roller table extension
- 20-in. bandsaw
- 14-in. bandsaw on casters
- 12-in. disc sander on casters
- 6-in. belt sander on casters
- Dehumidifier
- (A)
- Pedestal sander
- Veneer press (stored)
- 112 cardboard storage boxes
- Lumber racks, 2-in. square steel tube
- 13-in. planer
- 8-in. long-bed jointer
- Maple flooring over 1¼-in. plywood
- Saw-table extension
- All surfaces are 34 in. high.
- Movable work table
- Shaper
- Filler table
- Unisaw
- Clamp storage in stairwell
- Stairs to basement
- (A)
- 324 plastic storage bins
- 112 cardboard storage boxes
- Storage for portable tools on shelves below counter
- Radial-arm saw
- Two rolling scrap bins are stored below sanding table.
- Airtight drawers below table are vented to exhaust duct.
- Desk
- (A)
- Overhead door
- Radial-arm drill
- Planer, mounted flush with countertop, motor below
- Dust pickups
- Slotted sanding table
- Exhaust duct
- Note: Racks are arranged so long material worked on the jointer, table saw and planer can pass between lumber.
- 26 in.
- 34 in.
- Polishing stand
- Concrete floor in wood storage area

Scale: 0 2 4 8

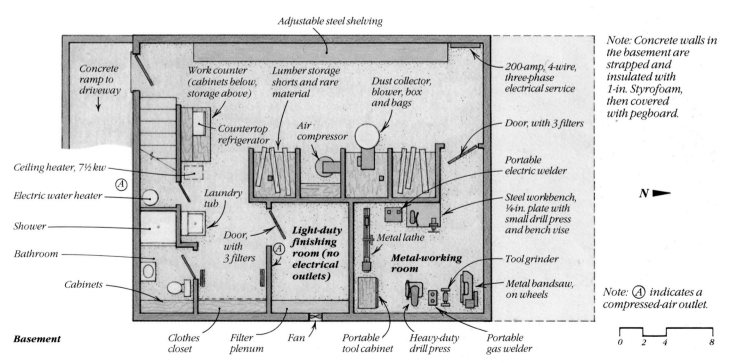

Basement

- Adjustable steel shelving
- Concrete ramp to driveway
- Work counter (cabinets below, storage above)
- Lumber storage shorts and rare material
- Dust collector, blower, box and bags
- 200-amp, 4-wire, three-phase electrical service
- Countertop refrigerator
- Air compressor
- Door, with 3 filters
- Portable electric welder
- Ceiling heater, 7½ kw
- (A)
- Electric water heater
- Laundry tub
- Steel workbench, ¼-in. plate with small drill press and bench vise
- Shower
- Door, with 3 filters
- **Light-duty finishing room (no electrical outlets)**
- (A)
- Metal lathe
- Bathroom
- **Metal-working room**
- Tool grinder
- Cabinets
- Metal bandsaw, on wheels
- Clothes closet
- Filter plenum
- Fan
- Portable tool cabinet
- Heavy-duty drill press
- Portable gas welder

Note: Concrete walls in the basement are strapped and insulated with 1-in. Styrofoam, then covered with pegboard.

N ▶

Note: (A) indicates a compressed-air outlet.

Scale: 0 2 4 8

racks, shown on p. 157.) In the working area of the shop is a gleaming expanse of ¾-in. hard-maple flooring, solidly supported by 2x12 joists and a 1¼-in. plywood subfloor. The bottom half of the shop walls is sheathed with ¾-in. plywood and the top is strapped and covered with pegboard. Downstairs, a three-quarter basement (with a separate outside entrance) houses a finishing room, a metalworking room and a full bathroom and shower, where Silke can clean up before going home.

Western Oregon is well known for its mild climate, but Silke wasn't taking any chances. He used 2x6 studs in the walls and sprayed-foam insulation, as well as stuffing the drywall ceiling with 12 in. of fiberglass. (The insulation also helps buffer his neighbors from the shop noise.) The basement walls are strapped and insulated with 1-in. foam panels, while double-glass windows and a dehumidifier (for winter use) help maintain a stable atmosphere. The shop is heated with three 7,500-watt electric heaters suspended from the ceilings, two upstairs and one in the basement. To vent the building or to clear the air of residual dust, Silke opens a window and a trap door in the ceiling and turns on a large attic fan.

As you might expect of a retired electrical contractor, Silke spared no effort when it came to shop wiring. Due to the proximity of outside power lines, he was able to get three-phase power delivered right to the shop. (Silke is a great advocate of three-phase power, but he dismisses home-built converters as hopelessly inefficient.) Wires are run entirely in metal conduit, with both three-phase and single-phase power available at every wall outlet. Outlets are spaced every 4 ft. along the walls for maximum flexibility. Two overhead cords descend from the ceiling above the sanding table and three bronze floor stanchions deliver electricity to the table saw, jointer and shaper. (The stanchions have 120-volt, single-phase outlets on one side and a three-phase outlet on the other.) In case he missed anything, Silke distributed several strips of Plugmold around the shop and installed a power bar on the apron of his assembly table for hand-held sanders, drills and other small equipment.

"One of the mysteries to me is how early woodworkers did such beautiful work with the meager lighting they had," Silke notes. His shop is bathed in fluorescence and you have to look hard to find shadows. Window light is augmented with three rows of 8-ft. long, high-output fluorescent lamps.

The joys of a life-long hobby

The care (and pride) Paul Silke lavished on his shop is evident, but I couldn't help wondering about the origins of Silke's love of wood and the role of the workshop in his life. When I asked him to explain, Silke composed this thoughtful history. On different levels, it speaks of one man's quest for the perfect shop and the meaning of craft. (Photo by Michael K. Lowery.)

In 1929 I entered Parrish Junior High School, where I excitedly signed up for my first class in woodworking. It was quite a thrill to be assigned to my own workbench and have access to all the tools. Mr. Barker took a liking to me right away. The students sharpened their own tools, and he would put mine away between classes so none of the other kids could get to them. Our first assignment was to take a small block of wood and make all the corners and edges absolutely square. I was through with the footstool project and working on the fern stand while a lot of kids were still trying to square their block.

The very first thing I learned in class was that you had to have a good vise to hold the work. We didn't have any kind of vise at home, but my dad had a makeshift workbench in the barn. I cut a couple of 3-ft. pieces off of

a heavy plank and used a large gate hinge and a heavy bolt with a long thread to build my own vise.

When I was 16 years old, my folks got me a job in a large hardware store. This was the worst of the Depression so the pay was small, but the experience was great. It wasn't long before the store owners let me take care of the tools, and soon I was in charge of the whole department. I couldn't afford to buy any of the tools myself, but I did inherit some later on.

I got married in 1939 and rented a tiny house with an interior stairway to the basement. Somehow I managed to finance a table saw and a 4-in. jointer. A year later, I was able to finance a house and lot — I built the cabinets for the house myself. There was enough money for a Delta Unisaw, which I had had my eye on

ever since they went on the market. I was working for an electrical-supply house at the time, and when we needed a couple of hand trucks in the warehouse, I gathered up some oak and fir, some leftover pecan flooring from the house and a few wheels and built them. They're still in use today, 50 years later.

I sold the new house and was able to buy an old house and some property with the money. The old house had a partial basement with an outside entrance, but I managed to turn it into a shop. I entered a night class in woodworking at the local high school to gain access to power tools I didn't have at home. Besides remodeling the house, I built a few things that I still own and use, including the workbench in my shop.

In 1950, we sold the old house so that I could buy an electrical-contracting

Silke's floor-to-ceiling, tube-steel lumber racks carry a lot of wood and are easily accessible through the overhead garage door at one end of the shop. The 2-in. sq. stock is butt welded where the cross members meet the uprights, with welded nuts and threaded leveler feet at the bottom (shown at left). Silke devised a clever method of attachment to the ceiling that allows for settling of the building. A section of pipe is welded above each upright to receive a slip-fit length of smaller-diameter pipe, which threads into a pipe flange on the ceiling. An oak ceiling brace provides a good bearing surface and a place for the flange screws.

business of my own. For a couple of years we lived in a rented house (with my workbench) until we could afford to buy another home. An opportunity came along to acquire a large colonial house that had to be moved from commercial property. We moved the house onto a nice new basement with an outside entrance, and I turned half the basement into what I thought was the ideal workshop. I had plenty of tools by this time, including a 13-in. planer and a 20-in. Delta bandsaw. I tore out the kitchen and utility room and made them into one beautiful kitchen, with solid walnut cabinets, a luminous ceiling and custom pine trim around the windows and doors.

In 1979, my wife Dorothy passed away, and everything suddenly changed. For a while, all of my interest in woodworking was gone. I put things aside in the shop and

went back to playing golf. When I married Lenna, she was building a new house for herself. I moved in with her and decided to put my own place up for sale, not knowing what to do about the shop. Two days later, I received earnest money on the house and, at the bottom of the agreement, they added that I could keep the shop in their home for one year, no charge. When I went over there to work, Maudie [the new home owner] sent coffee and cookies down. It was wonderful to have someone buy my home who appreciated it so much. At the end of the year I still didn't have a place to put my shop, so they let me keep it there another year.

By the end of the next year, I could see that they wanted the space but didn't want to ask me to move. I decided to store the tools in the basement of my business until I could build another

shop on the vacant lot next door to our house. There I built my last ideal workshop. I did a lot of planning with the city building-codes department to come up with a shop that met their requirements (and mine) and still could be turned into a home when I was through with the shop. I landscaped, decorated the building a bit and built a wrought-iron fence with a gate at the driveway entrance. Very few of my neighbors know that it's not another home.

At 75 years old, I'm still planning for the future. In my lumber rack is $768 worth of 5/4 ponderosa pine, 16½ in. and 20 in. wide. I'm building dowry chests for my eight granddaughters and one for my friend, Bill, who helps me in the shop. I have rough plans for a game table to be made out of the myrtlewood that I hauled out of the woods in 1941. The wood is stored in the

basement, just waiting to be used. I've started a spinning wheel made of some beautiful walnut that blew down during the infamous Columbus Day storm of 1962. Then there is the osage that the city cut at the airport, which I painted with beeswax and stored downstairs, along with the big maple burl and pieces of driftwood I picked up at the coast. If I look at this wood long enough I get inspired to make something special. Since junior high school, I've never made anything from a purchased plan.

All that I hope for now is to live long enough to build the things I've planned. In the meantime, I'll enjoy my shop. Sometimes I just sit in my shop chair and admire the rough wood and try to see something inside of it.

The twin-bulb fixtures run the length of the shop ceiling and two shorter units provide extra task lighting at the workbench. The only incandescent lights are in the basement stairwell, where they are turned on and off more frequently than the fluorescents; mercury-vapor safety lamps provide light outside.

Over the years, Silke has collected a full complement of vintage machinery, and his inventory reads like a Delta catalog, circa 1940 to 1950. (He paid about as much for a

Silke rigged up a metal junction box as a pickup and blast gate on his radial-arm saw. A microswitch attached to the box triggers the dust collector when Silke swings the door open. At the sanding station to the left of the saw, dust is sucked down through the slots in the table and carried off through a plywood plenum. Two large rolling bins beneath the table hold offcuts.

Unifence he recently purchased as for his 1940 Unisaw.) Despite its age, or maybe because of it, the machinery looks like it's been mothballed for decades. It forms an archipelago across the middle of the shop, anchored at one wall by the 20-in. bandsaw and by the radial-arm saw at the other. In the center of the shop is a large island workstation, containing the table saw, the shaper and their auxiliary tables. Several smaller tools, such as a 14-in. Rockwell bandsaw, a vertical belt sander and a disc sander, are mounted on wheels and can be rolled around as necessary. All major machine tables are 34 in. high, and with 18 ft. of infeed and outfeed clearance it's hard to imagine a board too long or a panel too wide to handle. Even the lumber-rack shelves are oriented so they won't interfere with long stock.

Silke's air compressor and 5-hp dust collector are located downstairs, where the noise will be least offensive. PVC dust-collection pipe is routed through the overhead floor joists to all of the shop machinery, leaving a minimum of exposed pipe upstairs. (Whenever he needed an adapter or plug, he simply turned one on the lathe.) The magnetic switch for the dust-collection system is wired to a clever shop-built blast-gate installed in the pipe beneath each machine. In Silke's latest "foolproof" design (shown on p. 107), a pair of brass bullet catches are connected with low-voltage bell wire to the starter relay.

Like most woodworkers I know, Paul Silke is a pack rat. "I never throw anything away," he says, and his assortment of screws, bolts and electrical fittings would rival the offering at my local hardware store. "But if you don't have a good system for storing this stuff," he adds, "you might as well forget it." Along one entire basement wall, large open shelves handle everything from paints and hardware to cherished chunks of wood put aside for special projects. Upstairs, three floor-to-ceiling cases hold several hundred small cardboard bins filled with hardware, while another case behind the bench contains yet more hardware in more than 300 clear plastic tubs.

The divider that separates Silke's bench and the basement stairs is loaded with plastic storage bins. A metal-lath screen keeps them from falling into the stairwell and allows sunlight to filter through from behind.

Not all of Silke's efforts have been lavished on his shop. Throughout the house are signs of shop activity—a carved headboard for the bed, a grandfather clock with egg-and-dart carving, curio cabinets, kitchen cupboards, and there are lots more projects underway. The consummate amateur, he explains, "I have fun, and I never sold a nickel's worth of woodwork in my life."

Mark Duginske's expanding garage shop

Dreams, and dream shops, rarely spring to life full-grown. Once the idea is planted or the first sketch is made, it is buffeted by changing needs and interests and tempered with reality. Mark Duginske's workshop grew in just such a fashion, suiting his budget and allowing him to tinker with the dream. "One of the more creative things you can do is build your own shop," Duginske says, "which, in a way, is your biggest tool."

Duginske's dream took root in a humble 14-ft. by 18-ft. uninsulated garage behind his house in Wausau, Wisconsin. (The garage was lit by a single 25-watt bulb and powered by an electrical outlet and a circuit so feeble that anything larger than a drill would blow the fuse.) It was of a piece with the unadulterated 1933 bungalow that he and his wife, Kate, took over in 1977. Sharing workspace in downtown Wausau, where he built furniture and architectural woodwork, Duginske long dreamed of moving his shop home, but only an experienced eye for renovation could have seen the potential in a derelict shack.

The metamorphosis took place over several years, but was concentrated in two major building spurts, as shown in the photos and drawing on p. 160. In the first phase, Duginske sliced the garage in half and stretched it lengthwise to 28 ft. He used a Milwaukee Sawzall to remove all the wood between a pair of wall studs and roof rafters on both sides of

You would never guess that Mark Duginske's handsome workshop started out as an old one-car garage.

Mark Duginske's expanded garage shop

Duginske transformed his garage shop in stages. First, he cut the building in half and rolled one half to the end of a new concrete slab. Then he enclosed the space between the sections with walls, windows and a roof. About a year later, in the final and most dramatic stage, the building sprouted up and out, creating a separate bench room and a second-floor storage loft. (Photos above by Mark Duginske.)

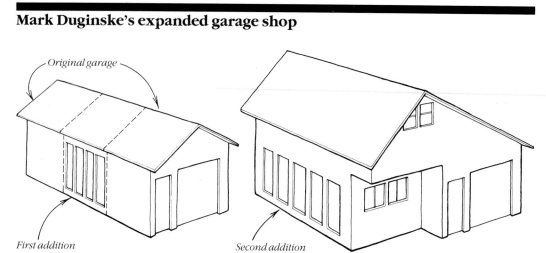

Original garage

First addition

Second addition

Stage 1

Stage 2

the building, thereby creating about 22 in. of space between the two segments. Next, he cut the bolts that anchored the rear section to the concrete slab and rolled it forward on 2-in. dia. PVC water pipes. This closed the gap between the two halves and provided enough working room to attach a 10-ft. by 14-ft. concrete extension to the back of the slab. Then he rolled the rear section back and filled in the open space with walls, roof and windows.

If this process sounds unusual, it was common practice in central Wisconsin, where Duginske's grandfather enlarged barns in the same manner. As Duginske explained, it saves a lot of time and uses materials more efficiently, since a gable end is much harder to construct than a straight wall or roof and requires lots of short pieces and angled cuts.

The shop molted again about a year later when Duginske nearly doubled its width and added a second story. He peeled off the entire south side of the roof, added a heavy-duty box beam for support under the original ridge and extended the north slope of the roof to a new peak. (The box beam consists of a cross-braced 2x4 stub wall sheathed on both sides with ¾-in. plywood, with holes drilled for ventilation.) Along with the construction, Duginske upgraded his household electrical service to 200 amps and put a 100-amp subpanel in the shop.

Duginske works in the enlarged downstairs and, for the moment, uses the upstairs for storage. A 6-ft. by 10-ft. shed at the back of the shop holds garden tools, and the large overhang in the southeast corner protects bicycles in the summer and firewood in the winter. (To support the overhang, which extends almost 6 ft. beyond the building, Duginske built a hefty plate beam for the south window wall out of two 2x10s and a ¾-in. plywood core, glued and nailed together.) Apart from its functional advantages, the idea for the roomy overhang is borrowed from the Prairie School of design that was popular around town during the early 1900s.

The shop is painted the same color as the house, and with a combination of clapboard and asphalt-shingle siding and plenty of surrounding foliage, it blends easily into the neighborhood. A lush garden, tended by Kate, completes the effect and offers a bucolic vista from the bench. The garden was a "happy accident" made possible by the location of the shop on the north edge of the property.

Inside, much of the finishing took place incrementally. The wood-paneled ceiling was added one summer, windows the next, and so on until all the doors, benches and cabinets were in place. The only major additions that remain to be completed are a new and enlarged retractable stairway to the second floor and a dormer in the north slope of the

The inside of Duginske's shop is as inviting to woodworkers as the outside is agreeable to neighbors. The large machines reside in the original garage, near the overhead door, while various benches and smaller machines occupy the pine-paneled addition. Duginske does most of his sharpening with Japanese waterstones at the window bench. The 33-in. high surface is low enough for him to exert some pressure without bending over too far, and the natural light is ideal.

roof, both of which would make the upstairs more functional. "But for now," Duginske says, "it's livable."

"The building is absolutely as big as I could make it and still stay within the local zoning guidelines," he explains. According to local regulations, the structure had to be less than 26 ft. wide (it's 25 ft. wide) and the roof peak could not exceed the height of his neighbor's house. Moreover, if he had made the upstairs knee walls just 2 in. higher, the second story would have been included in the "official" floor footage of the shop, putting it well above the 900-sq. ft. limit for an auxiliary garage.

The combined cost of both phases of construction came to about $5,000, including windows, plywood and the concrete slabs. "This is a lot of building for five or six grand," Duginske says, adding that it could only have been done with recycled materials. The wood for the ceiling and the large sheets of window glass were new, but they were on sale; all the other materials were secondhand. He did most of the work himself, with the help of a friend who did all the wiring and some of the concrete. It took hundreds of hours to complete, and he explains that "there's no way we could afford to have someone else do the work."

"There may be more efficient ways to build," Duginske says, such as hiring a backhoe to knock the old building down and dig a new foundation, but there's a real appeal to prolonging the life of an old building. Duginske is one of the few woodworkers I know who can draw a direct line to the craft tradition. His father was a patternmaker and his grandfather built bridges, barns and dams in the surrounding countryside. This sense of personal history carried over to the workshop construction itself, as he decided to leave as much of the original building intact as possible, and to complete the rest of it in such a way that it would not "offend" his house. As Duginske explains, even the original garage

Mark Duginske's expanded garage shop

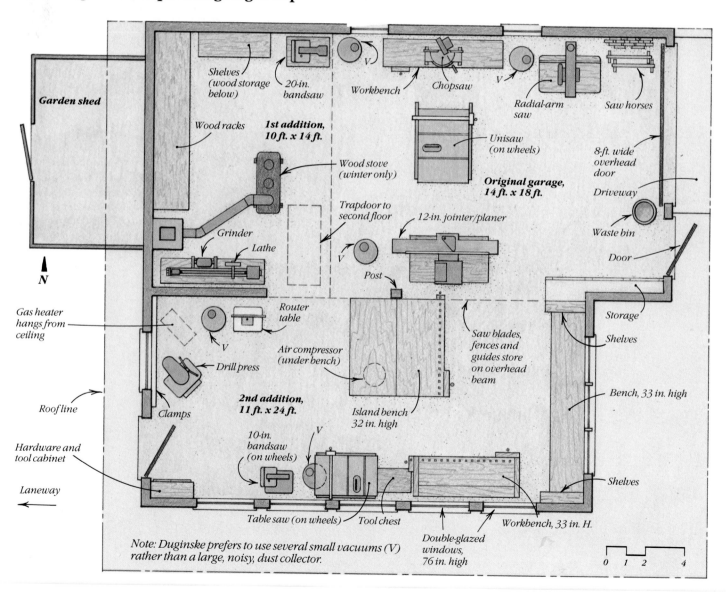

Note: Duginske prefers to use several small vacuums (V) rather than a large, noisy, dust collector.

sheathing has its own history, since it probably was sawn from "deadheads" that escaped the log drives on the Wisconsin River, which once fed the booming mills only blocks from Duginske's house. (One of his great-grandfathers died in one of those log drives.)

Heat and light   Sandwiched between Minnesota and Lake Michigan, Wisconsin receives the brunt of a northern winter. Heat loss and light deprivation are important issues almost everywhere, but they are critical in a northern workshop, where their prolonged effects can seriously influence physical safety, state of mind (fatigue and depression) and the quality of work.

Duginske's workshop is designed to weather the storm in comfort. The combination of a low north wall and long sloping roof, the high south wall of double-glazed windows and the concrete floor amount to a passive-solar design. The warmth is enhanced by the tongue-and-groove paneling in the bench room (drywall in the machine room) and plenty of fiberglass insulation throughout. Duginske augments the solar heat with a Sterling gas-fired heater and a small cast-iron wood stove, which he uses only in winter.

The wall of glass sacrifices a lot of potential storage space, but he gets more than a good view in return. In the winter, the sunlight streams in the large windows to the middle of the original garage floor. The concrete acts as a heat sink and is warm to the touch by the end of a sunny day. (It gets warmer, Duginske notes, if it's kept clean.) On all but the coldest days in December or January, the place hovers around 70°F, with little or no help from the stoves. During the summer months, when the sun is high in the sky, the 3-ft. overhang of the southern roof provides plenty of shade. Unlike some woodworkers I met, Duginske has no complaints about direct sunlight, although he wouldn't leave a piece of work sitting on the window bench for very long.

Turning on overhead bulbs around the shop, Duginske explains that the shop has got "the two most important prerequisites—lots of light and good cross-ventilation." (He considered painting the paneled walls and ceiling white, but if it were any brighter, he'd need to wear sunglasses in the bench room.) Fluorescent lights give him eye fatigue and headaches, so he installed 11 incandescent bulbs (250-watt) instead, each with its own pull. Strong cross-shop ventilation is easily accomplished by opening the garage door and the back door.

Shop layout   "When you look at a shop, it all seems natural," Duginske says, "but it takes a long time for things to evolve to a maximum efficiency." His layout provides for a partially isolated bench room and an easily accessible space for heavier machine operations. "It's actually two shops in one," he explains. "Everything I have is duplicated, except for the jointer/planer." He doesn't keep any full-time employees, but occasionally a brother or nephew will help out, in which case the separate areas can be dedicated to different functions.

Working alone in the shop, as he usually does, Duginske uses the original garage area for roughing out and fin-

When the weather is nice, Duginske opens the garage door and extends the workshop outside onto a recycled-brick driveway.

ishing; the wood-paneled addition is used mainly for bench work and finer machine operations. "The bandsaw is my favorite tool," he explains, "so it's nice to have two for different setups." (He had gained a third by the time of my last visit.) For a production run, he sets up one group of tools to make the final cuts, and uses the others to prepare stock. Hand planing and sharpening are done at the window bench, and the large island bench is used mainly for final preparation— cleaning, sanding and assembly.

The flexible layout allows Duginske to move things around within the shop and to work outside as much as possible. It's easy to cart a small bench and the chopsaw, bandsaw or table saw onto the driveway, and he simply wheels the table saw out of the way if he needs to use the space for photography. (He could even get a vehicle inside the garage if he had to.) "What I can't do in this space, I just won't do," he says.

The shop has come a long way in the last few years, and there is little Duginske would change, even if he were doing it all over from scratch. "In a perfect world, you'd have plumbing and a wood floor, but I think I'd have other options first," he says. Coming from the functional "old-school" perspective, Duginske's father thought he was nuts to put so much effort into the shop. "Are you going to live here?" his father asked. "But I haven't seen any shops I would trade it for," Duginske says. After working all day, he sometimes returns to the shop to enjoy a quiet beer in front of the wood stove. At such times, he often muses, "Boy, I could spend the rest of my life here."

Donald Kinnaman packs the contents of an entire workshop into a 90-sq. ft. metal shed next to his Phoenix, Arizona, home. He rolls the machines he needs out onto the covered patio behind his house and goes to work.

Donald Kinnaman's "vest-pocket" workshop

I've seen lots of compact shops, but in almost every one, the small size comes at a price. It leaves little or no room for power tools. Don Kinnaman's "vest-pocket" workshop is an exception. Kinnaman keeps a shop full of power tools in a 9-ft. by 10-ft. steel garden shed in Phoenix, Arizona. He packs the space as you would an overgrown toolbox, with a table saw, jointer, drill press, cut-off saw, lathe, bandsaw, air compressor, scrollsaw, router table, several stationary sanders and a workbench. A list of machinery and hand tools he gave me continues for 11 typewritten pages and covers everything from files and scrapers to waterstones. Until he recently completed the inventory, Kinnaman says, "I didn't realize I had so much stuff in such a little space."

Kinnaman couldn't build a boat or a dining-room table in his shop, but he wouldn't try. For any major operation, he simply rolls the required machinery onto the covered patio behind his house and is up and running in a matter of minutes. Even with all the equipment stowed inside the shop, he has complete access to the workbench, drill press and hand tools, and there's still some room to sit down. For greater comfort, he covered the shop floor and patio with indoor/outdoor carpeting.

There are two things that make this shop work. The first has to do with Kinnaman's choice of small, lightweight machinery, and the second is Phoenix itself. Like most small southwestern homes, Kinnaman's has no basement or usable attic space, so he naturally looked outdoors for his shop. And because of the warm, dry climate, he can work outside in comfort all year. Kinnaman's setup won't appeal to everyone, and it certainly won't work in Nome, Alaska—at least, not in the winter. But it makes a lot of sense for a part-time woodworker with more time than space and more ingenuity than money. What's more, you don't have to live in the Sunbelt to find indoor applications for Kinnaman's economical layout and storage tips.

A 9-in. combination Delta table saw/jointer is the only name-brand "professional" machine in the shop. It was also the first piece of equipment Kinnaman acquired and remains his favorite. A Duracraft lathe and a drill press came next, followed by a Black & Decker three-wheel bandsaw. He shops the discount catalogs for most of his machinery, such as the King Feng Fu drill press, which is an offshore clone of a Rockwell model. "It may be undersized," Kinnaman says, "but it does what I need it to do."

All the machines are mounted on shop-built stands with retractable casters, modeled after an illustration in Rosario Capotosto's *Woodworking Wisdom* (see the Bibliography on p. 208). Kinnaman modified the design of the casters by adding chained pins that lock the wheels in their rolling or stationary mode. The stands carry most of the blades, wrenches and accessories for each tool and are wired with a shutoff switch.

After 40 years of teaching high-school shop, you might expect Kinnaman to feel constrained by all this hobby equipment. But he expresses no regrets. To the contrary, he enjoys a "back-to-basics" philosophy and overcomes any limita-

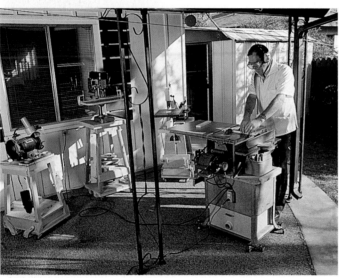

Donald Kinnaman's shop in a shed

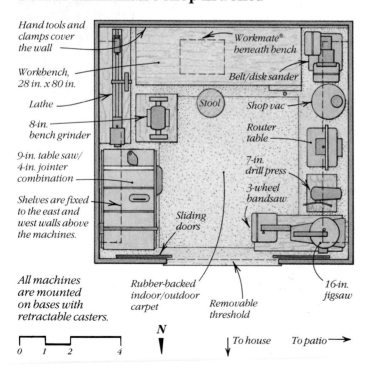

Hand tools and clamps cover the wall

Workbench, 28 in. x 80 in.

Lathe

8-in. bench grinder

9-in. table saw/ 4-in. jointer combination

Shelves are fixed to the east and west walls above the machines.

Workmate® beneath bench

Belt/disk sander

Stool

Shop vac

Router table

7-in. drill press

3-wheel bandsaw

Sliding doors

All machines are mounted on bases with retractable casters.

Rubber-backed indoor/outdoor carpet

Removable threshold

16-in. jigsaw

N

0 1 2   4

To house   To patio →

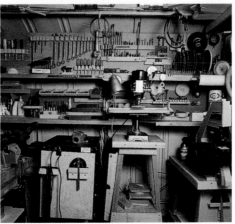

Kinnaman's power tools nest along the east and west walls of the shop, with a rolling workbench at the far end on the south wall (above). Hand tools are organized according to function on a plywood panel behind the bench. These spill over onto more shelves and panels on the west wall (at left), while routers, sanders and other hand-held power tools are assigned to their own compartments on the opposite wall (far left). The plywood-lined sliding doors carry a fire extinguisher, paper towels, extension cords and other shop accessories. Dowels, bandsaw blades and less frequently used paraphernalia are stored overhead on a shelf in the gable.

Dream Workshops 165

Something borrowed, something new

When it came to building his new shop, Arkansas conservator Rick Parker referred naturally to old forms. The distinctive architecture of a local turn-of-the-century railroad freight depot inspired the design. Most of the doors, windows and interior fittings came from other depots or local structures. Mixing historic references, Parker inlaid the entryway floor in a parquet pattern of 6-in. cherry squares with mitered beech borders, modeled after the parlor floor at Thomas Jefferson's Monticello. Parker did most of the work on the 1,000-sq. ft. superinsulated structure himself, and his reliance on secondhand materials enabled him to build the shop for about $8,500, not including the climate-control system or his own labor.

After doing floor plans for years, the actual construction took four months of full-time work and another six months part-time to complete. "I never dreamed it would take this long," Parker reports. "I wasn't ready for one-tenth of what I put up with," from skeptical building inspectors to termite-infested materials. But now that he's in, he adds, "it's going to be worth it."

Whether you lay out cash or sweat equity, you get what you pay for. And Peter Axtell didn't cut many corners when he built his Sonoma County furniture shop shown on the facing page. From the inside, clerestory windows and a vaulted, paneled ceiling (supported by huge laminated beams) make the place look more like a ski lodge or a small hockey arena. But the 1,500-sq. ft. space is loaded with

Rick Parker based his workshop on the old depot at Gentry, Arkansas, shown in the photo above. The modified-scissor truss he used for his roof provides more than 11 ft. of clearance from floor to ceiling in the center of the shop. The ⅞-in. elm paneling on the walls came from a neighbor's tree, which Parker felled, hauled to a mill and stored for more than a decade. 'It kills me to cut the openings for outlets,' he says.

high-end woodworking machinery, from a sliding table saw and a vertical panel saw to a large Hema bandsaw and several workstations. It also includes an 11-ft. by 12-ft. ventilated spray booth with a concrete floor, a drying room and a small office. The dust-collection pipe runs beneath the floor from every major machine to a cyclone collector located outside the building.

Axtell told me that there's little he would change if he had it to do over. "I don't know if I would build it as fancy, and I'd move the office to the house," he said, adding after a moment's pause, "...and build it about a 1,000 ft. larger."

tions of the equipment by developing all sorts of jigs and fixtures (which he calls "kinks") to enhance the capabilities of each machine. His designs for push sticks, featherboards and router jigs have been published in several magazines.

The shop structure itself is an Arrow Building Kit, which Kinnaman erected himself in one day, only 4 ft. from the side door of his house. To raise the shed door, which was only 65 in. to the header, he set the entire building on a 2x8 sill, caulked and fastened to the concrete slab with hanger bolts. The doors slide on an overhead track and are guided by a grooved threshold, which he made removable so it wouldn't obstruct the rolling equipment. The threshold is held in place with several more hanger bolts anchored in the slab. (He extended the sliding doors to fit the larger opening with 8-in. plywood panels, edged with a strip of hardwood to run in the threshold.) Three vertical 2x2s are screwed to each wall and the sills to support the interior shelves and tool panels; once the shelving was installed, the structure was stiffened considerably. (Kinnaman also erected another Arrow building next to the first to store wood and general overflow from the house.)

For power, Kinnaman ran a 12-2 grounded line from an empty circuit in the breaker box of his house. He wired an outlet on each wall (with two more behind the bench) and drove three 8-ft. long copper poles into the ground for additional lightning and short-circuit protection. Overhead, he suspended a twin-bulb fluorescent fixture in the center of the shop and added a couple of clip-on task lamps. Kinnaman grounded all his machinery with a separate wire, but ground-fault circuit interrupters (GFCIs or GFIs) would provide an extra measure of safety in an indoor-outdoor workshop.

I visited Kinnaman's shop in January, when the temperature was an almost chilly 65°F. But an uninsulated metal shed in Phoenix could become a solar oven in July, and I wondered how he kept from getting cooked. Kinnaman admitted that when it's 100°F in the shade, it's not much better inside the shop, but he plans to insulate the ceiling with Styrofoam, which will also reduce condensation, a more serious problem than heat. Eventually, he would like to pitch another roof above the shop to reflect the sun and carry off the rain, and perhaps add a breezeway that would tie the shop to the house. For now, he keeps his tools sprayed with WD-40 and covers the major machinery with plastic.

Kinnaman's tiny shop hasn't limited the size of his woodworking projects, which include all of his kitchen and bathroom cabinets. Hauling tools out to the patio and packing them away in the shop is as routine at home as it once was in school, but I wondered if Kinnaman didn't experience an occasional wave of claustrophobia, born of so much equipment and so little elbow room. "Nope, never," he said simply. "I can always work outside."

Peter Axtell's custom-built workshop in Sonoma County, California, was a great improvement on his previous shop in a three-car garage.

Bristling like a giant pincushion, Larry Smotroff's screwdriver rack is practical to use and pleasing to behold. Hung individually, Smotroff's collection of drivers, awls and assorted hand tools would cover most of a wall. Piled in drawers, they would be out of sight, out of mind and hard to find.

Storage

Every cubic inch of space is a miracle. —Walt Whitman, *Leaves of Grass*

Chapter 8

oodworkers are pack rats of the highest order. We hoard hand tools, wood, hardware, clamps, more wood and still more tools as if they were going out of style. (In the case of some woods, that's not far wrong.) In a throwaway society, we are also model recyclers, which requires even more storage space. Many woodworkers I know reuse, burn or give away all their scrap. Some operate a considerable salvage business in spare machine parts; quite a few others save their sawdust for the garden.

Given our obsession, it's no surprise that the woodworkers I met have come up with many clever storage solutions. Dozens of handy space-saving, organizational devices occupy the backgrounds of photo after photo in the previous chapters. These unsung racks, chests and other specialized containers help wring order out of chaos. Without them, the shops would be hopelessly overrun by clutter.

Storage occupies the foreground in this chapter. Here I've included some of the best storage contraptions I found. They fall in three categories—tools, hardware and wood—and may be further subdivided from there (e.g., lumber, sheet goods, shorts and odd stock). As wonderfully creative and practical as all these devices are, however, they are not final solutions. New storage problems, or old ones in new forms, will always crop up. In fact, you might even say that efficient storage only makes room for more stuff.

Tool cases

Michael Fortune's tool chest is a model of good planning and good organization, keys to success in any small space. As Fortune has moved from shop to shop, the chest has grown. The upper section was built first, in 1972, as a wall-hung cabinet for small measuring instruments, planes, chisels and the like. Ten years later Fortune added the bottom section to accommodate a burgeoning supply of hand-held power tools, as well as saws and larger planes, which hang on the doors. The midsection between the two cases holds a supply of frequently used hardware and a bin for goggles, masks and other safety gear. Fortune hung his original chest on the wall, but in a freestanding space you could mount more tools or a corkboard on the back.

The construction is simple, consisting of Baltic-birch plywood dadoed, glued and screwed together. (If he built it today, Fortune says, he'd put the case together with biscuit joints.) For added flexibility, Fortune made the shallow trays half the height of the drawers so that one drawer can be substituted for two trays or vice versa.

Michael Fortune's tool chest

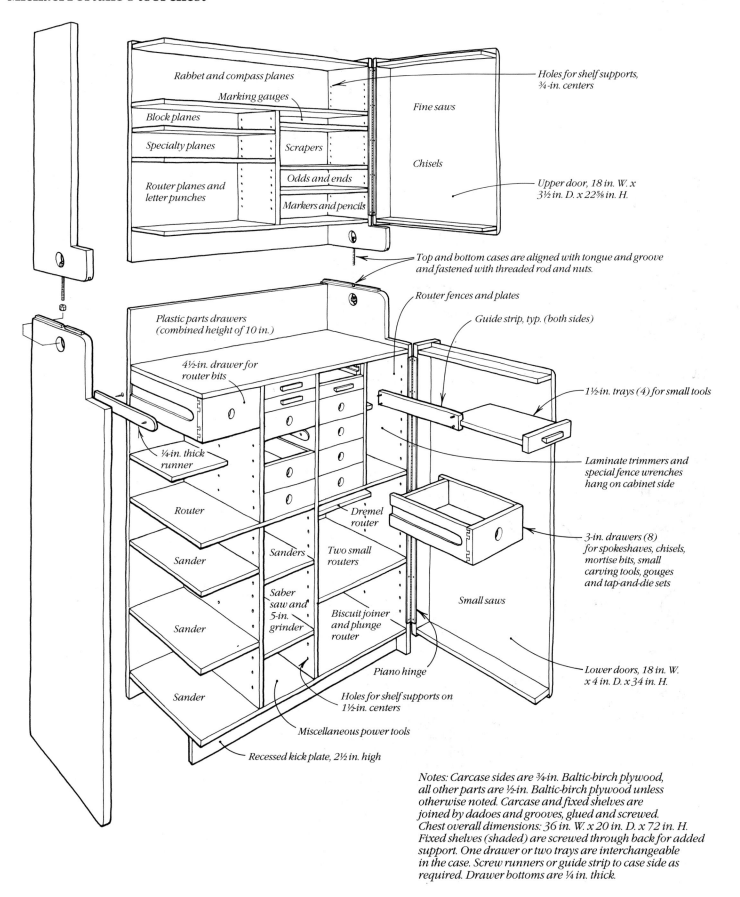

Rabbet and compass planes

Marking gauges

Block planes

Specialty planes

Router planes and letter punches

Scrapers

Odds and ends

Markers and pencils

Fine saws

Chisels

Holes for shelf supports, ¾-in. centers

Upper door, 18 in. W. x 3½ in. D. x 22⅝ in. H.

Top and bottom cases are aligned with tongue and groove and fastened with threaded rod and nuts.

Router fences and plates

Guide strip, typ. (both sides)

Plastic parts drawers (combined height of 10 in.)

4½-in. drawer for router bits

¼-in. thick runner

Router

Sander

Sander

Sander

Sanders

Saber saw and 5-in. grinder

Two small routers

Dremel router

Biscuit joiner and plunge router

Piano hinge

Holes for shelf supports on 1½-in. centers

Miscellaneous power tools

Recessed kick plate, 2½ in. high

1½-in. trays (4) for small tools

Laminate trimmers and special fence wrenches hang on cabinet side

3-in. drawers (8) for spokeshaves, chisels, mortise bits, small carving tools, gouges and tap-and-die sets

Small saws

Lower doors, 18 in. W. x 4 in. D. x 34 in. H.

Notes: Carcase sides are ¾-in. Baltic-birch plywood, all other parts are ½-in. Baltic-birch plywood unless otherwise noted. Carcase and fixed shelves are joined by dadoes and grooves, glued and screwed. Chest overall dimensions: 36 in. W. x 20 in. D. x 72 in. H. Fixed shelves (shaded) are screwed through back for added support. One drawer or two trays are interchangeable in the case. Screw runners or guide strip to case side as required. Drawer bottoms are ¼ in. thick.

Cabinetmaker Martha Collins
built these tool chests for herself and her
husband, luthier Richard Schneider.
They're about 72 in. high and 48 in. wide,
with a 17-in. deep top section and a 22-in.
bottom section. Both are made of oak—solid
white oak for the drawers and oak-veneered
plywood for the rest. Collins varied the
layout of drawers and shelves to suit the
demands of their respective occupations.
Her tool chest has plenty of open cubbies
for hand-held power tools; Schneider's is
loaded with shallow drawers to handle all
the specialized clamps, files and assorted
paraphernalia of the guitar-maker's trade.

Curtis Erpelding rarely devotes time to building workshop fixtures unless they're related to a particular job. But this tidy hand-tool cabinet, which he built around 1985, gets a lot of use. He has hung it between his bench and drill press in three successive workshops in and around Seattle. The drawers carry all manner of drill bits, countersinks, hole saws, router bits and other small tools. Erpelding stores sharpening stones and his collection of custom-made wooden planes and plane-making floats on the open shelves above the drawers. "If I hadn't made it," he says, "I'd still have things scattered all over."

Erpelding hung the doors on piano hinges for strength and recessed the shelves and drawers to allow room for squares and other flat tools on the inside of the doors. (He eventually decided to put the tools on the outside of the case instead, where they won't flop around.) The carcase is 36 in. tall, 24 in. wide and 16 in. deep inside and was built from some leftover red-oak plywood. The dovetailed drawers are made from local northwest cherry, and the quartersawn ash door frames surround vertical-grain Douglas-fir panels, which mimic the striated effect of the quartered ash.

A tool tote

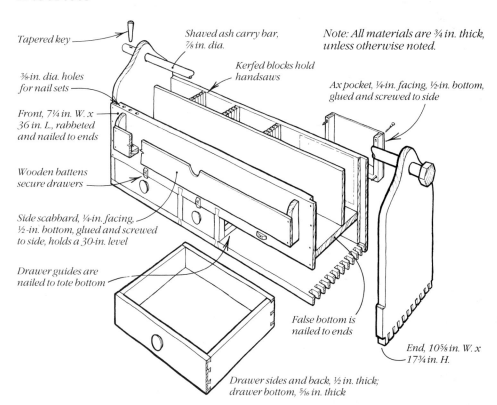

Tapered key

Shaved ash carry bar, ⅞ in. dia.

Note: All materials are ¾ in. thick, unless otherwise noted.

Kerfed blocks hold handsaws

⅜-in. dia. holes for nail sets

Ax pocket, ¼-in. facing, ½-in. bottom, glued and screwed to side

Front, 7¼ in. W. x 36 in. L., rabbeted and nailed to ends

Wooden battens secure drawers

Side scabbard, ¼-in. facing, ½-in. bottom, glued and screwed to side, holds a 30-in. level

Drawer guides are nailed to tote bottom

False bottom is nailed to ends

End, 10⅝ in. W. x 17¾ in. H.

Drawer sides and back, ½ in. thick; drawer bottom, ⁵⁄₁₆ in. thick

Peter Murkett's carpenter-style toolbox is as central to his workshop as any fancy tool chest or wall-hung cabinet. He built the box around 1975 to tote tools to the job, but he uses it inside the shop, too, where it rests on a pair of wall-mounted brackets alongside the bench. The box is made entirely of pine, except for the shaved ash handle, which has been broken and replaced several times.

"It's riddled with dovetails," Murkett says, "which pretty much have been obliterated with use." The dovetails may

have been overkill, but they've helped hold the box together under some serious loads. The drawers hold an impressive collection of small tools, including a spokeshave, several small planes, scrapers, screwdrivers, a compass and files, all sorts of measuring and marking instruments, a drill index, punches, allen wrenches, chisels and an awl. On the road, Murkett packs the open bin with saws, hammers and a mallet, large chisels, a staple gun, a chalkline, long tape measures, a glue bottle, a framing square, wrecking tools, wrenches and a "toad

stabber" (a drywall keyhole saw). Nail sets reside in drilled holes in the top of the box, and wooden scabbards on both sides carry a 30-in. level and a small hand ax.

"It's a ball breaker to carry," Murkett says, "but I've never broken a handle carrying it." He lifts the box with both hands, placed near the ends, and supports it with his knee while carrying it upstairs. "When I'm loading up after a job, the thing I think about most," he adds, "is at what point do I want to move the box and will it be a two-man carry?"

"The toolbox was the cabinetmaker's resume," Carlyle Lynch once told me. Indeed, a toolbox was Lynch's first woodworking project and it had the first key he ever owned. Jerry Blanchard, who teaches high-school wood and metal shop in Monterey, California, used Lynch's tool-chest design (available from Garrett Wade, see Sources of Supply on p. 210) as a point of departure in designing his own "resume." As Blanchard says, "it's not the same if you buy it from somebody else." The overall dimensions of Blanchard's chest were determined not by Lynch's plan, but by the length of his saws and the wood he had available. "I kind of have to see what the wood says first," he explains.

"I like things simple and solid," Blanchard continues, "engineered, if you like." The sides of the chest are single, $\frac{3}{16}$-in. thick Peruvian walnut boards, dovetailed at the corners and reinforced at the top and bottom with dovetailed 1-in. thick straps. The dovetails are reversed on the straps to resist any tendency for the sides to spread. The whole case is "glued and screwed to a fare-thee-well" with bronze fastenings and finished with exterior-grade Watco oil. The frame-and-panel top permits wood movement, but the solid bottom could present some problems. Blanchard has had no trouble — perhaps because of his stable climate or because he use well-seasoned wood and oiled it thoroughly. It would be safer however, to use plywood or to house the bottom in a rabbeted grove and allow space for expansion and contraction.

All but one of the removable sliding trays inside the chest are made of black walnut. (Blanchard had not finished the hinged tray covers when the photos were taken.) A stickler for details, Blanchard added an engraved name plate and a monogrammed hasp, and attached wheels to the bottom and silicon-bronze trunk handles to both ends so he could move the chest around.

"We've moved a lot, so everything that's important is in a case," Blanchard says. The tool chest sits next to the workbench in Blanchard's living room, which serves as a hobby shop when he's not at school. The chest is a tribute to Blanchard's childhood mentor, Rae Warren Phillips, the machinist and craftsman who cast the original Oscar awards. (Phillips worked in a barn and kept his own toolbox covered with saddle blankets; Blanchard's tool chest resides on a plush carpet and is covered with an heirloom quilt when not in use.) Blanchard recalls that, in the tradition of many old carpenters' chests, Phillips's toolbox was plain on the outside but had an extravagant interior, with complex geometric patterns of inlaid woods collected from around Southern California. "History means a lot to me," Blanchard says, noting that many of the tools in the trunk belonged to his father (who was a carpenter) or to his grandfather, and will someday belong to his kids.

Jerry Blanchard's traditional tool chest

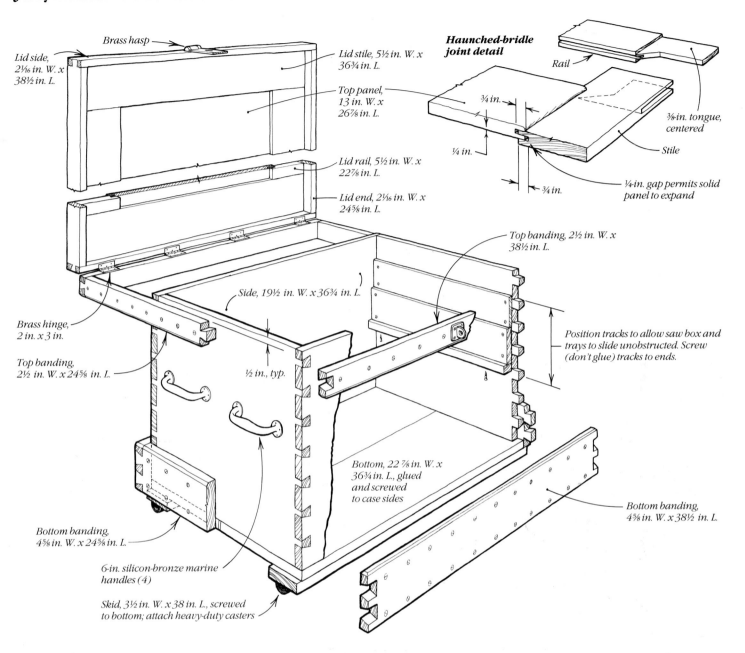

Brass hasp

Lid side, 2¹⁄₁₆ in. W. x 38½ in. L.

Lid stile, 5½ in. W. x 36¾ in. L.

Haunched-bridle joint detail

Rail

Top panel, 13 in. W. x 26⅞ in. L.

¾ in.

¾ in.

¼ in.

⅜-in. tongue, centered

Stile

Lid rail, 5½ in. W. x 22⅞ in. L.

Lid end, 2¹⁄₁₆ in. W. x 24⅝ in. L.

¼-in. gap permits solid panel to expand

Top banding, 2½ in. W. x 38½ in. L.

Side, 19½ in. W. x 36¾ in. L.

Brass hinge, 2 in. x 3 in.

Top banding, 2½ in. W. x 24⅝ in. L.

½ in., typ.

Position tracks to allow saw box and trays to slide unobstructed. Screw (don't glue) tracks to ends.

Bottom, 22 ⅞ in. W. x 36¾ in. L., glued and screwed to case sides

Bottom banding, 4⅝ in. W. x 38½ in. L.

Bottom banding, 4⅝ in. W. x 24⅝ in. L.

6-in. silicon-bronze marine handles (4)

Skid, 3½ in. W. x 38 in. L., screwed to bottom; attach heavy-duty casters

Saw box and trays

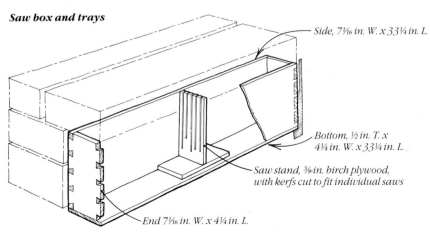

Side, 7¹⁄₁₆ in. W. x 33¼ in. L.

Bottom, ½ in. T. x 4¼ in. W. x 33¼ in. L.

Saw stand, ⅜-in. birch plywood, with kerfs cut to fit individual saws

End 7¹⁄₁₆ in. W. x 4¼ in. L.

Notes: Banding is screwed to the chest side and ends with #8 by 1½-in. flathead brass screws. All materials are solid wood ⅞ in. thick, unless otherwise noted. Saw box and trays are the same dovetail construction: solid ½-in. thick stock is used throughout, except for ⁵⁄₁₆-in. thick tray bottom, glued and screwed in place.

Mac Campbell's rolling tool chest (below) is a valuable asset in his crowded basement shop—he can roll it right up to his work or move it out of the way with a strong shove. The chest is 23 in. deep, 30 in. wide and 50 in. high, and has room for eight 4¾-in. high drawers, which hold most of Campbell's collection of bits, planes, chisels, files and rasps. Some of the most frequently used router bits, chisels and screwdrivers are mounted in racks on the top and one side of the case. (Marking gauges hang on the opposite side.)

The rolling chest is the result of Campbell's first "bank job"; he rescued the walnut-front teller drawers on their way to the dump. The overall construction is simple: "Just a couple of pieces of plywood wrapped around the drawers," Campbell says. The interior drawer dividers, which once separated $5, $10 and $20 bills, are removable, allowing Campbell to organize the space to fit his tools. With the locks removed from the drawer fronts, the empty holes serve as convenient finger pulls.

Handsaw rack

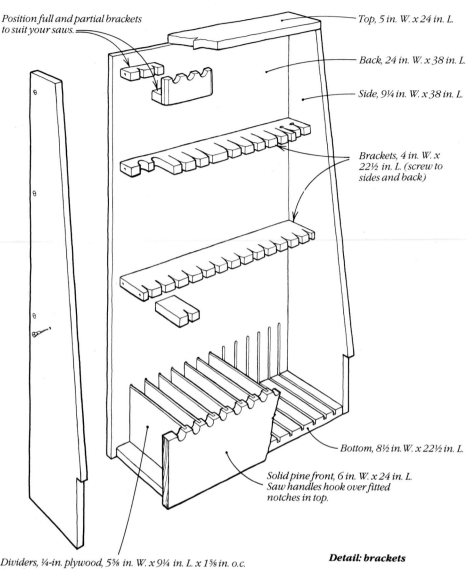

Position full and partial brackets to suit your saws.

Top, 5 in. W. x 24 in. L.

Back, 24 in. W. x 38 in. L.

Side, 9¼ in. W. x 38 in. L.

Brackets, 4 in. W. x 22½ in. L. (screw to sides and back)

Bottom, 8½ in. W. x 22½ in. L.

Solid pine front, 6 in. W. x 24 in. L. Saw handles hook over fitted notches in top.

Dividers, ¼-in. plywood, 5⅝ in. W. x 9¼ in. L. x 1⅝ in. o.c. Dividers separate saw handles and are housed in ⅜-in. dadoes in the front, bottom and back.

Note: All parts are made of ¾-in. plywood, glued, nailed and screwed throughout, unless otherwise noted.

Detail: brackets

Cut ⅛-in. wide saw kerfs to hold saw blades; chamfer for easy entry.

Handsaws can be tough to store, yet their teeth are just as easily dulled as any plane blade or chisel. They take up a lot of valuable space if they're hung flat on the wall, and they're difficult to squeeze into a small cabinet. To solve this problem efficiently, Clifford Metting built this benchtop saw stand, which protects and presents his collection of 21 assorted handsaws in a compact space 24 in. wide by 38 in. high. To make the notches for the saw handles, Metting bored a row of holes in a pine board, then ripped it in half and rounded the semicircular scallops with a file. He reinforced the horizontal brackets that support the sawblades with a screw between each pair of slots driven from the back side of the case.

If the toolbox is a microcosm of the workshop, it's no wonder that so many of them are bursting at the seams. "Basically, this is my shop," Luca Valentino says, patting his backpack toolbox with one hand and a Black & Decker Workmate® with the other. Inspired by a camping trip in the Grand Canyon, Valentino built the box shown above in 1978 and bolted it to an aluminum Camp Trails pack frame, which transfers most of the load to his hips, rather than to his shoulders or his arms. A handle on top and casters below enable him to roll it around his house and shop in New York City. (The load is hard on the casters; he's gone through four sets.) On the road, Valentino lays the toolbox gently in the back of his station wagon. "Things rattle around, but they don't fall out," he says. "And when I stand it up again everything basically falls back into place."

The case is made of ¾-in. oak-veneer plywood joined with splined miters at the corners, and the back is ¼-in. plywood. The door is secured with L-shaped knife hinges, a touch-latch and a barrel cabinet lock. The drawers are built of ½-in. Baltic-birch plywood, with mahogany-veneered fronts and ¼-in. plywood bottoms, which slide in dadoes in the case sides and partitions. Drawer design is sturdy and consumes no

extra space in the box—the bottom is simply glued and nailed to the sides and back and to a shallow rabbet in the front.

The dimensions and layout of the box are determined mainly by its contents. In addition to the small bits, measuring tools, sharpening stones and the like, which fit in the drawers, the box holds Valentino's favorite 22-in. 1902 Bailey jointer plane and is wide enough to carry a framing square. The seemingly bottomless bottom drawer carries at least 16 files, a doweling jig, a mallet, a Yankee push drill and roughing chisels. "It gets to be quite a process fitting everything in," he says, "but it's satisfying to know that everything's got a place."

This is one backpack I wouldn't tote to the Grand Canyon, and the kit is still growing. Valentino recently added the hinged side panel (shown in the photo above) to carry saws. With the toolbox on his back, Valentino's bathroom scale tops 300 lb.—about half pack and half him. Since the box spends most of its time in one place, he has considered hanging it on the wall, where it would be more convenient to use and he wouldn't risk a hernia every time he hits the trail.

As a construction coordinator for the film industry, Martin Bernstein has built everything in his shop to travel—most of it in large rolling plywood packing chests. But Bernstein keeps a small selection of his most frequently used hand tools in the telephone-lineman's case shown below. The indestructible hard-shell exterior protects the contents, which are tucked away in canvas pockets in the lid and on the interior divider. The divider lifts up to reveal a deeper well in the bottom for larger tools.

Tools on the wall

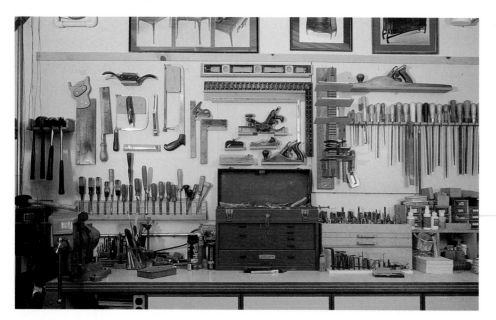

Everyone hangs tools on the wall, but rarely with the attention to detail that is reflected in Roger Heitzman's shop. Close examination of the photo at left reveals that the plywood shelves beneath each plane are relieved to eliminate wear and tear from contact with the cutter. As Heitzman notes, "I like 'em razor sharp."

The "reference library" of shapes provided by Norm Vandal's 19th-century molding planes (below) inspires and informs his reproduction furniture and architectural woodwork. In the almost two decades that he's been in business, Vandal has bought, sold and bartered truckloads of antique molding planes, keeping some of the finest for his own collection.

Free-hanging tool shelves

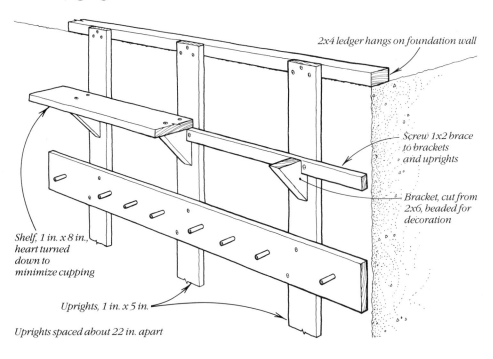

2x4 ledger hangs on foundation wall

Screw 1x2 brace to brackets and uprights

Bracket, cut from 2x6, beaded for decoration

Shelf, 1 in. x 8 in., heart turned down to minimize cupping

Uprights, 1 in. x 5 in.

Uprights spaced about 22 in. apart

Rob Tarule has moved his shop six times in the last 15 years, and in the process has solved one of the dilemmas of most basement workshops: how to hang shelves a concrete or cinder-block wall. Tarule screws them to a simple frame that hangs from the top of the foundation, so he needn't bore holes in the concrete or use special anchors. The weight of the tools keeps the free-hanging shelves securely in place, yet they can be moved easily to another location. Tarule makes his shelves and brackets from standard-dimension lumber and assembles them with drywall screws. (The size of the lumber may be varied for light or heavy loads, and the width of the triangular shelf-supports is determined by the width of the shelves.) At last count, Tarule had seven such units around his shop, holding everything from planes and chisels to saws.

Bob Stocksdale's swivel pipe rack (shown at left) keeps a wide range of bits within easy reach of the drill press. The horizontal pipe that holds the drill indexes swings on a threaded right-angle elbow, and the rack is screwed to the wall with a standard pipe flange.

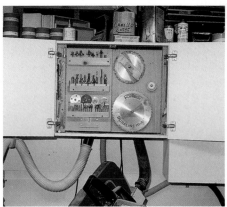

A double set of doors (above) provides ample room to hang sawblades and shaper bits in Randall Ores's California workshop. The interior plywood panels swing open on piano hinges to gain access to more bit shelves (on the left) and dowels (on the right), which hold the blades. (Photo by Scott Arfsten.)

Clamps

Clamps, like other hand tools, live on the wall in many workshops. Hanging his clamps was one of the first projects Bob Allen undertook when he set up his new workshop in Raleigh, North Carolina. Allen's open layout (shown at right) makes it easy to find the right clamp in a hurry, but to speed the process, he also marked each clamp with its maximum clamping distance. (Photo by Bob Allen.)

Allen's layout is attractive if you have the space, but clamps may be needed anywhere in the shop, wherever the action is. For that reason, a lot of woodworkers store their clamps on rolling carts. Many clamp carts hold one or two types of clamps well, but Ken Bishop's rolling clamp caddy seems as comfortable with long pipe and bar clamps as with wooden handscrews and small C-clamps. Bishop's caddy (far right) is built from standard 2x4 lumber, mounted on a plywood base and 2-in. casters. All the horizontal components, which carry the clamps, are 24 in. long. The plastic bucket contains an assortment of hardwood glue blocks. (Photo by Ken Bishop.)

Robert Markee, of Iowa City, designed the rotary clamp rack shown in the drawing at right to hang from the joists of his workshop ceiling. "It's nothing but a lazy Susan, hung from the top," he explains. Markee has four of them in his shop, two filled with clamps (93 on each one, at last count) and the others draped with hammers, screwdrivers, wrenches and various other hand tools. The rack is suspended by bolts through the top and bottom of the central conduit, and is held in place by the weight of the tools. "Heavens," Markee says, "I think I've got 50 lb. on there!"

Clamp racks don't get much simpler than Lewis Judy's galvanized clamp can (far right). Judy bored concentric rings of 1-in. dia. holes in a plywood disc and jammed it inside the top of a garbage can to receive bar clamps. He spaced the holes about 3 in. apart, staggering them as they radiate out from the center. The bottom of the can is filled with sawdust to protect it from the long bars. "I don't know how many it holds," Judy says, "but I can't lift it."

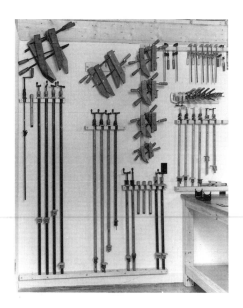

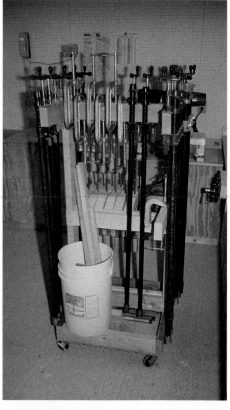

A rotary tool rack

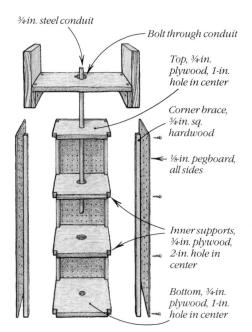

¾-in. steel conduit

Bolt through conduit

Top, ¾-in. plywood, 1-in. hole in center

Corner brace, ¾-in. sq. hardwood

⅛-in. pegboard, all sides

Inner supports, ¾-in. plywood, 2-in. hole in center

Bottom, ¾-in. plywood, 1-in. hole in center

Assemble pegboard box with glue and screws

Lazy-Susan bearing (3 in. or 4 in.) screwed to rack bottom

¾-in. plywood washer, same size as bearing, fits between conduit bolt and bearing

Bolt through conduit

Note: Conduit may be suspended from a 6-in. wide plywood crosspiece between ceiling joists, as shown, or though-bolted directly to the joist.

Hardware

You're short one screw, the hardware store is closed and you wish you'd bought a box on the last trip to town. But how much stuff can you afford to keep on hand and where can you store it so that you have a reasonable chance of finding it again? The answer depends on how much you're willing to spend and how long you're willing to wait. Here are a number of solutions that range from simple to elaborate.

Don Anderson, of Sequim, Washington, stores staples, tacks and other small hardware in a rack of film cans (shown at right). He glues or otherwise fastens a sample of the contents to the lid of each can. The Masonite trays stand on three ¾-in. long dowels, which keep the containers from falling out when the trays are placed on the bench. (Photo by Ross Hamilton.)

Harold Payson installed a few rows of angled shelves (shown at left) between the peeled-log studs of his Maine workshop to hold boxes of screws and bolts at an easy-to-read angle.

Using old cafeteria trays for shelves, Michael Fortune built two plywood racks to provide a home for wayward hardware. The trays slide completely out of the rack (shown below), and their shallow depth makes it easy to scavenge odds and ends of screws, nuts and bolts, organized roughly according to type. Likewise, Fortune's wall-mounted plywood rack (at left) helps keep many different grades and sizes of sandpaper readily available.

Bruce Lee Gross keeps more hardware than many hardware stores in these three reinforced plywood trunks. I visited Gross behind the scenes at a sound stage in New York, where he was the "set dresser" for Spike Lee's movie "Mo' Better Blues." Considering the size of Gross's boxes, you would think he'd never run out of hardware, and that's precisely the idea. Gross explained that with all the high-priced help on the set, he can't afford to be short a roll of tape or the right-sized staple in the middle of a shoot. "Nobody takes 'no' for an answer in this business," he says. "The correct answer is 'give me five minutes.'"

Lumber and plywood

At last count Lewis Judy was sitting on about 60,000 board feet of local walnut, stacked in flitch sequence in several metal sheds around his Oregon workshop. (This particular shed holds only 15,000 board feet.) Judy mills most of his own furniture wood from salvaged trees that would otherwise wind up in the stove, and he dries it in one of two Ebac kilns. The gravel floor of his metal woodshed is covered with a plastic vapor barrier, and the pile rests on 6x6 sleepers placed on 2-ft. centers, with the boards separated by 1x1 kiln-dried stickers. The shed has a continuous roof vent, and Judy keeps the doors open and air moving to reduce fungal activity.

These heavy-duty lumber racks (above) consume one wall of Mark Duginske's Wisconsin workshop. Duginske designed the shelf supports around a windfall supply of ⅛-in. thick galvanized brackets, which he extended with two strips of perforated angle iron. To install the racks, he bolted the brackets to the vertical 2x6 braces and lag-screwed the braces to the wall studs on 2-ft. centers. Finally, he ripped two 4x8 sheets of ¾-in. plywood in thirds and used the 16-in. wide strips to make the shelves.

A wall-mounted lumber rack

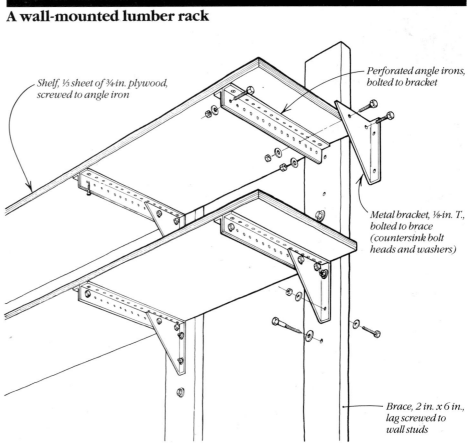

Shelf, ⅓ sheet of ¾-in. plywood, screwed to angle iron

Perforated angle irons, bolted to bracket

Metal bracket, ⅛-in. T., bolted to brace (countersink bolt heads and washers)

Brace, 2 in. x 6 in., lag screwed to wall studs

Roger Heitzman stores most of his lumber on pipe racks, lag-screwed to the studs of his California workshop wall. The 18-in. long sections of iron pipe (1⁵⁄₁₆ in. o.d.) slip into a three-layer lumber sandwich, nailed together from both sides and lag-screwed to the studs on 32-in. centers along the wall. Heitzman used standard 2x4 and 2x3 lumber and planed down the center strips to match the outside diameter of the pipe. He cut a 2° angle on the ends of the center strips, above and below the pipe, so wood sits more securely on the rack and the load is effectively transferred to the wall. "They're probably level now, with the full weight of the wood," Heitzman notes, "but it's held up to an earthquake."

Pipe rack

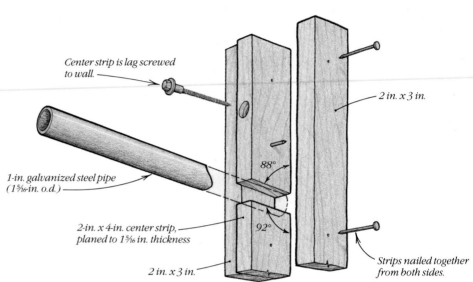

Center strip is lag screwed to wall.

1-in. galvanized steel pipe (1⁵⁄₁₆-in. o.d.)

2-in. x 4-in. center strip, planed to 1⁵⁄₁₆ in. thickness

2 in. x 3 in.

2 in. x 3 in.

88°

92°

Strips nailed together from both sides.

Richard Starr used 6x6 fir uprights and 1¾-in. thick oak support arms for the lumber rack in his middle-school workshop. The arms are attached to the uprights by a mortise-and-tenon joint, with a ½-in. shoulder top and bottom. Two drawbored 1-in. dia. dowel pins pull the joint together. To keep the rack in place, Starr lag-screwed the top of each upright into the rafters and nailed a 2x6 pad to the bottom of the uprights and the concrete floor.

As an afterthought, Starr added a long tapered wedge on top of each horizontal arm, as shown in the photo, which makes the rack a little safer. (The proper way to do it, he explains, would be to angle the arms or to shape them with a taper.) "You have to be careful with open racks," he explains. "I keep the kids back when I'm taking lumber off." The wood comes off the rack parallel to the radial-arm saw and in position for crosscutting. "When I'm working with the kids," Starr says, "it's really important to get wood out to them quickly and efficiently."

An adjustable rack

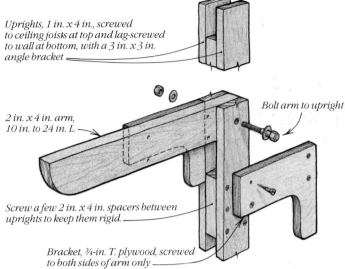

Uprights, 1 in. x 4 in., screwed to ceiling joists at top and lag-screwed to wall at bottom, with a 3 in. x 3 in. angle bracket

2 in. x 4 in. arm, 10 in. to 24 in. L.

Bolt arm to upright

Screw a few 2 in. x 4 in. spacers between uprights to keep them rigid.

Bracket, ¾-in. T. plywood, screwed to both sides of arm only

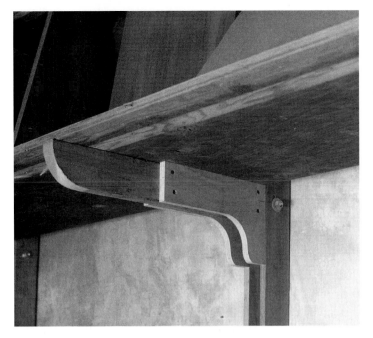

Wood-storage requirements are volatile in many workshops. They may increase dramatically with the arrival of a load of lumber or be depleted quickly at the end of a job. When he's making a batch of chairs, John Nyquist clears his racks of lumber (shown above), moves the shelves up and puts the chairs underneath. A single bolt holds the horizontal arm to the uprights, and the load is carried almost entirely by the plywood brackets screwed to both sides of the arm.

"It's about the cheapest and easiest cantilevered rack you can make," Nyquist says. The Douglas-fir uprights are screwed into the ceiling joists, which they straddle at the top of the rack, and the bottom of each upright is screwed to the wall with a 3x3 right-angle metal bracket. (Nyquist uses screws and bolts throughout, so the unit can be taken apart and reshuffled.) A few 2x4 spacer blocks between the uprights keep them rigid. Nyquist has a variety of support arms, from 10 in. to 24 in. long, depending on the load. "I had a good 500 ft. of red oak on one set of three brackets. So it had a good test," he says.

Free-standing plywood rack

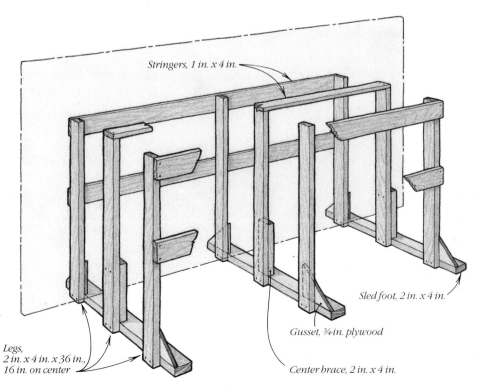

Stringers, 1 in. x 4 in.

Sled foot, 2 in. x 4 in.

Gusset, ¾-in. plywood

Legs, 2 in. x 4 in. x 36 in., 16 in. on center

Center brace, 2 in. x 4 in.

In most shops I visited, plywood is stacked against the wall, behind a machine or anywhere there are a few free inches of space. But C. Wayne Joslin's rack (at left) will keep full and partial sheets of plywood and other flat stock upright anywhere in the shop, without the aid of a wall or other prop. It would be handy to have near the saw, where you could load it up with sheets before a job.

Shorts and odd stock

Short stock is the nemesis of most workshops: The stuff seems too good to throw away, but impossible to keep straight. To organize the short stock in his Vermont workshop, Frank Perron built the rack shown below almost entirely from scrap . He assembled the shelves first, using two 2x6 main braces, a ⅝-in. piece of plywood and three 1x4 cross braces, shot together with drywall screws. (Perron substituted 2x6s for the 1x4s below the bottom shelf.) Next, he added the 2x3 uprights and sheathed the two sides of the bin that face the corner with ¼-in. plywood. Finally, he added a few extra pieces of lumber and plywood (and vertical 1x3s shown in the drawing) to keep the short chunks from falling out. Larger pieces of plywood are stored between the rack and the wall. Despite all the storage space, Perron told me, "I've got to get down there and hoe it out. You save every little jewel." (Photo by Sandor Nagyszalanczy.)

A three-way scrap-wood rack

Closed side (optional), ¼-in. plywood

Upright, 2 in. x 3 in. x 76½ in.

Main brace, 2 in. x 6 in. x 48 in.

Cross brace, 1 in. x 4 in. x 36 in.

Bin wall, ½-in. plywood, 11 in. x 39 in.

78 in.

Side slats, 1 in. x 3 in. x 63½ in.

Shelf, ⅝-in. plywood, 36 in. x 48 in.

Footing, 2 in. x 6 in. x 39 in.

Note: All parts, dimensional lumber and plywood, are fastened with drywall screws.

A multipurpose wood rack

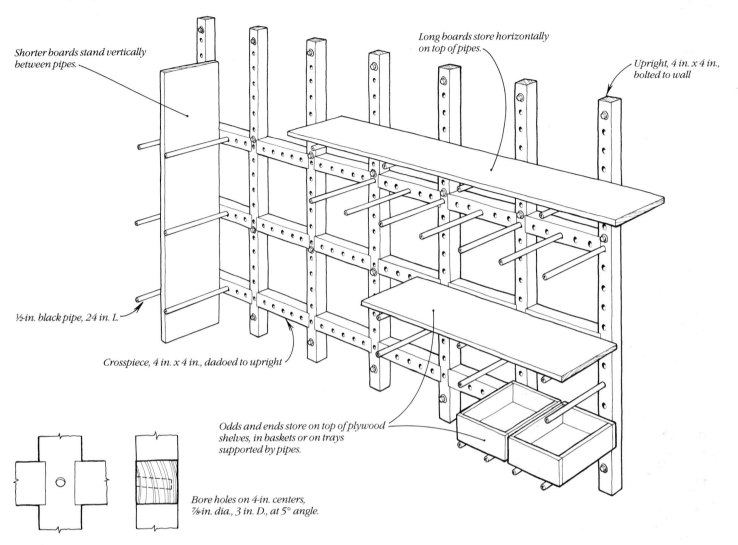

Shorter boards stand vertically between pipes.

Long boards store horizontally on top of pipes.

Upright, 4 in. x 4 in., bolted to wall

½-in. black pipe, 24 in. L.

Crosspiece, 4 in. x 4 in., dadoed to upright

Odds and ends store on top of plywood shelves, in baskets or on trays supported by pipes.

Bore holes on 4-in. centers, ⅞-in. dia., 3 in. D., at 5° angle.

To keep his unruly lumber pile in check, C. Wayne Joslin installed this multipurpose wood rack in the furnace room of his Ontario basement. Joslin attached a 4x4 grid to the wall, riddled with 3-in. deep holes, bored 5° above horizontal in all the uprights and stringers. The more than 200 holes (on 4-in. centers) give Joslin great flexibility in positioning the 24-in.

lengths of ½-in. black-iron pipe that he uses for shelf supports and dividers. Long boards are placed horizontally on the pipes, and short boards (up to 6 ft. long) stand upright between the pipes. Odds and ends and carving blocks are stored on plywood shelves or in wire baskets and old bakery trays, which rest on the pipe supports.

A well-known photograph of George Nakashima shows the master fondling huge flitches of live-edge lumber stacked on end in his Pennsylvania studio. Although several woodworkers I met spoke nostalgically of Nakashima's vertical-storage arrangement, the fact is that very few of them can spare the room. It may be easier to leaf through a pile of vertical lumber in search of the right color or ideal grain match, but it takes up a lot of space, and you need a tall ceiling to accommodate long boards.

Short stock is a different story. Small pieces are more easily buried in a horizontal pile, and a surprising volume of short stock can fit in a narrow vertical space. Robert Weisman stores his short stock on end between the exposed studs of his basement bench room in Ann Arbor, Michigan (photo at right). The material is organized according to length and held in place with ¾-in. dowels, which snap into gripper clips screwed to the studs. If he wants a 3-ft. board, he simply goes to the area that's 3 ft. high and leafs through the stack in search of the appropriate width, thickness and species. "It's space that would otherwise be wasted," Weisman notes, "and as a former submariner, I can't stand wasted space." (Photo by Darragh Humphrey Weisman.)

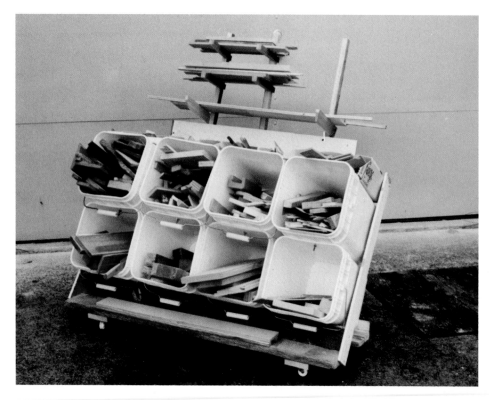

Don Anderson assembled a rolling cart for short stock from eight 5-gallon square plastic tubs he picked up at a local hot-dog stand. The tubs are bolted together and braced at both ends with a strip of ¼-in. plywood, 3 in. wide. A plywood shelf on top provides extra room for longer boards. (Photo by Don Anderson.)

A dowel-storage can

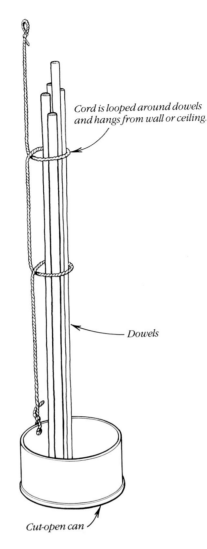

Cord is looped around dowels and hangs from wall or ceiling.

Dowels

Cut-open can

Long, skinny material—dowels, moldings or odd bits of metal rod—call for some innovative storage solutions. Carlyle Lynch just stuffed these items between the ceiling joists of his basement shop and held them in place with a couple of nailed-on straps, as shown in the photo at left.

Don Anderson's cord-and-can arrangement (drawing, left) is another low-tech solution to this common problem. The weight of the contents keeps the looped cord tight when the rig is hanging; lift the can slightly and the cord may be easily loosened.

C. Wayne Joslin went to a bit more trouble to devise the freestanding dowel rack (drawing, far left), which is filled with 80 3¼-in. dia. cardboard tubes from the center of IBM photocopier-paper rolls. Each tube is 8½ in. long, and Joslin stacked and glued them end-to-end to make four rows in the rack, from 8½ in. to 34 in. high.

Dowel rack

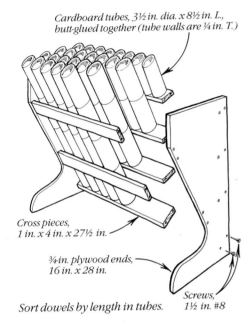

Cardboard tubes, 3½ in. dia. x 8½ in. L., butt-glued together (tube walls are ¼ in. T.)

Cross pieces, 1 in. x 4 in. x 27½ in.

¾-in. plywood ends, 16 in. x 28 in.

Sort dowels by length in tubes.

Screws, 1½ in. #8

You think you've got storage problems... Several woodworkers I visited had storage problems that almost defy description, if not solution, but none matched Tom Phillips's problem. "I am my woodpile," he told me, sitting atop the inventory of "twigs" in his Adirondack workshop. The sprawling pile is 6 ft. high, 12 ft. wide and 20 ft. long and takes up part of a large garage adjacent to Phillips's twig-furniture shop in upstate New York. "I carry a running inventory in my head," Phillips says, "and much of this stock is still on the stump."

Cliff Friedlander rigged up portable sidefeed and outfeed support for the table saw in his compact California cabinet shop. Long pieces slide along the top edge of a board mounted on bracket feet; the board sits on a nearby sanding/assembly table. To pick up the outfeed material, Friedlander installed a series of multidirectional, steel-ball transfers (large bearings) on top of an adjustable horse.

Fixtures

Triumphs over time and space... —Albert Tennyson, *Locksley Hall Sixty Years After*

Chapter 9

 ike any well-made tool, a good shop seems to improve with use. The structure, benches, machinery, tools and storage racks are just the beginning. Inspired by new projects or new ideas, you'll constantly make improvements that will help you work quicker or better, or in less space. Many of these improvements can be gathered under the general heading of fixtures—accessories and gadgets that fine-tune a machine or the workshop in general.

Many of us comb tool catalogs for accessories, and you can plow almost as much money into souping up some tools as you paid for the tools themselves. Saws alone benefit from fences, outfeed tables, push sticks, dust collectors, blade guards and crosscut sleds. Fortunately, you can make many of these and dozens of other fixtures yourself—without spending a lot of money.

This chapter includes some of the most interesting and useful homemade fixtures I found in my workshop visits. Some are simple and others are quite complex, but the total cost of the materials required to build them all probably amounts to less than that of a good table saw—a small price to pay for the added convenience and capacity they will add to your shop.

Each of these fixtures reflects the needs and resources of the person who built it. Don't hesitate to adapt them to suit yourself and use them to fine-tune your own dream. In a sense, the whole workshop is a jig or fixture that you constantly modify. Have fun exploring the boundaries.

Sharpening

Japanese waterstones are replacing India and Arkansas oilstones in more and more workshops. They cut quickly, and water is a lot cleaner than oil. The stones are usually submerged in a "pond" (a container of water) when not in use and may be removed for sharpening. I found several different sharpening setups designed for waterstones.

Jeff Elliott built a wooden carriage to hold three stones inside a plastic container (shown below) with a tight-fitting lid to keep out dust. The stones are held in position—either flat or on edge—in notches cut in the carriage. (Elliott keeps the water level at, or slightly above, the surface of the stones, and he adds a dash of dish detergent to discourage mold.)

Pieces of laminated particleboard provide a smooth platform for the rolling blade guide; the height of the platform determines the angle of the bevel.

Roger Heitzman keeps his waterstones in a Micarta box stored on a sliding shelf beneath his bench. The Plexiglas lid is sealed tightly with a foam gasket and two thumb latches to keep water in and dust out. Each stone has its own wooden frame, which is submerged when not in use and rests on a narrow ledger along the back of the box when Heitzman sharpens. Heitzman machined the Micarta with a router and butt-joined the box with machine screws—but without any sealant or adhesive. To his surprise, it never leaked. "I knew it was a good fit," he says, "but I expected it to leak a little."

Mark Duginske also stores his waterstones in a plastic pond, but he removes them to his workbench for sharpening. To protect the bench and to keep the stone from sliding around, Duginske made a plywood sharpening platform covered with a piece of 240-grit wet-or-dry sandpaper. The plywood is varnished, and the sandpaper is attached with double-sided tape. A ledger strip on the bottom of the plywood clamps in the face vise of the bench. When the stones get worn, Duginske trues them roughly on the concrete shop floor and then smooths them on his sharpening platform, using another sheet of sandpaper.

For all the mystique of sharpening—the bevel guides, sharpening "systems" and so forth—there's no substitute for experience. Japanese timber framer Makoto Imai does his sharpening on the floor, with but a few rudimentary aids—an elevated platform for the stone, a tub of water and a strong directional light.

Every now and then, you'll have to true your blades and chisels on a grinder. The blade guide on most grinders pivots to allow for adjustment of the bevel angle, but Curtis Erpelding varies the bevel by raising and lowering his grinder (shown at left) instead—the more the stone protrudes from the slot in the bench, the steeper the angle. The benchtop provides a large flat surface, which is ideal for sharpening spokeshave irons and other small blades securely. Two L-shaped brackets attached to the end of the bench support the grinder. The motor platform is hinged to the rear bracket. Erpelding moves the grinder up or down by turning two short lengths of threaded rod that pass through T-nuts in the forward bracket and bear on the underside of the platform. He "jam-nutted" a wing nut on the end of each rod to give him something to grip. "There's probably a much more elegant way of doing it," Erpelding says, and he has considered a sliding-wedge arrangement. "But it works," he adds, "and with the material at hand."

Robert Weisman's rolling sharpening station carries four grinders on top—a 3,450-rpm bench grinder (at the right corner of the cart, in the photo at right), a slow, 10-in. waterstone grinder (its white wheel is visible at the rear of the cart), a 1-in. by 42-in. belt sander (at the left rear of the cart) and a 1,725-rpm Baldor grinder (in the foreground). Drawers below house extra wheels and stones. Weisman redesigned the bench grinder's tool rests to make use of the miter gauge from the waterstone grinder, which helps maintain a square sharpening angle. The sliding wooden rest at left handles turning tools. (Photo by Darragh Humphrey Weisman.)

Years ago, when I worked in a shop without electricity, I had a hand-cranked grinder. It did the job, and I liked the slow speed, but I found it irritating to hold the tool with one hand and crank with the other. Fred Matlack converted his hand-cranked grinder to foot power by adding a rope and a hinged pedal. He gets the wheel going with the crank, then keeps it going with the pedal. The arrangement frees both hands to guide the tool.

Benches and horses

Below are two folding benches that were designed for tight spaces. Both are made of 2x4s and plywood. In Kent, Washington, R.L. Tunnard's flip-top bench opens up to form an 18-in. high by 4-ft. wide assembly table (shown below left). James E. Brown installed the 2-ft. by 8-ft. folding workbench (below right) along one wall of his garage/shop in Jacksonville, Florida. The bench is the same height as a Black & Decker Workmate®, which enables Brown to

harness extra support. Folded flat against the wall, Brown's bench consumes almost no space and does not accumulate clutter.

David Hartka's bench (shown in the photos below) explores the limits of convertibility in the tradition of the "gentleman's" tool chest. Three removable vises attach to the case, which functions as a workbench and tool chest. A set of drawers on the front of the bench carries chisels, planes and other small tools; a hinged panel on the back holds

saws and large squares. (The disassembled vises store in the end of the upper case, between the legs.) Used separately, the base serves as a shaving horse, saw bench and shooting board, and doubles as seating furniture. Hartka's combination bench proved to be a stimulating design exercise, since it incorporates a variety of joints and at least ten different kinds of wood. Buttoned up and not in use, the bench masquerades as a sideboard in Hartka's Baltimore living room.

A convertible bench/ low assembly table

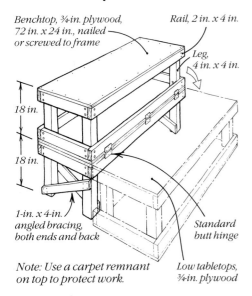

Benchtop, ¾-in. plywood, 72 in. x 24 in., nailed or screwed to frame

Rail, 2 in. x 4 in.

Leg, 4 in. x 4 in.

18 in.

18 in.

1-in. x 4-in. angled bracing, both ends and back

Standard butt hinge

Note: Use a carpet remnant on top to protect work.

Low tabletops, ¾-in. plywood

A folding bench

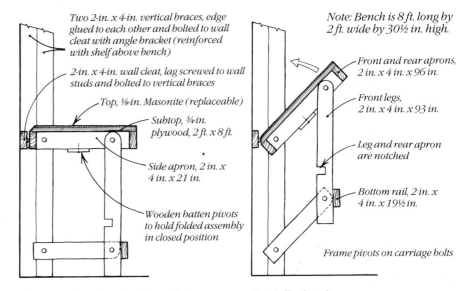

Two 2-in. x 4-in. vertical braces, edge glued to each other and bolted to wall cleat with angle bracket (reinforced with shelf above bench)

2-in. x 4-in. wall cleat, lag screwed to wall studs and bolted to vertical braces

Top, ⅛-in. Masonite (replaceable)

Subtop, ¾-in. plywood, 2 ft. x 8 ft.

Side apron, 2 in. x 4 in. x 21 in.

Wooden batten pivots to hold folded assembly in closed position

Note: Bench is 8 ft. long by 2 ft. wide by 30½ in. high.

Front and rear aprons, 2 in. x 4 in. x 96 in.

Front legs, 2 in. x 4 in. x 93 in.

Leg and rear apron are notched

Bottom rail, 2 in. x 4 in. x 19½ in.

Frame pivots on carriage bolts

Open — section at centerline, end view

Partially closed

The lathe lends itself better than any machine in the shop to combination with a workbench. It is long and narrow, and unlike most saws or planers, it tends to be used heavily for specific projects and then left idle for long periods. These factors (as well as a lack of space) inspired the two "swinging" lathe benches shown in the drawings at right and below.

Alan Hamilton, of Utica, Michigan, mounted his lathe (at right) on a pivoting arm, which is held in place with two locator pins when the lathe is in use. (The lathe motor is installed on the stationary, rear portion of the bench.) Otherwise, it rests out of the way on the floor, providing access to the other tools on the bench.

A swinging lathe

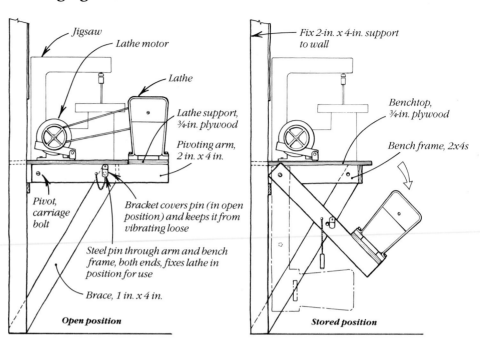

Jigsaw

Lathe motor

Lathe

Lathe support, ¾-in. plywood

Pivoting arm, 2 in. x 4 in.

Pivot, carriage bolt

Bracket covers pin (in open position) and keeps it from vibrating loose

Steel pin through arm and bench frame, both ends, fixes lathe in position for use

Brace, 1 in. x 4 in.

Open position

Fix 2-in. x 4-in. support to wall

Benchtop, ¾-in. plywood

Bench frame, 2x4s

Stored position

A flip-top lathe bench

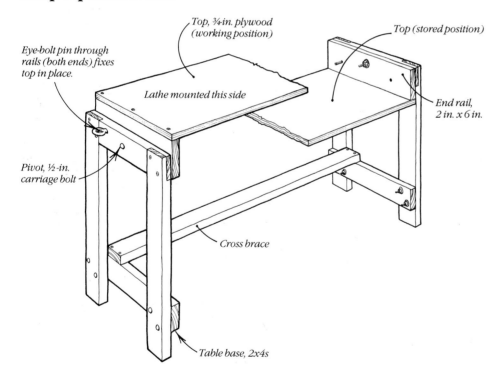

Top, ¾-in. plywood (working position)

Top (stored position)

Eye-bolt pin through rails (both ends) fixes top in place.

Lathe mounted this side

End rail, 2 in. x 6 in.

Pivot, ½-in. carriage bolt

Cross brace

Table base, 2x4s

David Peterson, of Jacksonville, Florida, took a somewhat different approach when he designed his flip-top lathe bench (shown above). The lathe is bolted to one side of a plywood bed, which pivots on a ½-in. carriage bolt at both ends. Peterson's workshop shares space in the garage with a washer and dryer and assorted garden tools, so when the lathe is out of action, he simply pulls the ¼-in. eye-bolt pins that secure the plywood bed at each end and flips the lathe over to provide a convenient shelf for stacking laundry baskets.

No other shop fixture is as versatile and portable as the humble sawhorse. Inside the shop, as well as on the job, the sawhorse is the invisible hero of many woodworking activities. Below and on the facing page are three functional designs that can be made to any size you need.

Peter Murkett often works outside of his shop, so he built the two-legged (three-footed) horse shown below to provide a stable platform on any surface. The wide foot makes it a little harder to get up and down stairs than a conventional sawhorse, but Murkett reports that "it's always steady." The horse is made of chestnut salvaged from old house parts. Pinned tenons at the top of the legs and in the foot hold the horse together, and keyed through-tenons in the base allow Murkett to tighten the joints as they work loose or if the wood shrinks with seasonal changes.

Sawhorses don't get any simpler or more compact than Mark Duginske's interlocking knock-down horses. The crossbar and the legs tighten together as weight is applied, but the joint is easily disassembled when the crossbar is lifted. (The slots in the crossbar are angled 5° from vertical.) "After a while, you get used to lifting it by both ends," Duginske says. He made his horses of 1-in. thick die board (a high-grade, heavy-duty plywood used in the tool-and-die trade), but any good grade of plywood will do, and he relieved the bottom of the legs to create a stable footprint.

For its combination of strength, light weight, compact design and ease of assembly, Martin Bernstein's theatrical sawhorse is a marvel of economy. Working backstage on about three films (and numerous commercials) each year, Bernstein applies those criteria to all of his equipment, as well as to his on-camera productions. Everything that isn't built to roll must be folded and trucked from sound stage to sound stage, or to some pretty unlikely shooting locations. Bernstein built this horse out of 1x3 lumber, reinforced with ½-in. plywood gussets at the corners. Hinges at the top and at the ends and center of the bottom brace allow the horse to be folded flat. (Bernstein has used string at the bottom in place of the hinged brace, but the locking action of the rigid crossmember is what makes this design so successful.)

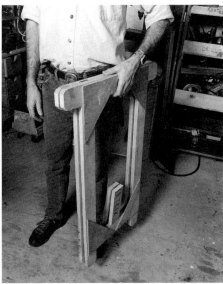

Auxiliary machine tables

The most elaborate accessory tables I saw were made by Roger Heitzman. Fully arrayed, they provide a great deal of support at his table saw for wide and long stock. Folded away, they take up little space. The photos show how he unfurls the setup. Three tables fold together in a 30-in. wide sandwich at the rear of the saw. Heitzman begins by lifting the sandwich and releasing a pair of hinged legs to support the main outfeed table (the middle one in the sandwich), which is hinged to the rear of the saw. Next, he flips the top table (an 18-in. wide outfeed extension) into position on another pair of legs, as shown in the center photo

below. He can also simply continue rotating this table and let it hang vertically off the end of the main outfeed table.

The 24-in. by 28-in. sidefeed table is hinged to the underside of the main outfeed table and is supported by an independent leg frame (below right) that extends along the left side of the saw. To complete the assembly, Heitzman covers the exposed part of the leg with a particleboard box beam, which provides additional bearing surface. (The beam is shown upside down on the edge of the saw table in the photo below right.)

Heitzman used a form of torsion-box construction for the tables, with an

internal grid of 1x4 poplar, sheathed on top with a ¼-in. Kortran skin. He made the mistake of using single-sided Kortran, however, and during humid weather, the tables sometimes warp so badly he can't close them. Two-sided Kortran or a similar particleboard material that is coated on both sides would solve the problem.

Heitzman designed the unit in his head and built it in a couple of evenings. The trickiest part, he says, was figuring out the special wood-and-plastic hinges he built to join the top two tables (see the drawing below). They could not protrude above the surface of either table, yet had to permit the top table to swing almost

Double drop-leaf hinge

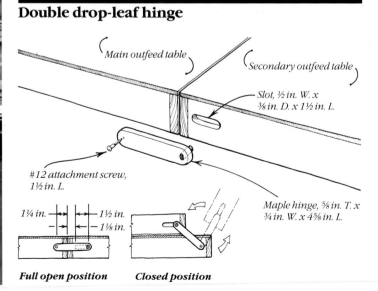

Main outfeed table

Secondary outfeed table

Slot, ½ in. W. x
⅜ in. D. x 1½ in. L.

#12 attachment screw,
1½ in. L.

Maple hinge, ⅝ in. T. x
¾ in. W. x 4⅝ in. L.

1¼ in. — 1½ in.
— 1⅛ in.

Full open position   ***Closed position***

270° from its folded position to its vertical drop-leaf position. When the second outfeed table is extended for use, a couple of small suitcase latches underneath the tables hold them tightly together. It seemed like a lot of work for a bunch of outfeed tables, but in Heitzman's busy workshop, the versatility pays off. With a minimum of fiddling around, he can use only the extensions he needs and save valuable floor space for other activities. "I sure love it," he says. "Now anybody can cut sheet stock here without a helper."

A folding outfeed table was likewise a necessity when Michael Fortune worked in a cramped backyard shop, but he had even less room than Heitzman to spare. Fortune's extension (at right) is hinged to the back of his saw, and a pair of adjustable threaded leveler feet locate in two shallow pockets bored in the lower batten. To keep sawdust from clogging the pockets, Fortune chiseled out the wood on the "down-hill" side of the bored holes and installed a small metal bracket, which supports the feet.

Folding outfeed table

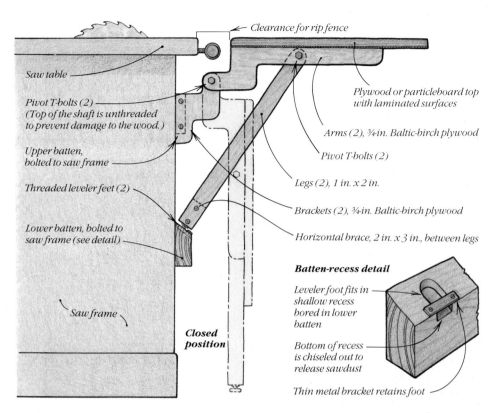

Clearance for rip fence

Saw table

Pivot T-bolts (2)
(Top of the shaft is unthreaded to prevent damage to the wood.)

Upper batten, bolted to saw frame

Threaded leveler feet (2)

Lower batten, bolted to saw frame (see detail)

Saw frame

Closed position

Plywood or particleboard top with laminated surfaces

Arms (2), ¾-in. Baltic-birch plywood

Pivot T-bolts (2)

Legs (2), 1 in. x 2 in.

Brackets (2), ¾-in. Baltic-birch plywood

Horizontal brace, 2 in. x 3 in., between legs

Batten-recess detail

Leveler foot fits in shallow recess bored in lower batten

Bottom of recess is chiseled out to release sawdust

Thin metal bracket retains foot

A sawhorse bench

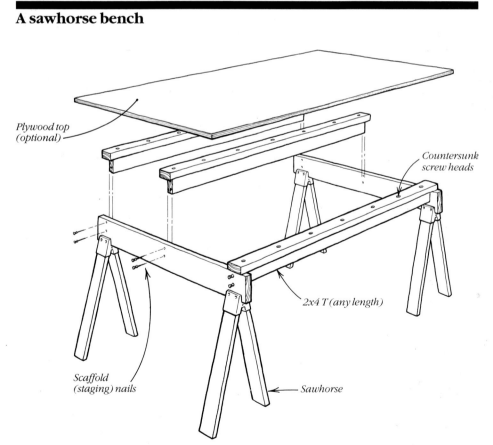

Plywood top (optional)

Countersunk screw heads

Scaffold (staging) nails

2x4 T (any length)

Sawhorse

With the addition of three 2x4 T's, Maine cabinetmaker Lee McGinley converts two sawhorses into a sturdy outfeed table for his saw or a job-site workbench. He clamps work directly to the T's, or adds a 4x8 sheet of plywood or particleboard for a benchtop. The bench is sturdy, easy to move and stores in very little space.

C. Wayne Joslin flanked the portable radial-arm saw in his crowded basement shop with a pair of drop-leaf extension tables (at right), adapted from a design in R.J. DeCristoforo's *Complete Book of Power Tools*. The male half of the wooden slide is hinged to a cleat mounted on the side of the saw table, and the sliding female half is attached to the underside of the extension table. To extend one or both tables, Joslin simply lifts the table, allowing the hinged, 12-in. wide leg frame to drop into position. With both tables fully extended, he has 6 ft. of support on either side of the blade.

To handle long boards, Paul Silke attaches a pair of infeed and outfeed roller tables to his bandsaw (shown below). He mounts the infeed tables only when he's resawing heavy stock. The square steel arms on the roller tables are slotted to fit over bolts on the sides of the saw table, and they're supported at the ends by a pair of steel legs with leveler feet.

Thomas Durney's auxiliary tables provide him with a 39-in. square worksurface on two sides of his bandsaw (below right). The side and rear tables hinge to wooden brackets bolted to the edges of the saw table, and are supported by thin scrap-wood braces jammed between the tables and the floor. A third section rests on wooden pads screwed to the underside of the two hinged tables and bolts to two T-nuts in each of the adjacent tables. Durney outfitted the groove in the sidefeed table with an adjustable circle-cutting jig that can handle a 30-in. radius. (Photo by Thomas Durney.)

A folding extension table for a radial-arm-saw

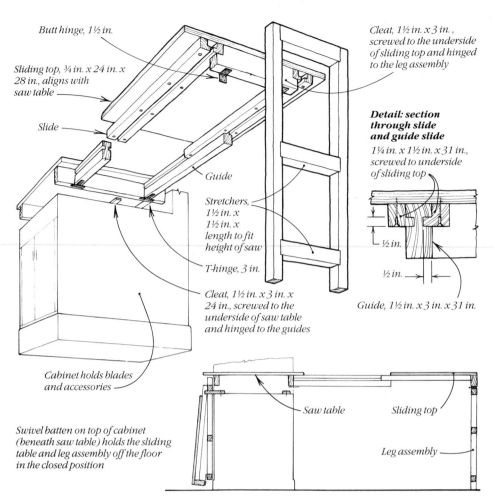

Butt hinge, 1½ in.

Sliding top, ¾ in. x 24 in. x 28 in., aligns with saw table

Slide

Guide

Stretchers, 1½ in. x 1½ in. x length to fit height of saw

T-hinge, 3 in.

Cleat, 1½ in. x 3 in. x 24 in., screwed to the underside of saw table and hinged to the guides

Cleat, 1½ in. x 3 in., screwed to the underside of sliding top and hinged to the leg assembly

Detail: section through slide and guide slide

1¼ in. x 1½ in. x 31 in., screwed to underside of sliding top

½ in.

½ in.

Guide, 1½ in. x 3 in. x 31 in.

Cabinet holds blades and accessories

Swivel batten on top of cabinet (beneath saw table) holds the sliding table and leg assembly off the floor in the closed position

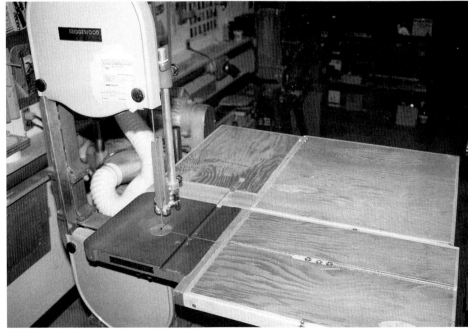

Saw table

Sliding top

Leg assembly

A sawhorse can be modified to provide convenient outfeed support for machines of varying heights. Curtis Erpelding mounted an adjustable roller support on a three-legged sawhorse (shown above). The bracket slides up or down and is held in place by two large handscrews on the horse.

John Kelsey, of Bethel, Connecticut, keeps a stack of interchangeable brackets of different heights, which mount on the top rail of his sawhorse (above right). Each bracket serves a different machine or working surface in the shop, and they hang on the sides or stack on the lower crossbar of the horse when not in use. A shallow shoulder near the bottom of each vertical leg helps support heavy loads, and the horizontal brace at the bottom resists racking. The horses are assembled with drywall screws driven into the end grain with a brace and power-drive bit. "I don't mean to make too much of it," Kelsey says. "The technology of making rigid horses is trivial, but it's critical."

Like the horses, Kelsey's brackets are made of scrap lumber with leftover plywood flooring slabbed on both sides. The top of the bracket is crowned slightly and waxed to minimize resistance. It may be planed slightly to lower the height, or the brackets may be doubled and even tripled for tall support.

Workbench outfeed

Chamfered batten

Bench dog

Workbench

Table saw

In many small shops, the workbench provides outfeed support for the table saw—there's just no room for nifty folding tables. New York carpenter Scott McBride positioned his bench behind the saw, but its top surface is lower than the saw table. To make up the difference, McBride places a wooden batten a little more than half the stock's length away from the sawblade, backed up by two bench dogs. The benchtop has parallel rows of dog holes. To make sure that boards ride up and over the batten without getting stuck, McBride chamfered the top edge. This setup has an unexpected advantage—he needn't clear the bench every time he rips a board. "The stock just sails over the squares, router bits and accumulated flotsam on the bench," he reports.

Workstations

Workstations come in all shapes and sizes, depending on what work you do and the space you have to do it in. The ones shown here explore the range of the form.

Thomas Durney's compact cluster of hand-held power tools (shown at right) is mounted on the wall behind a radial-arm-saw bench that runs the entire length of his shop. The tools are positioned at a convenient angle and kept on short cords to avoid a tangle on the bench. (Photo by Thomas Durney.)

In the compact assembly station shown below, Randall Ores combines a 2-ton press (24 in. by 54 in.) with an impressive deployment of screw guns, hammer drills and miscellaneous tools and materials. "It's tight for space here," Ores says, "and I can see what I have." (Photo by Scott Arfsten.)

At the large, carpeted assembly station near the loading door of Lewis Judy's Oregon workshop, employees Hector Santana and Raymond McLaughlin put the finishing touches on a small table. Well known for his prodigious production, Judy points to the line-up of routers on the top shelf of the station (he keeps more than 20 in the shop) and jokingly says: "We don't keep wrenches."

Portable workstations are a blessing in both large and small shops, but often for different reasons. In a small shop, rolling tool carts and movable stands make the space more flexible, while in a large shop, the carts simply help move materials around. In Michael Elkan's Oregon shop (at left), Sue Marcoe glues and clamps boxes on lightweight assembly stands that can be moved out of the way until the glue dries. Likewise, Jeff Elliott's swivel-stool assembly station (below), can be pulled right up to the bench to work on a guitar and moved safely out of the way when the job is done.

A shop-built veneer press

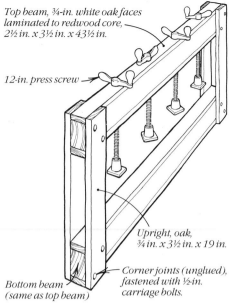

Top beam, ¾-in. white oak faces laminated to redwood core, 2½ in. x 3½ in. x 43½ in.

12-in. press screw

Upright, oak, ¾ in. x 3½ in. x 19 in.

Bottom beam (same as top beam)

Corner joints (unglued), fastened with ½-in. carriage bolts.

Note: Maximum press capacity is 36 in. x 59 in. with frame, spaced 9 in. apart.

Paul Silke sets up his portable veneer press on an island workstation in the middle of the shop and packs it away in a corner when not in use. To save weight, Silke laminated the frames out of ¾-in. white oak, with a redwood core, and joined them at the corners with carriage bolts and no glue. Allowing for two 1-in. thick plywood cauls, the inside height of the press makes the most of the 12-in. long screws Silke used.

Roger Heitzman brings his compact sanding caddy (above) right to the job. The rolling cart carries all the paper and accessories for the pneumatic sanders he uses around the shop. The side of the cart in the foreground of the photo holds a series of bins in which Heitzman organizes different grits of sandpaper in quartered sheets that fit his pad sander. The interior holds 100-sheet reams of sandpaper and sanding belts, which are accessible on open shelves from the opposite side of the cart. Two random-orbit pneumatic sanders are usually stored on top, along with boxes of self-adhesive sanding disks. It's hard to measure the value of such a simple fixture, but Heitzman figures he's saved himself a lot of wasted steps.

The portable fixture shown above, right, links several workstations together in Bill and Jim Kochman's cavernous cabinet shop. The Kochman brothers use several rolling carts like this one to keep all the parts for a cabinet job together as they circulate between machines for different operations. The plywood box rests on a heavy-duty rolling dolly and is outfitted with removable Masonite dividers that organize the parts of individual cabinets.

Routers don't need a lot of space, and they are often installed in compact or portable workstations. Michael Fortune's minimalist router table amounts to a cantilevered shelf bolted to the edge of his bench. The mounting arms are slotted to receive two stove bolts that are screwed into threaded inserts in the underside of the bench and tightened with wing nuts. (You could use hanger bolts instead.). Under the router table, two battens pivot to capture segments of the router base and hold it in its routed recess. Fortune stretches a length of rubber inner tube over the router to keep it in position while he's removing the battens; it also supports the weight of the router while he's adjusting the depth of cut.

A simple router table

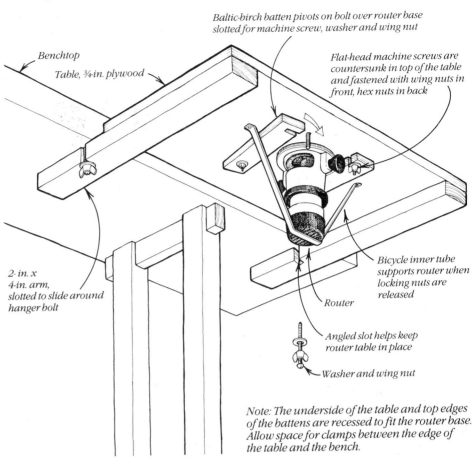

Baltic-birch batten pivots on bolt over router base slotted for machine screw, washer and wing nut

Flat-head machine screws are countersunk in top of the table and fastened with wing nuts in front, hex nuts in back

Benchtop

Table, ¾-in. plywood

2-in. x 4-in. arm, slotted to slide around hanger bolt

Bicycle inner tube supports router when locking nuts are released

Router

Angled slot helps keep router table in place

Washer and wing nut

Note: The underside of the table and top edges of the battens are recessed to fit the router base. Allow space for clamps between the edge of the table and the bench.

Jim Whetstone built the two-part router table at left with a hinged top to provide easy access to his plunge router. To accommodate large work, Whetstone removes the top section from the base and places it on his bench. (Photo by Jim Whetstone, Quality Cabinetry.)

Safety accessories

A well-designed push stick is a critical safety fixture at the table saw and jointer. It interposes wood between your fingers and the blade, and it improves control at the same time. Each of the push sticks shown here has its own appeal and application.

Tired of "trashing" his push sticks, Roger Heitzman built the hot-rod jointer push stick (shown at top right) to last. It is easy to hold, easy to find and has survived nearly a decade in his shop.

Kelly Mehler's "stretch" push stick (middle right) enables him to apply even pressure over a long board. Its sculpted handholds afford a safe and comfortable grip.

John Nyquist uses two push sticks when ripping narrow stock (below left)—one to hold the wood against the fence and the other to feed the material. Several of these push sticks are always available in a box attached to the side of Nyquist's table saw. The handle on Nyquist's two-piece plywood jointer push stick (below right) is cut out on the bandsaw and glued into a rabbet in the base.

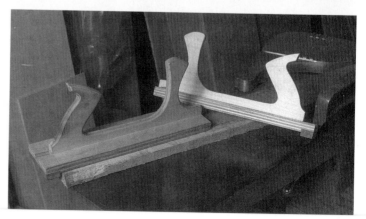

A multipurpose table-saw sled

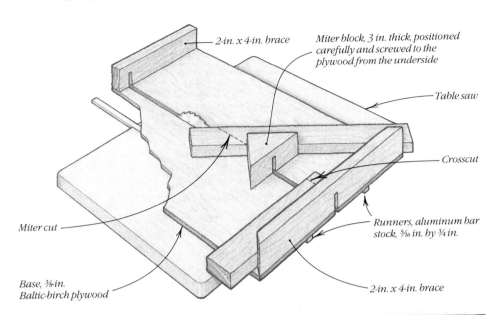

2-in. x 4-in. brace

Miter block, 3 in. thick, positioned carefully and screwed to the plywood from the underside

Table saw

Crosscut

Miter cut

Runners, aluminum bar stock, 5/16 in. by 3/4 in.

Base, 3/8-in. Baltic-birch plywood

2-in. x 4-in. brace

A sled for small parts

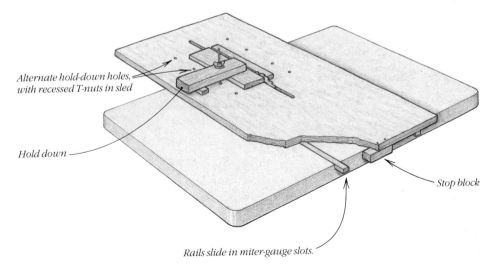

Alternate hold-down holes, with recessed T-nuts in sled

Hold down

Stop block

Rails slide in miter-gauge slots.

Table-saw sleds greatly enhance safety and crosscut accuracy by providing good sliding support—even for small stock. And they reduce the risk of kickback, since thin offcuts are unlikely to jam in the narrow sawblade slot. The rear brace on most sleds also provides a surface to clamp the work or to attach guide blocks for repeated cuts.

Like push sticks, there is an endless variety of sled styles, a few of which are shown here. Dick Sellew designed the sled shown in the drawing at left to handle both right-angle and mitered crosscuts. The two-point support for the mitered stock is much more substantial than a standard miter fence.

Cabinetmaker Charlie Mastro's large, open-ended sled (middle photo) stores flat and can handle wider panels than most two-sided sleds. It is made of ½-in. Baltic-birch plywood and is grooved to receive the guide bar that slides in the slotted table. Its free-form, roughly triangular shape is easier to handle (and takes less plywood) than a large rectangular sled and, with only one brace, it stores easily against the wall.

Don Anderson built the sled shown in the drawing below to cut parts for small models and miniatures, as well as hard-to-hold materials like plastic and dowels. The work is held securely to the sled—at any angle to the blade—beneath a wooden batten, so his hands are well away from the action. (Anderson uses a V-block beneath the batten to hold round stock.) He places a piece of scrap the same thickness of the stock beneath the opposite end of the batten, which is fastened to the sled with a wing nut. Anderson bored a series of holes in the plywood sled to enable him to reposition the hold-down bolt for different operations. The sled is about a foot longer than the saw table, and has two hardwood runners that ride in the miter-gauge slots. Stop blocks are attached to the underside of the sled at both ends to prevent him from accidentally sawing it in half.

Bibliography

Historical Background

Diderot, Denis. *Rameau's Nephew and Other Works.* Translated by Jacques Barzun and Ralph H. Bowen. Indianapolis: Bobbs-Merrill, 1964.

Diderot, Denis and Jean d'Alembert, eds. *Encyclopédie, ou Dictionnaire Raisonné des Sciences, des Arts et des Métiers, par un Société de Gens de Lettres.* 17 vols. Paris: Briasson et al., 1751-65.

Félibien, André. *Des Principes de l'Architecture.* Vols. 1 and 3. Paris: Chez Jean-Baptiste Coignard, 1676.

Forman, Benno M. *American Seating Furniture 1630-1730.* N.Y.: W.W. Norton, 1988.

Gardner, John. *Building Classic Small Craft.* Camden, Maine: International Marine Publishing, 1977.

Gilbert, Christopher. *The Life and Work of Thomas Chippendale.* N.Y.: Macmillan, 1978.

Goodman, W.L. *The History of Woodworking Tools.* London: G. Bell and Sons, 1964.

Gusler, Wallace B. *Furniture of Williamsburg and Eastern Virginia, 1710-1790.* Richmond: Virginia Museum, 1979.

Hastings, Scott E., Jr. *The Last Yankees: Folkways in Eastern Vermont and the Border Country.* Hanover, N. H.: University Press of New England, 1990.

Hayward, Helena and Pat Kirkham. *William and John Linnell: Eighteenth Century London Furniture Makers.* London: Cassell, 1980.

Hindle, Brooke, ed. *America's Wooden Age: Aspects of Its Early Technology.* Tarrytown, N.Y.: Sleepy Hollow Press, 1975.

Hubbard, Frank. *Three Centuries of Harpsichord Making.* Cambridge, Mass.: Harvard University Press, 1965.

Hume, Ivor Noël. *Williamsburg Cabinetmakers: The Archaeological Evidence.* Williamsburg, Va.: The Colonial Williamsburg Foundation, 1971.

Hummel, Charles F. *With Hammer in Hand: The Dominy Craftsmen of East Hampton, New York.* Charlottesville: The University Press of Virginia, 1968.

Jobe, Brock and Myrna Kaye. *New England Furniture: The Colonial Era.* Boston: Houghton Mifflin, 1984.

Kebabian, Paul B. and William C. Lipke. *Tools and Technologies: America's Wooden Age.* Burlington, Vt.: Robert Hull Fleming Museum, University of Vermont, 1979.

Lamoureux, Louis A. "Ben Thresher's Mill: for 120 years a Peacham institution." *Vermont Life* (Spring 1969): 5-7.

MacCarthy, Fiona. *The Simple Life: C.R. Ashbee in the Cotswolds.* Berkeley and Los Angeles: University of California Press, 1981.

Manley, Atwood. *Rushton and His Times in American Canoeing.* Syracuse, N.Y.: Syracuse University Press and The Adirondack Museum, 1968.

Moxon, Joseph. *Mechanick Exercises. Or the Doctrine of Handy-Works.* 3rd ed. London: Printed for Dan Midwinter and Tho. Leigh, 1703.

Nicholson, Peter. *Mechanical Exercises.* London: J. Taylor, 1812.

Pye, David. *The Nature and Art of Workmanship.* Cambridge: Cambridge University Press, 1968.

Roubo, Jacques-André. *L'art du Menuisier.* 4 vols. Paris: L.F. Delatour, 1769-75. Reprint. 4 vols. in 3. Paris: Léonce Laget, 1977.

Sturt, George. *The Wheelwright's Shop.* Cambridge: Cambridge University Press, 1923.

Vandal, Norman. *Queen Anne Furniture.* Newtown, Conn.: The Taunton Press, 1990.

Viires, A. *Woodworking in Estonia.* Translated by J. Levitan. Jerusalem: Israel Program for Scientific Translations, 1969. Reprint. Springfield, Va.: U.S. Department of Commerce.

Wamsley, James S. *The Crafts of Williamsburg.* Williamsburg, Va.: The Colonial Williamsburg Foundation, 1982.

Dust Collection

Berendsohn, Roy. "Clearing the Air." *Fine Woodworking* 67 (November 1987): 70-75.

Campbell, Mac. "Return-Air Dust Collection." *Fine Woodworking* 25 (November 1980): 58-59.

Johnson, Doyle. "Dust Collection System." *Fine Woodworking* 12 (September 1978): 76-78.

Stodola, Rick. "Sucking up the Small Stuff." *Fine Homebuilding* 60 (April 1990): 63.

Urban, Harry. "OSHA Takes New Steps Towards Wood Dust Rule." *Wood & Wood Products* (June 1987): 75-76.

Electrical

Alternative Energy Sourcebook 1990. Ukiah, Calif.: Real Goods Trading Company, 1990.

Campbell, Mac. "Converting to 3-Phase Power." *Fine Woodworking* 24 (September 1980): 57-59.

Miller, Rex and Mark Richard Miller. *Fractional-Horsepower Electric Motors.* N.Y.: Bobbs-Merrill Co. (Theodore Audel & Co.), 1984.

Murkett, Peter. "Running a shop on a thimbleful of power." *Fine Woodworking* 63 (March 1987): 114-116.

Richter, Herbert P. and W. Creighton Schwan. *Practical Electrical Wiring.* 12th ed. New York: McGraw-Hill, 1982.

Ross, Joseph A., ed. *The National Electrical Code Handbook.* 2nd ed. NFPA No. SPP-6C. Quincy, Mass.: National Fire Protection Association, 1981.

Sloan, David. "Working Wood Without Electricity." *Fine Woodworking* 56 (January 1986): 72-75.

Machinery

Corneil, William. "Shopmade Bandsaw." *Fine Woodworking* 65 (July 1987): 60-63.

DeCristoforo, R.J. *Complete Book of Power Tools, Both Stationary and Portable.* N.Y.: Popular Science Books, 1972.

Fine Woodworking on Woodworking Machines. Newtown, Conn.: The Taunton Press, 1985.

Duginske, Mark. *Band Saw Handbook.* N.Y.: Sterling Publishing Co., 1989.

——"Tuning-Up Your Tablesaw." *Fine Woodworking* 78 (September 1989): 69-73.

Heitzman, Roger. "Metalworking in the Woodshop." *Fine Woodworking* 79 (December 1989): 84-87.

——"Building a Stationary Sander." *Fine Woodworking* 79 (December 1989): 88-89.

Kriegshauser, John. "Alvin Weaver: A shop full of home-built machines." *Fine Woodworking* 65 (July 1987): 57-59.

Rekoff, M.G., Jr. "Stroke Sander." *Fine Woodworking* 3 (Summer 1976): 46-51.

"Sources of Supply: Combination machines, domestic and imported." *Fine Woodworking* 24 (July 1980): 84-87.

Safety

Bertorelli, Paul. "Keeping Ten Fingers." *Fine Woodworking* 42 (September 1983): 76-78.

Code of Federal Regulations (29 Labor, Parts 1900 to 1910). Washington, D.C.: U.S. Government Printing Office, 1988.

Justis, Dr. E. Jeff. "Woodworking Injuries." *Fine Woodworking* 36 (September 1982): 84-86.

Podmaniczky, Michael S. "Ripping, grooving and molding safely." *Fine Woodworking* 42 (September 1983): 77.

Robinson, Charley. "Tablesaw Safety Devices." *Fine Woodworking* 81 (March 1990): 84-88.

Workshop Accessories

Campbell, Mac. "The Finishing Room." *American Woodworker* 2, No. 1 (1986): 52-53.

Capotosto, Rosario. *Woodworking Wisdom.* N.Y.: Popular Science Books, 1983.

Dresdner, Michael. "Compressed-Air Systems." *Fine Woodworking* 82 (May 1990): 56-61.

Landis, Scott. *The Workbench Book.* Newtown, Conn.: The Taunton Press, 1987.

Payson, Harold H. "Dynamite". "Keeping a Cutting Edge: Power Saws." *WoodenBoat* 48 (1982): 44-49.

"Shop Notes." *Popular Mechanics* 37 (1941): 99-101.

Workshop Designs and Planning

Baldwin, J. "One Highly Evolved Toolbox." *The Essential Whole Earth Catalog.* Garden City, N.Y.: Doubleday, 1986, 152-155.

——"One Highly Evolved Toolbox Evolves Some More." *Whole Earth Review* (July 1985): 76-79.

——"The Compleat Country Workshop." *Country Journal* (November/December 1989): 59-64.

Bahrman, Neal. "Camper-Shell Toolbox." *Fine Homebuilding* 57 (December 1989): 71.

"Build PM's Work-and-play camper." *Popular Mechanics* (January 1978): 76-77.

Burrowes, John. "My first shop." *Fine Woodworking* 24 (September 1980): 36-37.

Fine Woodworking on The Small Workshop. Newtown, Conn.: The Taunton Press, 1985.

Frid, Tage. "Start with a table saw." *Fine Woodworking* 24 (September 1980): 48-49.

Gottshall, Franklin H. "High ceiling, wood floor, good light." *Fine Woodworking* 24 (September 1980): 50.

Hiltebeitel, J.A. "Woodworking in Seventy-Five Square Feet." *Fine Woodworking* 24 (September, 1980): 54-55.

Jones, Henry. "Leave room in the middle." *Fine Woodworking* 24 (September 1980): 47-48.

Kern, Ken and Barbara Kern. *Ken Kern's Homestead Workshop.* North Fork, Calif.: Owner Builder Publications, 1981. (Available from Barbara Kern, Box 817, Owner Builder Publications, North Fork, CA 93643.)

Kern, Ken. *The Owner Built Home Revisited.* North Fork, Calif.: Owner Builder Publications 1984. (Available from Barbara Kern, Box 817, Owner Builder Publications, North Fork, CA 93643.)

Klausz, Frank. "Build around bench and hand tools." *Fine Woodworking* 24 (September 1980): 52-53.

Manners, David X. *Complete Book of Home Workshops.* N.Y.: Popular Science Publishing, 1969.

Marlow, Andy. "Get a big band saw and a jigsaw too." *Fine Woodworking* 24 (September 1980): 51.

McNair, Don. *Building & Outfitting Your Workshop.* Blue Ridge Summit, Pa.: Tab Books, 1983.

Modern School Shop Planning. 7th ed. Ann Arbor, Mich.: Prakken Publications, Inc., 1978.

Payson, Harold H. "Dynamite". "A Boatbuilding Shop." *WoodenBoat* 85 (1988): 27-35.

"PM's Gardening and Outdoor Living Guide." *Popular Mechanics* (March 1980): 140-143.

"Set Up Your Home Workshop." *Workbench* (September 1990): 37-51.

Walker, Lester. *Tiny Houses.* Woodstock, N.Y.: The Overlook Press, 1987.

Westlake, Cy. "A Mobile Workshop." *Fine Homebuilding* 8 (April 1982): 58-59.

Wheeler, Anthony. "Mobile-Home Wood Shop." *Fine Woodworking* 24 (September 1980): 56.

Miscellaneous

Dawson, Sheila Rose. *I Can Build It Myself.* San Diego, California: Children's Woodshop Publications, 1984. (Available from Sheila Dawson, Box 178451, San Diego, CA 92177.)

——"That's Not Dandruff, That's Sawdust." *Tradeswomen* (Spring, 1985): 14-18.

Krenov, James. *The Fine Art of Cabinetmaking.* N.Y.: Van Nostrand Reinhold, 1977.

Starr, Richard. *Woodworking with Kids.* Newtown, Conn.: The Taunton Press, 1982.

Stone, Michael. *Contemporary American Woodworkers.* Layton, Utah: Gibbs M. Smith, 1986.

Watson, Aldren A. *Hand Tools: Their Ways and Workings.* N.Y.: W.W. Norton, 1982.

Woodworker's Logbook. Ottawa, Ont.: Veritas Tools, 1986.

Sources of Supply

Aair Purification Systems
1250 Pierre Way
El Cajon, CA 92021
(619) 588-2825
(800) 777-6746
Electrostatic and media air cleaners

Airflow Systems, Inc.
10755 Sanden Drive
Dallas, TX 75238-1336
(214) 272-3003
Dust collectors and free-hanging air cleaners

Airstream Dust Helmets
16 Division Street W.
Box 975
Elbow Lake, MN 56531
(218) 685-4457
(800) 328-1792
Air-filtration helmets

Arrowsmith & Lang-Borne
Washington and Main Street
Box 126
Lumberport, WV 26386
(304) 584-4246
(800) 544-4283
Dust-collection accessories

Biesemeyer Manufacturing Corp.
216 S. Alma School Road, Suite 3
Mesa, AZ 85210
(602) 835-9300
Aftermarket saw fences, blade guards and extension tables

Blue Sky Filters
2833 N.E. Sandy Boulevard
Portland, OR 97232
(503) 232-9281
(800) 648-2247
Air/liquid filtration products (dust-collector filter bags)

B.R. Gale Co.
81 Hano Street
Boston, MA 02134
(617) 254-2813
Dampers, blast gates, Y-joints, flexible hose, floor pickups and other dust-collection equipment

Bridge City Tool Works, Inc.
1104 N.E. 28th Avenue
Portland, OR 97232-2498
(800) 253-3332
Elegant hand tools and accessories

C. Goodman and Co., Inc.
75 Spruce Street
Box 2777
Paterson, NJ 07509
(201) 278-1303
Custom-made, dust-collection fabric filter bags

Chiswick Trading, Inc.
33 Union Avenue
Sudbury, MA 01776-0907
(800) 225-8708
Rubber fatigue mats and large plastic bags for dust collectors

Direct Safety Co.
7815 South 46th Street
Phoenix, AZ 85044
(602) 968-7009
(800) 528-7405
Dust masks, respirators, rubber fatigue mats, metal paint cabinets and a full range of other safety products

D-M International, Inc.
61 Malcolm Road, Unit 2 and 3
Guelph, Ontario
Canada N1K 1A7
(519) 821-8830
Zincken and Mini-Max machinery

EBAC Systems
106 John Jefferson Road
Suite 102
Williamsburg, VA 23185
(804) 229-3038
(800) 433-9011
Wood-drying kilns

Fisher Hill Products
Fisher Hill
Fitzwilliam, NH 03447
(603) 585-6883
Ripstrate table-saw hold down

Garrett Wade
161 Avenue of the Americas
New York, NY 10013
(212) 807-1757
(800) 221-2942
Inca machinery, hand tools, safety equipment and shop accessories

Gilliom Manufacturing, Inc.
Box 1018
St. Charles, MO 63302
(314) 724-1812
Plans, patterns and parts for shop-built machinery

Grizzly Imports, Inc.
Box 2069
Bellingham, WA 98227
(206) 647-0801
(800) 541-5537
Dust collectors and other discount machinery

Harbor Freight Tools
3491 Mission Oaks Boulevard
Camarillo, CA 93011-6010
(800) 423-2567
Dust collectors, discount equipment and hand tools

H. Gerstner & Sons, Inc.
Box 517
Dayton, OH 45402
(513) 228-1662
Wooden carving chests and rolling benches and chests

Highland Hardware
1045 N. Highland Avenue, N.E.
Atlanta, GA 30306
(404) 872-4466
(800) 241-6748
Machinery, safety equipment, tools and shop accessories

Holz-Her U.S., Inc.
5120 Westinghouse Boulevard
Charlotte, NC 28273
(704) 523-5250
Cabinet shop machinery, vertical panel saws and edge banders

Homestead Energy Systems, Inc.
Route 25A
Orford, NH 03777
(603) 353-9207
Consultants for water-powered and wood-powered electric systems

HTC Products, Inc.
Box 839
Royal Oak, MI 48068
(313) 399-6185
(800) 624-2027
Mobile machine bases and table saw Brett-Guard

Kaddies, Inc.
1601 North Main Street
Suite 203
Walnut Creek, CA 04506
(415) 934-4488
Lightweight, portable and rolling tool chests

Laguna Tools
2081 Laguna Canyon Road
Laguna Beach, CA 92651
(714) 494-7006
(800) 234-1976
Robland combination machines, workbenches and other shop accessories

Lee Valley Tools Ltd.
Box 6295, Station J
Ottawa, Ontario
Canada K2A 1T4
(613) 596-0350
Hand tools, safety equipment, barrel-stove kits and shop accessories

Leichtung Workshops
4944 Commerce Parkway
Cleveland, OH 44128
(216) 831-6191
Antikickback hold-down guide system for the table saw and other shop accessories

Manufacturers Service Co., Inc.
5 Lunar Drive
Woodbridge, CT 06525
(800) 367-3828
(800) 535-0425 in CT
Air-handling systems

Mooradian Manufacturing Co.
1752 East 23rd Street
Los Angeles, CA 90058
(213) 747-6348
Idler and drive drums for shop-built sanders

Murphy-Rodgers, Inc.
2301 Belgrave Avenue
Huntington Park, CA 90255
(213) 587-4118
Cyclone centrifugal dust separators

Nauset Engineering and
Equipment, Inc.
578 Lincoln Road
Lincoln, MA 01773
(617) 259-0160
Polyester-felt filter bags for dust-collection systems; standard or custom-made bags

Pangborn Corp.
Box 380
Hagerstown, MD 21741
(301) 739-3500
Blowers for dust-collection systems

Parks Repair Parts, Inc.
Box 586
201 Johnson Street
Covington, KY 41011
(606) 581-7511
Replacement parts for Parks machinery

Parts Company of America
1250 Busch Parkway
Buffalo Grove, IL 60089
(800) 323-0620
Wholesale distributor of replacement parts for machine motors, power tools, electrical hardware, safety equipment and other shop accessories

Plymovent
375 Raritan Center Parkway
Edison, NJ 08837
(201) 417-0808
Electrostatic and media air cleaners, vacuums and fume extractors

Radiantec
P.O. Box 1111
Lyndonville, VT 05851
(802) 626-8045
(800) 451-7593
Radiant floor-heating systems

Real Goods Trading Co.
966 Mazzoni Street
Ukiah, CA 95482
(707) 468-9214
(800) 762-7325
Compact fluorescent bulbs, photovoltaics and other alternative energy systems

Shopsmith Inc.
3931 Image Drive
Dayton, OH 45414-2591
(513) 898-6070
(800) 762-7555
Shopsmith machinery, safety kit and accessories

Tech Paper, Inc.
64 Euclid Avenue
Pittsfield, MA 01201
(413) 499-3351
Air-filtration units, kit plans and filter media

Torit Division/Donaldson Co., Inc.
Box 43217
St. Paul, MN 55164
or
2399 Cawthra Rd.
Mississauga, Ontario
Canada L5A 2W9
Cyclone centrifugal separators for dust collection

Trend-Lines, Inc.
375 Beacham Street
Box 6447
Chelsea, MA 02150-0999
(617) 884-8951
(800) 767-9999
Workshop machinery, hand tools, accessories and supplies

Trion, Inc.
101 McNeill Road
P.O. Box 760
Sanford, NC 27331-0760
(919) 775-2201
Tepco electrostatic and media air cleaners and electronic air cleaners

Vega Enterprises Inc.
R.R. #3, Box 193
Decatur, IL 62526
(217) 963-2232
Table-saw fences, push sticks and stock feeders

Western Commercial Products
Box 238
Tulare, CA 93275
(209) 688-7409
Shophelper antikickback stock feeders

Wilke Machinery Company
3230 Susquehanna Trail
York, PA 17402
(717) 764-5000
Dust collectors and machinery

Wirsbo Co.
5925 148th Street W.
Apple Valley, MN 55124
(612) 469-4800
Radiant floor-heating systems

Woodcraft Supply Corp.
210 Wood County
Industrial Park
Box 1686
Parkersburg, WV 26102-1686
(800) 535-4482
Machinery, safety equipment, hand tools and shop accessories

Woodworkers Machinery
and Supply
2822 East Olympic Boulevard
Los Angeles, CA 90023
(213) 263-7111
Aluminum idler and drive drums for shop-built sanders

Woodworker's Supply of
New Mexico
5604 Alameda Place, N.E.
Albuquerque, NM 87113
(505) 821-0500
(800) 645-9292
Wirth Machine II (Matchmaker 95-200) horizontal router/mortiser and other tools and workshop accessories

Index

Credits

Chapter 1

Page 4, photo: Courtesy Tate Gallery, London/Art Resource, N.Y.

Page 5, quote: George Sturt. *The Wheelwright's Shop.* Cambridge: Cambridge University Press, 1963, p. 31.

Page 5, quote: Denis Diderot. *Rameau's Nephew and Other Works.* Translated by Jacques Barzun and Ralph H. Bowen, N.Y.: Bobbs-Merrill, 1964.

Page 6, excerpts: Benno Forman. *American Seating Furniture 1630-1730.* N.Y.: W.W. Norton, 1988, p. 42, p. 45.

Page 7, photo: Courtesy Duncan McNab.

Page 8, photo: Courtesy The Winterthur Library: Printed Book and Periodical Collection.

Pages 8-9, excerpt: Reprinted by permission of the publishers from Jacques-André Roubo's *L'art du Menuisier,* Paris, 1769-1774, as translated and reprinted in *Three Centuries of Harpsichord Making* by Frank Hubbard, Cambridge, Mass: Harvard University Press, ©1965 by the President and Fellows of Harvard College, p. 195-197.

Page 9, drawing: Redrawn with permission of Macmillan Publishing Company from *The Life and Work of Thomas Chippendale* by Christopher Gilbert. ©1978 by Christopher Gilbert. Originally published by Studio Vista Ltd.

Page 12, photo: Courtesy Virginia State Library and Archives.

Page 13, top left photo: Courtesy Henry Francis du Pont Winterthur Museum.

Page 13, top right photo and floor plan: From the Historic American Buildings Survey, 1940, courtesy of the Library of Congress.

Pages 18-20, drawings: By the Historic American Engineering Record (HAER), courtesy of the Library of Congress.

Page 20, photos: Courtesy Billings Farm & Museum, from the collection of Billings Farm & Museum, Woodstock, Vermont.

Chapter 2

Page 23, quote: Fiona MacCarthy. *The Simple Life: C. R. Ashbee in the Cotswolds.* Atlantic Highlands, N.J.: Humanities Press International, 1988.

Page 35: drawings at left and top right: Redrawn with permission of Charles Scribner's Sons, an imprint of Macmillan Publishing Company from *Ken Kern's Homestead Workshop* by Barbara and Ken Kern. ©1981 Barbara and Ken Kern. Drawing at lower right: Redrawn with permission of Charles Scribner's Sons, an imprint of Macmillan Publishing Company from *The Owner Built Home Revisited* by Ken Kern. ©1972, 1975 Ken Kern.

Chapter 3

Page 59, computer printouts: Courtesy Maurice Gordon.

Chapter 4

Page 67, quote: Sigvard Strandh. *A History of the Machine.* AB Nordbok, Gothenburg, Sweden. 1979.

Page 68, photo: Courtesy The Campden Trust.

Page 76, photo: Courtesy Richard H. Vonderheide.

Page 87, printout: Courtesy Kochman Woodworking.

Chapter 5

Page 96, charts: Charts first appeared in *Fine Woodworking* magazine, September 1980, No. 24. Redrawn with permission of The Taunton Press. ©1980 the Taunton Press, Inc. All rights reserved.

Page 103, top right photo: Courtesy Biesemeyer Manufacturing Corporation.

Page 109, drawing: Drawing first appeared in *Fine Homebuilding* magazine, April 1990, No. 60. Redrawn with permission of The Taunton Press. ©1980 the Taunton Press, Inc. All rights reserved.

Page 113, quote: Courtesy of The Coolidge Collection of Thomas Jefferson Manuscripts: architectural notebook, Nichols #146 and Massachusetts Historical Society #81, p. 19.

Page 116-117, excerpt: Reprinted with permission of Real Goods Trading Company from *Real Goods Trading Company's Alternative Energy Sourcebook 1990,* Ukia, Calif.: Real Goods Trading Company, 1990.

Chapter 6

Page 124, photo: Courtesy Peter Murkett.

Page 126, photo: Courtesy The Adirondack Museum, Blue Mountain Lake, New York.

Page 127, top photo: Courtesy The Adirondack Museum, Blue Mountain Lake, New York.

Page 139, photo at right: Courtesy Lester Walker.

Page 141, photos at left: Photos first appeared in *Whole Earth Review.*

Page 166, top right photo: Courtesy Rick Parker

Chapter 7

Page 153, quote: Christopher Alexander. *The Timeless Way of Building.* N.Y.: Oxford University Press, 1979, p. 9.

Chapter 9

Page 200, drawing: Redrawn courtesy Meredith Press®

Editor: Roger Holmes

Designer/Layout Artist: Henry Roth

Copy/Production Editor: Pam Purrone

Illustrators: Vince Babak (floor plans)

Heather Brine Lambert (all other drawings)

Typeface: Garamond

Paper: 70-lb. Warren Patina matte, neutral pH

Printer and binder: Arcata Graphics, Kingsport, Tennessee